W9-CBM-861

Peacekeeping in Transition

A Twentieth Century Fund Report

PEACEKEEPING in TRANSITION

THE UNITED NATIONS IN CAMBODIA

Janet E. Heininger

The Twentieth Century Fund Press * 1994 * New York

The Twentieth Century Fund sponsors and supervises timely analyses of economic policy, foreign affairs, and domestic political issues. Not-for-profit and nonpartisan, the Fund was founded in 1919 and endowed by Edward A. Filene.

BOARD OF TRUSTEES OF THE TWENTIETH CENTURY FUND

Morris B. Abram, *Emeritus*
H. Brandt Ayers
Peter A. A. Berle
José A. Cabranes
Joseph A. Califano, Jr.
Alexander Morgan Capron
Hodding Carter III
Edward E. David, Jr.
Brewster C. Denny, *Chairman*
Charles V. Hamilton
August Heckscher, *Emeritus*
Matina S. Horner
Lewis B. Kaden

James A. Leach
Richard C. Leone, *ex officio*
P. Michael Pitfield
Don K. Price, *Emeritus*
Richard Ravitch
Arthur M. Schlesinger, Jr., *Emeritus*
Harvey I. Sloane, M.D.
Theodore C. Sorensen
James Tobin, *Emeritus*
David B. Truman, *Emeritus*
Shirley Williams
William Julius Wilson

Richard C. Leone, *President*

Library of Congress Cataloging-in-Publication Data

Heininger, Janet E.
    Peacekeeping in transition : the United Nations in Cambodia, 1991–1993 / Janet E. Heininger.
        p. cm.
    "A Twentieth Century Fund report."
    Includes index.
    ISBN 0-87078-362-9 :
        1. United Nations--Armed Forces--Cambodia.   2. United Nations. Transitional Authority in Cambodia.   3. Cambodia--Politics and government--1975–   I. Title.
JX1981.P7H45   1994
341.5'8--dc20   94-31673
                                                                       CIP

Cover Design: Claude Goodwin
Manufactured in the United States of America.
Copyright © 1994 by the Twentieth Century Fund, Inc.

JX
1981
.P7
H45
1994

To C. Ross Wagner

a gifted teacher who introduced me to East Asia

FOREWORD

When historians reflect on international relations during the years immediately following the cold war, they may be considerably more generous than are commentators today in their assessment of the performances of leaders around the world. The disarray and unevenness that are currently criticized may well be judged an inevitable and immediate by-product of the radically altered state of global politics. After all, the West's principal adversary in the cold war, the Eastern Bloc, has crumbled into a group of nations, each struggling with revolutionary political and economic transformations; at the same time, the "winning" coalition is struggling with the disharmony that results from the reassertion of individual national politics and priorities.

Each nation in the newly expanded "free world" must discover, by trial and error it seems, where its central international interests now lie, what foreign activities its people will support, and how its goals can be most effectively pursued.

The major international institutions, too, are in the process of shedding their former skins and inventing new roles to play. Preeminent in this category is the United Nations, an organization forged by the winners of World War II, constrained by the frozen certainties of the cold war for most of its history, and suddenly the seemingly logical choice to play an active part in virtually every world crisis as it develops.

Prominent among the new activist pursuits of the United Nations is the placement of its peacekeeping forces in a host of countries, often nations where such involvement would have been impractical, if not impossible, in the past. To be sure, between 1945 and 1980, fourteen UN peacekeeping missions were sent into the field (half in the Middle East), but these efforts were puny compared to the dispatch of UN forces to trouble spots around the globe in recent years. By 1993, the United Nations had such forces in seventeen countries, totaling 75,000 personnel at a cost of $3.29 billion annually. The most extensive involvement was its peacekeeping mission in Cambodia.

In many ways, the painful recent history of Cambodia reflects that of the world itself in the decades following World War II. It became a major battlefield in the cold war after escaping from colonial domination. The long struggle between the superpowers and their proxies for influence in Cambodia culminated in the ascension of an indigenous political force—a political movement marked by stark extremism that engaged in genocide on an immense scale. Indeed, the universal revulsion generated by the death and destruction brought by the Khmer Rouge in Cambodia transcended cold war rivalries, laying the foundation for the large-scale peacekeeping effort that has been in place since 1991.

With the salience of the United Nations' role in Cambodia in mind, the Twentieth Century Fund decided to support Janet Heininger's study of the UN peacekeeping mission. She emphasizes its effort to organize a democratic vote, and searches for general lessons from the Cambodian experience for other UN missions.

Heininger's study is one of the first to assess this experience comprehensively. Indeed, Heininger's in-depth analysis of the Cambodian case helps us to understand the extent and nature of the United Nations' successes and shortcomings—and it offers lessons for future peacekeeping enterprises.

On behalf of the Trustees of the Twentieth Century Fund, I thank her for this contribution to the work we have been and are continuing to sponsor on the new missions of international organizations. Two Fund projects, *Beyond Charity*, Gil Loescher's study of the role of the United Nations in dealing with refugees, and *U.S. Policy and the Future of the United Nations*, a collection of essays, were published in the past year; *Utopia Lost*, Rosemary Righter's analysis of the future of the United Nations, will be released this fall.

Richard C. Leone, *President*
The Twentieth Century Fund
September 1994

CONTENTS

ACKNOWLEDGMENTS

At a dinner hosted by the Aspen Institute's Indochina Policy Forum in 1991, Pauline Baker reminded me that I had been trained as an academic and encouraged me to go back and start writing again. Little did either of us know that this monograph would result from that conversation.

It has been my great pleasure to work with the Twentieth Century Fund toward the publication of this work. Harry Ozeroff persuaded the Fund to support it; Michelle Miller provided valuable suggestions for revising it; and Steven Greenfield's superb editing immeasurably improved it.

I wish to thank the people whose brains I picked and off whom I bounced ideas as I was preparing to write: Elizabeth Becker, senior foreign editor at National Public Radio; Fred Brown, director, Southeast Asian Studies Program, at Johns Hopkins University's Nitze School of Advanced International Studies; Maureen Steinbruner, president of the Center for National Policy; Ken Quinn, deputy assistant secretary of state in the Bureau of East Asian and Pacific Affairs; Richard Bush, committee liaison for the House Committee on Foreign Affairs; Steven Kentwell and Michael Smith, first secretary and minister for political affairs, respectively, at the Australian Embassy; and Jennifer Hills, UN district electoral supervisor in Battambang province. These people were exceedingly helpful in shaping my thinking about UNTAC.

I want to thank Richard Solomon, now president of the United States Institute of Peace, for clearing up an important point, and Jeanne Dixon and Joan Luke Hills at the United Nations Information Centre for their unfailing courtesy and helpfulness in tracking down important details on UN operations. Rick Kessler, of the Senate Foreign Relations Committee, graciously provided me with a copy of the committee's report on UN peacekeeping. Bill Durch, senior associate at the Henry L. Stimson Center, repeatedly helped clear up details about UN peacekeeping issues. Bob Sutter, senior specialist in the Foreign Affairs and National Defense Division of the Congressional

Research Service, made available CRS materials and wrote recommendations in support of my grant proposals (as did Fred Brown). Bill Herod, director of the Indochina Project, not only made the Project's files available to
me, but gave me valuable advice as well. Robert Muller, executive director of the Vietnam Veterans of America Foundation, provided useful information about the Cambodia Mine Action Centre.

I was privileged to hear Yasushi Akashi on numerous occasions during and after UNTAC's implementation when he came to Washington to report
in a variety of forums about UNTAC. I was also privileged to attend a lunch
with Lt. General John Sanderson, who spoke off-the-record, near the end
of UNTAC's mission, about his evaluation of the United Nations' experience
in Cambodia. Peter Swarbrick, who had been Akashi's assistant in Cambodia,
delved into his files to clarify details about the electoral process.

I particularly want to thank Jim Schear, now senior associate at the Henry
L. Stimson Center, who was policy consultant to Akashi in Cambodia. Not
only did he provide me with copies of all the most important UN documents,
but he was always available to clarify points, discuss matters pertaining to
UNTAC, as well as share his candid assessments. I am very grateful to
him for all his assistance.

I want to express my deep gratitude to the General Accounting Office,
and specifically Tetsuo Miyabara, senior evaluator with the National
Security and International Affairs Division, who made available GAO's
enormous cache of documents used to compile its report, *UN Peacekeeping:
Lessons Learned in Managing Recent Missions*, of December 1993. That material included GAO interviews and original UNTAC documents, as well as
GAO's own preliminary analyses.

I want to thank my children, Caroline and Theodore, who patiently
put up with the diversion of my attention while I was writing. Five-year-
old Theodore did tell me, however, that seven chapters was too many. I should
stop with the four I then had written, he said, because writing was making
me grumpy.

This monograph could never have been written without my hus-
band, James A. Reuter, who, though he knew little about Cambodia, took
the time to edit every draft of every chapter, even on nights when he would
come home at 1:00 a.m. during the mark-up of health-care reform legislation, and plunge, bleary-eyed, into yet another revision. His lack of
knowledge about Cambodia made him my best editor. If I couldn't make
it clear to him, it certainly wasn't going to fly elsewhere.

PEACEKEEPING IN TRANSITION

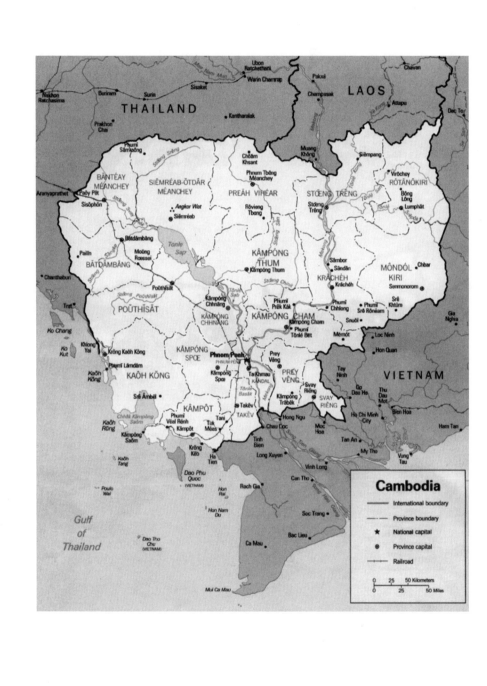

1

INTRODUCTION

A surprising thing happened in May 1993: the United Nations hosted an election in Cambodia, and the Khmer Rouge did not disrupt it. As little as ten days before the elections, it looked as if the 1991 peace accord might unravel through a violently disrupted or boycotted election. Contrary to most predictions, and in abrupt reversal of its actions leading up to the elections, the Khmer Rouge did not engage in a sustained campaign of terror and intimidation against Cambodia's voters. To the surprise of the international community—and probably to many Cambodians—the May 23–28 elections went off without any serious hitch. As a *New York Times* editorial put it: "In a surprising democratic triumph, more than 90 percent of eligible Cambodians braved death threats to cast their votes in an election that monitors certify as free and fair."[1]

What made the May elections so striking was that the effectiveness—and success—of one of the United Nations' largest, most ambitious, and costliest peacekeeping operations turned on the outcome of those elections. Had they not been certified as free and fair, or had they been violently disrupted by the Khmer Rouge, the UN operation would have been deemed a failure. Coupled with the increasing difficulties with UN operations in Bosnia-Herzegovina and Somalia, a failure in Cambodia would have been a serious blow for the United Nations. It would also have been a blow for the international community, which has increasingly turned to the United Nations to resolve problems that countries have neither the will nor the funds to tackle unilaterally or in regional coalitions.

On the surface, the UN mission in Cambodia must be judged a success. The elections were free and fair. The winner of the elections, Prince Norodom Sihanouk, established an interim coalition government. His son, Prince Norodom Ranariddh, and his rival, Hun Sen, who had been the

1

prime minister of the Vietnamese-installed Phnom Penh regime, joined together as cochairmen of the Interim Joint Administration, or Provisional National Government.[2] Even the Khmer Rouge president, Khieu Samphan, suggested in mid-July as he returned to Phnom Penh after a three-month, self-imposed exile, that the Khmer Rouge might call off its fourteen-year insurgency if it were guaranteed a formal role in the coalition government and if its troops were merged into a national army.[3]

The transition to a new government went more smoothly than had been expected. The newly elected Constituent Assembly began work on June 14, 1993. On September 21, it adopted a constitution that permitted Sihanouk to become king and effectively blocked Khmer Rouge participation in the new government by requiring that ministers and vice-ministers be chosen only from parties represented in the Assembly. Since the Khmer Rouge had refused to participate in the May elections, it had no elected representatives.[4]

The United Nations technically ended its eighteen-month operation on September 26, 1993, meeting the timetable set by the 1991 agreement that brought it to Cambodia.[5] The first contingent of peacekeeping troops withdrew on August 2, and the remainder by November 30, 1993.[6] Many of the United Nations' civilian workers had left by the middle of August.[7]

Yet, it is unclear whether the new government and King Sihanouk will be able to bring true peace to Cambodia. The Khmer Rouge's intentions remain suspect. As Marvin C. Ott of the National War College noted, "The current leadership of the Khmer Rouge is identical, to a man, to that which produced the killing fields. . . . If political maneuvers prove unfruitful, they will act upon the Maoist dictum that all political power grows out of the barrel of a gun. Having kept their military stockpiles and fighting units intact, the Khmer Rouge will get down to the business of the real 'election'—and this one will be conducted with weapons instead of ballots and terror instead of speeches."[8]

Khmer Rouge violence did not cease with the May 1993 elections. A series of sporadic attacks and government counterattacks took place throughout the rest of the year. In early December 1993, a Thai army unit was caught transporting largely Chinese-made weapons to the Khmer Rouge. The same day, Thai police raided a heavily guarded compound in Thailand's Chantaburi province and uncovered a vast arsenal in a dozen warehouses. A Cambodian arrested that day identified himself as a Khmer Rouge guerrilla and claimed that the weapons belonged to the Khmer Rouge. Senior Thai officials quickly attempted to hush up the episode and cover up the continuation of the close relationship between the Thai military and the Khmer Rouge.[9]

While some observers argue that continued Khmer Rouge violence is a strategy designed "to make it clear to the other factions that they will pay a terrible price in bloodshed if the Khmer Rouge are not given some sort of role in the Government," the group's longer-term objectives are unclear.[10] Although weakened by defections, the Khmer Rouge still controls parts of Cambodia with vast stocks of weapons and an army of an estimated 8,000 to 10,000 troops, and it has tens of millions of dollars stashed away in Thai banks.[11]

With the final verdict not in, therefore, the UN mission in Cambodia must be evaluated using criteria other than merely the conduct of the elections and the organization's success in meeting the timetable for conclusion of its mission.

THE EXPANSION OF UN PEACEKEEPING EFFORTS

In six years (1988–1993), the United Nations created eighteen new peacekeeping operations, compared with a total of thirteen in its first forty-three years. Five peacekeeping operations were established during 1988 and 1989, with an estimated cost of $629.8 million, 31 percent of which was paid by the United States. In 1991 and 1992, the UN Security Council created another nine operations.[12] In October 1993, there were seventeen active UN missions, compared to only five in 1987.[13] Sixteen were still active in January 1994.

In 1993, the United Nations spent $3.29 billion for seventeen missions and 80,000 peacekeepers on four continents.[14] This was more than twice the 1992 expenditure of $1.4 billion and nearly a sevenfold increase in the number of peacekeepers from just 11,500 at the beginning of 1992.[15]

The most ambitious of these operations was that in Cambodia. Called the United Nations Transitional Authority in Cambodia (UNTAC), it was established after the signing of a comprehensive peace plan in Paris by the various Cambodian factions and eighteen countries on October 23, 1991. UNTAC marked a major departure in UN peacekeeping. It was unique among UN peacekeeping operations in terms of its size, multidimensional mandate, complex administration, and unprecedented authority over a country. Despite its shortcomings, it sowed the seeds of democracy and human rights in Cambodia. Although authorized as a peacekeeping mission, it entailed far more.

PEACEKEEPING AND PEACE ENFORCEMENT MISSIONS

Traditional peacekeeping missions, like those in Cyprus, the Golan Heights, and Lebanon, interpose neutral UN military personnel between parties or governments that have agreed to stop fighting. In these operations, UN forces observe, monitor, supervise, or verify cease-fire and related agreements. Their purpose is to prevent further outbreaks of conflict and promote permanent settlement of disputes. They operate with the consent of the parties involved, tend to be lightly armed, and function under rules of engagement that permit them to fire back only in self-defense. One of the best definitions of how UN peacekeepers use force is William

Durch's description that "what constitutes appropriate self-defense will vary by mission, but because they are almost by definition outgunned by the disputants they are sent out to monitor, any recourse to force must be calibrated to localize and defuse, rather than escalate, violence."[16]

Traditional peacekeeping missions are authorized under Chapter VI of the UN Charter. Peacekeeping deployments are made after armed conflicts subside to ensure that agreements are implemented. They are premised on cooperation: their methods are inherently peaceful, and they help bridge the gap between the will to make peace and the achievement of it.[17]

At the opposite end of the spectrum are peace enforcement missions, like those in Somalia and the former Yugoslav republics. Peace enforcement missions are undertaken without the consent of the parties involved, when other strategies to deal with an armed conflict have failed and the international community concludes that armed intervention is warranted in response to an act of aggression or in order to maintain or restore international peace and security.

Historically, peace enforcement missions have been rare. During the entire cold war period, only two peace enforcement operations were undertaken by the United Nations: the Korean War in 1950 and the Congo mission in 1960. Since 1990, however, the United Nations has authorized four such missions.[18] In November 1990, the Security Council sanctioned military action, subsequently led by the United States, against Iraq's occupation of Kuwait. In December 1992, it approved an operation to restore order and permit delivery of food in Somalia—again, led by the United States. The third recent case was the authorization of measures to ensure safe delivery of humanitarian aid and freedom of movement of personnel in Bosnia-Herzegovina in 1992 and 1993. In July 1994, it authorized the United States to lead a multinational invasion of Haiti to drive out the military rulers and restore exiled president Jean-Bertrand Aristide to power.

In general, peace enforcement missions are authorized under Chapter VII of the UN Charter, which in Article 42 permits UN forces to "take such action by air, sea, or land forces as may be necessary to maintain or restore international peace and security."[19] Although neither Chapter VI nor Chapter VII explicitly mentions peacekeeping or peace enforcement, this language has been interpreted as permitting the use of force beyond self-defense to achieve the mission's objectives. Although neither the Korean War nor the Congo operation were authorized under Chapter VII, their mission definitions and extensive use of force qualify them as peace enforcement. The Korean War was undertaken to repel cross-border aggression, while the Congo operation was designed to prevent civil war.

Peace enforcement missions are dangerous, involve considerable risk to UN personnel, are exceedingly costly, and can be of long duration. By contrast with most traditional peacekeeping missions, UN personnel in peace enforcement operations may match the level of force arrayed against them, as in Korea, or outgun their opponents, as in Somalia. In cases where they are outgunned, though, as in the former Yugoslav republics, the enforcement side of the mission can easily run into trouble.

PEACE-BUILDING MISSIONS

Neither peacekeeping nor peace enforcement definitions fully describe the tasks undertaken by the United Nations in the wide array of missions embarked on since the end of the cold war. Mandates have become more complex, and the size, frequency, and makeup of peacekeeping missions have differed from the peacekeeping operations of the cold war period. In large part, this has been due to the international community's attempt to utilize peacekeeping for more than conflict management. In Namibia, El Salvador, Mozambique, the Western Sahara, Angola, and Cambodia, UN diplomatic efforts have been followed by peacekeeping operations with mandates that include conflict resolution.

Australian foreign minister Gareth Evans terms this departure "expanded peace keeping," describing it as a more activist, multifunctional move "to go far beyond traditional peace keeping by assisting the parties in implementing the settlement that they have arrived at in Stage II peace making, assisting them to bring about a genuine and durable solution."[20] In cases in which the mission involves containment or disarmament of belligerents, significantly more military force is needed than in traditional peacekeeping missions.

These new, multifaceted missions can include a variety of tasks: military, police, human rights, information, elections, rehabilitation, repatriation, and administration. They frequently involve facilitating the resolution of domestic conflicts or civil wars rather than cross-border disputes. Often, in situations where violence has been the result of ethnic conflicts or internal political struggle, the ultimate goal of these missions is the restoration of a stable democratic government, particularly if the conflict has caused the collapse of state institutions.

In his June 1992 report, *An Agenda for Peace*, UN secretary-general Boutros Boutros-Ghali used the term *peace-building* to describe these new tasks. Under this definition, postconflict peace-building is undertaken to prevent a recurrence of conflict by attempting to construct a new environment to consolidate peace. Measures to enhance a sense of confidence among the people may include "disarming the previously warring parties and the restoration of order, the custody and possible destruction of weapons, repatriating refugees, advisory and training support for security personnel, monitoring elections, advancing efforts to protect human rights, reforming or strengthening governmental institutions and promoting formal and informal processes of political participation."[21]

To rebuild societies that have been shattered by war or other major crises, the United Nations couples meeting basic humanitarian needs with activities to strengthen or reestablish institutions that engender confidence in a legitimate government. Peace-building also entails the education of a populace concerning its rights and responsibilities—a critical element in achieving a just and durable peace.

PEACEKEEPING AND PEACE-BUILDING IN NAMIBIA

The first UN operation to combine traditional peacekeeping with peace-building was the United Nations Transition Assistance Group (UNTAG) in Namibia from April 1989 to March 1990. UNTAG was designed to assist in the transition of Namibia to independence from South Africa. It performed traditional peacekeeping functions, including monitoring the cease-fire between the South African Defence Force (SADF) and the forces of the South West African People's Organization (SWAPO). But it also took on duties associated with peace-building by monitoring elections for a constituent assembly that were run by South Africa's administrator general and by monitoring the South African police to ensure that they were not being used for political intimidation.[22]

While UNTAG's peacekeeping functions were essential to the performance of its mission, its most important—and successful—roles fell into the category of peace-building. "UNTAG was to serve as a counterweight to South Africa's presence, to behave impartially, and to monitor and reinforce a climate of security. But most important, it was to build confidence in and to legitimize the peace process, the elections, and the result of the transition: the new state of Namibia."[23]

EXPANDING ON PEACEKEEPING AND PEACE-BUILDING IN CAMBODIA

At the time it was established, the operation in Cambodia was the most extensive and expensive UN peacekeeping effort ever.[24] Although subsequently exceeded in size and cost by the Somalia mission, which at its height had more than 28,000 troops, and by the nearly 28,000-person operation in the former Yugoslav republics, no mission has matched that in Cambodia for the scope of responsibilities, the number of countries represented in the staffing (more than one hundred, with thirty alone involved in the military component), or the degree of control exercised by the United Nations over the internal workings of a country.[25]

Unlike Namibia, where it oversaw the transition to independence and supervised elections held by South African authorities, the United Nations was mandated to assume the actual management of Cambodia and take it through the transition from civil war through free elections to the establishment of a democratically elected government. In Cambodia, the United Nations ran the elections, rather than merely monitoring them.

More than any previous or subsequent UN mission, UNTAC stretched the concept of peace-building to the limit.

At the same time, as a mission authorized under Chapter VI, it was a peacekeeping operation, designed to uphold an agreement to stop fighting. Although hostilities continued throughout UNTAC's tenure, the United Nations resisted pressure to turn the mission into one engaged in peace enforcement.

UNTAC's success or failure is widely believed to have profound implications not only for Cambodia's future peace and stability, but for future UN peacekeeping efforts overall. There has been no consensus, however, on what constitutes success in Cambodia, beyond the conduct of free and fair elections. The uneasiness about making judgments regarding UNTAC's long-term effect in Cambodia stems largely from the continued threat of the Khmer Rouge to the country's stability.

Nevertheless, by its very size, scope, and cost, UNTAC represented a turning point for the United Nations. The testing of a new model combining peace-building with peacekeeping held important lessons for the future. Demonstrating weaknesses, as well as strengths, in peace-building may be Cambodia's most useful contribution to the evolution of UN peace efforts. Given the problems encountered by the United Nations' peace enforcement mission in Somalia in 1993, its experience in Cambodia suggests that peace-building may be more realistic—and perhaps more important—than peace enforcement in the post-cold war world.

No one operation—UNTAC or any other—can be a complete model for future peacekeeping efforts. UNTAC's chief significance lies in how it can illuminate which aspects of the peace-building mission in Cambodia may be transferable or applied to future UN operations. In that sense, it is less important to determine whether UNTAC was a "success" than it is to evaluate why certain elements of UNTAC worked well. By the same token, an assessment of what did not work well in UNTAC can suggest areas to which the United Nations should devote particular attention in future operations. The focus of this examination, therefore, is less on whether UNTAC will bring peace to Cambodia than on what can be learned from UNTAC that can make future peacekeeping/peace-building efforts more effective.[26]

In the wake of the U.S. casualties in Somalia in October 1993, the Clinton administration pulled back from its initial emphasis on peacekeeping as a central feature of its foreign policy. In his campaign rhetoric, Bill Clinton called for a UN "'rapid deployment force . . . standing guard at the borders of countries threatened by aggression, preventing mass violence against civilian populations, providing relief and combating terrorism.'"[27] Multilateral action was to be the key to maintaining U.S. influence abroad in an era of scarce resources and budget cutbacks. But the turbulent American experience in Somalia, the intractable situation in Haiti, and the fear of bogging down in the war in Bosnia-Herzegovina amid unclear political and security goals and potentially high costs all contributed to the Clinton administration's decision to set high thresholds for the use of U.S. troops in UN missions in a presidential directive on peacekeeping drafted in early 1994.

In pulling back from greater reliance on UN peacekeeping, the Clinton administration risks throwing the baby out with the bathwater. UN peacekeeping can work. Missions in Mozambique and El Salvador are proving to be successful. It is not a panacea for conflict. But following a few guidelines—some of which can be drawn from UNTAC—can enhance the chances for success and increase the likelihood that the people of the United States will support peacekeeping and peace-building missions.

2

THE NEGOTIATION OF THE PEACE PLAN

A s with all negotiations, the path to the 1991 agreement on a peace plan for Cambodia, often called the Paris Accords or Paris Agreements, was circuitous, marked by fits and starts, and, more often than not, deemed by most observers as unlikely to lead to a fruitful settlement. The accords, shaped largely in 1990 but not finalized until October 1991, were not a solution to Cambodia's problems per se, but rather a face-saving framework that allowed the parties most immediately involved (the four factions: the Vietnamese-backed Communist regime and the three armies arrayed against it, those of Prince Sihanouk, Son Sann, and the Khmer Rouge) to jockey for control in a manner that met the needs of the international community in a changed political environment. Some would say that the 1991 agreement allowed the international community to wash its hands of the Cambodia problem in a universally accepted way. With the agreement in place, the problem was turned over to the United Nations, and outside parties, concerned but reluctant to be involved, could sit back and see how things worked out.

The Paris Accords became the stage on which the Chinese—supporting the three rebel factions, particularly the Khmer Rouge—and the Vietnamese could do their Kabuki act and slowly back off, matching each other step by step. Neither side could say it had won or lost. The decisions to withdraw, arrived at separately, established new ground rules for the Cambodian factions struggling for power: neither China nor Vietnam would get back in the game. These decisions made the framework for a peace agreement possible and allowed each foreign patron to end its military supply relationship with its surrogate. China and Vietnam saw it in their interest to make the peace agreement work and never wavered from that position.[1]

In many ways, the Cambodia problem shifted focus during the 1980s. Many observers agree that at the outset—after Vietnam's December 1978 invasion of Cambodia and the establishment of a pro-Vietnamese client regime in Phnom Penh—the Cambodia conflict was essentially a struggle between China and Vietnam for hegemony over Indochina. But even as it became an externally supported civil war, the main obstacle to a negotiated settlement lay in the inability of the Cambodian factions to share power, or even to conceive of the survival of their particular faction without the exclusion of all rivals.[2] Solution of the internal conflict over power sharing, however, was contingent on the outside powers ending their use of Cambodia as a pawn in their own struggles.

According to Douglas Pike,

> The central factor in the Cambodian peace process always has been governance, the institutionalisation of political power. Who is to govern and under what arrangements; how is power to be divided, and how are the divisions to be maintained. . . . The opposite of war in Cambodia is not peace; it is government. . . . [I]f there is government there can be peace; without government continued warfare is inevitable.[3]

What the Paris Accords attempted to provide was a means to attain a government that could resolve the debate over power-sharing and be recognized internationally as legitimate. Such a government, the international community hoped, would be able to attract the assistance needed to rebuild the country, which had been devastated by Khmer Rouge rule and fifteen subsequent years of warfare.

1980–87: STALEMATE

During the 1980s, the Phnom Penh government engaged in sporadic warfare with the Khmer Rouge and the two smaller, non-Communist resistance forces led by Prince Sihanouk and former prime minister Son Sann. All three resistance forces received assistance from China, although military aid went overwhelmingly to the Khmer Rouge. The non-Communist resistance received material support and political backing from the United States and the ASEAN countries (Thailand, Malaysia, Singapore, Indonesia, the Philippines, and Brunei). International support largely coalesced around the Coalition Government of Democratic Kampuchea (CGDK), a paper coalition of the non-Communist factions and the Khmer Rouge. The CGDK was formed at Western insistence in 1982 to prevent Cambodia's UN seat from falling into Soviet hands via the Vietnamese client regime in Phnom Penh.

Much of the stalemate of the 1980s owed to outside powers allowing their surrogates to fight their battle for them in Cambodia, with each side following an almost identical strategy designed to carry on a war of attrition. Each believed that time was on its side, that it would be able to outlast its opponent and profit politically from the other's exhaustion.[4]

The lines were firmly drawn. China backed the Khmer Rouge. Vietnam and the Soviet Union backed the Phnom Penh regime. ASEAN, the United States, and other Western countries supported the non-Communist resistance. The problem was defined by the United States and the West in cold war terms, with a determination to oppose Soviet influence in Indochina and to roll back Vietnamese aggression. For the most part, the United States did not view the Cambodia problem through the lens of regional competition for hegemony.

At the same time, the Vietnamese remained bogged down in support of their client, largely because Chinese military assistance enabled the Khmer Rouge to keep pressure on the Phnom Penh regime. The willingness of the Thai military to act as a conduit for weapons to the Khmer Rouge continued unabated, despite repeated requests by the Americans and others to stop. The Vietnamese invasion had reignited Thai fears of a resurgent Vietnam. Since Thailand wanted a neutral Cambodian buffer state, successive Thai governments turned a blind eye to the army's support for the Khmer Rouge.

China's goals were to reverse Vietnam's gain in Cambodia and to limit any further expansion of Vietnamese power. To that end, China's strategy was to pin down Vietnamese resources by maintaining military pressure on the Sino-Vietnamese border and by arming the Khmer Rouge to oppose Vietnam in Cambodia, effectively impeding Vietnam's economic growth by forcing it to devote a huge percentage of its GDP to defense spending.[5] As one Western diplomat noted, "The Chinese don't love the Khmer Rouge for themselves, they love them as a cheap weapon for bashing the Vietnamese."[6]

The Soviet Union's support for Vietnam was of long-standing duration, predating Vietnam's invasion of Cambodia, and predicated on its own competition with China. That support, however, was expensive. It took Mikhail Gorbachev's disenchantment with the costs—both monetary and political—of that support to start to alter the global environment and permit movement toward a Cambodian peace settlement.

As Gorbachev moved to cap the drain on Soviet resources (estimated at roughly $3 billion annually in Indochina alone), pressure increased on Vietnam. At the same time, the battlefield situation was at a stalemate, with fewer and fewer offensives of any consequence. The deterioration of Vietnam's economy, which accelerated in the mid-1980s, and the accession to power of a new generation of younger leaders in 1986–87, resulted in an atmosphere more conducive to compromise.

Attempts to mediate the conflict had been made sporadically throughout the 1980s by Japan, Australia, and Indonesia, particularly in

1984 and early 1985. The time, however, was not right. Vietnam still hoped for a battlefield victory, and, for the most part, the major actors seemed content with the status quo. Mediation attempts focused on extracting concessions from Vietnam in Cambodia but failed to deal with the underlying problem of Sino-Vietnamese competition for hegemony. Although these early mediation efforts were unsuccessful, one did lay some of the groundwork for the 1991 agreement. In 1984, a Japanese proposal set forth principles that, with some modifications, were eventually incorporated into the final settlement: 1) withdrawal of Vietnamese troops; 2) free elections supervised by an international peacekeeping force; and 3) large-scale international aid for the three Indochinese states.[7]

1988 AND 1989: THE PEACE PROCESS ACCELERATES

In mid-to-late 1987, an agreement by Vietnam and Indonesia launched a series of informal talks on Cambodia between the Cambodian factions and other interested parties. These talks were formalized during 1988 and 1989, although little apparent progress was made. Differences always remained within the same context: disagreement on the composition of a peacekeeping force, the timetable for Vietnamese withdrawal, and the nature of a transitional authority to oversee the elections.

In August 1985, Vietnam had announced it would withdraw all its troops from Cambodia by 1990. On April 5, 1989, feeling economically pressed as Soviet aid declined, Vietnam moved up the withdrawal date to September 1989, setting no conditions for progress on a political settlement.[8] There has been disagreement about whether all troops were withdrawn on that timetable, or whether some were reintroduced later as Phnom Penh's military stumbled in its solo efforts to combat the Khmer Rouge. Nevertheless, withdrawal of Vietnam's forces substantially altered the negotiating environment.

The United States had long used Vietnamese occupation of Cambodia (as well as unaccounted-for P.O.W.-M.I.A.s) as a rationale for refusing to normalize relations with Vietnam. Although the United States and the Western powers had been involved in the negotiating process during 1988 and 1989, their somewhat desultory and lackluster participation gave the appearance that the status quo remained acceptable. The situation changed in late 1989, when various pressures came to a head.

The international nongovernmental organizations operating in Cambodia had become increasingly dissatisfied with the country's continued diplomatic and economic isolation. They saw things changing for the better under the Phnom Penh regime. Some members of these organizations, Oxfam in particular, began to argue that the provision of international aid to reconstruct the country would do more than anything else to move Cambodia toward peace and help neutralize the Khmer Rouge threat. They were also concerned that half of the population was under the age of fifteen and thus had no personal recollection of the Khmer Rouge regime. As a result, they were more susceptible to the Khmer Rouge's appeal in the countryside as the military leader of the resistance against Vietnam's puppet regime in Phnom Penh. The relief agencies' sentiments were echoed in the press by commentators who also wanted to end Cambodia's diplomatic isolation for humanitarian reasons.

The Khmer Rouge was also setting off alarm bells in the United States. Congress began to express discomfort as the non-Communist resistance's increasingly close military coordination with the Khmer Rouge became exposed.[9] U.S. law made it illegal to provide aid to any organization cooperating with the Khmer Rouge. A debate between Congress and the Bush administration over Cambodia policy picked up steam. In 1989, the Bush administration toyed with the idea of providing military aid to the non-Communist resistance, but that trial balloon went nowhere in Congress.

Internationally as well, pressure increased to bring Cambodia back into the family of nations. In late 1989, Britain joined Australia with quasi-diplomatic representation in Phnom Penh. That move was protested by the United States, which had requested that Britain not initiate discussions with the Phnom Penh regime.[10]

Direct talks between Prince Sihanouk and Prime Minister Hun Sen had taken place as early as December 1987. As the negotiating process intensified in 1989, these talks became an important mechanism for moving the process forward. While the talks may not have been decisive in the eventual conclusion of an agreement, they were important in garnering Hun Sen legitimacy, both for himself and for the Phnom Penh regime. They also re-solidified Sihanouk's position as titular head of Cambodia, and made other interested parties somewhat nervous about the possibility of a separate peace that might fail to address their own concerns.

At this stage of the negotiating process, the most basic conflict revolved around the role of the Khmer Rouge in an interim government. ASEAN, the CGDK, China, and the United States endorsed Sihanouk's proposal for a quadripartite coalition government representing all factions in the period leading to elections. Vietnam and the Phnom Penh regime adamantly insisted that the Khmer Rouge not be permitted a role in the interim government. The Phnom Penh regime feared that a quadripartite interim government would supplant its own administration. Worse, it would grant legitimacy to the Khmer Rouge, allowing it to return to power someday, regardless of any promises of good behavior on its part.

1989 PARIS INTERNATIONAL CONFERENCE ON CAMBODIA

On July 30, 1989, an international conference on Cambodia convened for a month in Paris. This conference marked the point at which the efforts of the five permanent members of the Security Council (the so-called

Perm Five) superseded other negotiating tracks. At the opening ministe-
rial-level meeting, they reached consensus on a blueprint for peace and agreed
to dispatch a UN fact-finding mission to Cambodia. The blueprint laid out
goals for a settlement, including withdrawal of all foreign forces under international supervision; voluntary return of refugees; preparing for Cambodia's
economic reconstruction; restoration of its independence; guaranteeing
its sovereignty, territorial integrity, and neutrality; supporting peace and
national reconciliation; and self-determination through elections under international control. Working groups were established to determine how to reach
these goals. After the foreign ministers left, however, the conference
foundered on the central issue of the composition of an interim government and participation by the Khmer Rouge in it. The conferees failed to
reach agreement on a comprehensive peace plan or on international
supervision of the upcoming Vietnamese withdrawal. They also left unresolved the issue of whether to use the word "genocide" to describe Khmer
Rouge rule from April 1975 to Vietnam's invasion in December 1978.[11]
Although its goals ultimately were met by the Paris Accords, at its conclusion the conference was viewed largely as a failure.

While the Khmer Rouge issue had been festering for a long time, it became
acute in mid-1989 as the international community concluded that the
Vietnamese troop withdrawal would leave Cambodia vulnerable to intensified guerrilla attacks. Observers and Western diplomats warned that
civil war was likely to be renewed after Vietnam withdrew, since the Phnom
Penh regime had demonstrated little ability to combat the Khmer Rouge
effectively. Nor did it appear that Vietnam's nearly eleven-year occupation
and 200,000-plus troops had substantially eroded Khmer Rouge strength.[12]

As alarm grew about the Khmer Rouge as a military threat, a Khmer
Rouge role in an interim government increasingly became the chief obstacle in the negotiations. The Perm Five disagreed on Sihanouk's proposal
to include the Khmer Rouge. The Soviet Union backed Vietnam's and
Hun Sen's insistence on excluding the Khmer Rouge, while China supported
its client. While the Americans vehemently opposed a return to power by
the Pol Pot and his associates, if Sihanouk insisted that there was a better
chance for peace if the Khmer Rouge were included in an interim government,
then they would defer to his wishes. At a February 1989 press conference,
Sihanouk's son, Prince Norodom Ranariddh, defended Sihanouk's insistence on the inclusion of the Khmer Rouge. "Not only members of my family but a lot of Cambodian people were killed at that time. . . . But for the
time being . . . we have to talk about a real national reconciliation."[13]

The logic of national reconciliation with the Khmer Rouge as the
basis for a settlement struck numerous observers as ludicrous—dangerous
at minimum, naive at best. As Lorna Hahn wrote in a *Washington Post* op-
ed piece in January 1989:

Suppose that at the close of World War II, we Americans had argued that the Nazis should be included in the postwar German government. After all, a great many Germans had supported the Nazi Party; including it in a new coalition would constitute an act of national reconciliation, while preventing the Nazis from becoming an obstructionist force. Furthermore, as the Nazis were firmly opposed to the Soviet Union, their participation in the government would have helped to ensure that Germany would be a bulwark against Soviet expansionism.

Of course, no such argument was ever seriously considered. To the contrary; we vowed to eliminate all vestiges of a force whose conduct—including the slaughter and torture of vast numbers of Germany's own citizens—had violated the most basic norms of civilized behavior. Why, then, are we now considering the inclusion of an equally barbarous group in the government of a liberated Cambodia?[14]

Even the *Washington Post,* which had been less insistent than the *New York Times* on the need for the United States to distance itself from the Khmer Rouge, concluded after the July–August 1989 Paris International Conference on Cambodia that the future lay with Hun Sen instead of Sihanouk, if Sihanouk continued to link himself with the Khmer Rouge.

The United States went to Paris insisting that its overwhelming priority was to fence-out the Khmer Rouge. But American diplomacy has yet to grant the politically distasteful but undeniable fact that the vital instrument to achieve this goal is not the weak and uncertain non-Communist opposition of Prince Sihanouk and former prime minister Son Sann, but the tough and well-armed Communist opposition led by Vietnam's Cambodian choice, former Khmer Rouge officer Hun Sen. American officials sought to bridge the gap by encouraging the prince to deal with Hun Sen, but he had another game in mind and chose to stay in league with the deadly Khmer Rouge.

The terrible truth seems to be that unless and until the United States can bring itself to rely on Hun Sen, it will not have a relevant role in keeping the Khmer Rouge from bidding again for power.[15]

THE AUSTRALIAN PROPOSAL

To the surprise of many, the Vietnamese withdrawal took place as scheduled on September 26, 1989. It was, however, accompanied by the expected charges that withdrawal was not complete. Lacking an agreement for international verification of the withdrawal, most of the international community concluded that it was about as complete as could have been reasonably expected and that Phnom Penh had been left to sink or swim. As the Phnom Penh regime floundered, Vietnam probably sent advisers, and may have sent troops to assist, but it soon became a nonissue to all but the most rabid who claimed a continuing, clandestine foreign troop presence in order to stir up the countryside.

The more important issue was how to restart the stalled negotiations. The peace process was resuscitated by Australian foreign minister Gareth Evans when he resurrected an earlier proposal by U.S. congressman Stephen Solarz. Solarz had suggested an enhanced role for the United Nations in the transition process as a means of breaking the stalemate over the composition of the interim administration.[16] On November 24, Evans proposed that the United Nations be directly involved in the civil administration of Cambodia during a transition period leading to elections that the United Nations would organize and conduct. All four Cambodian factions would be allowed to take part in the elections and would agree to abide by the results. Evans proposed that Cambodia's UN seat be left vacant during the transition period.[17] Coming as it did when pressure to resolve the conflict was escalating in the wake of Vietnam's withdrawal, Evans's proposal neatly sidestepped the issue of power-sharing by giving the United Nations the task of running the country. His efforts set the negotiations on the track to completion.

The Australian proposal offered something for everyone. The Khmer Rouge would be allowed to participate in elections, although many observers believed that it would get minimal support and thus would be unlikely to figure in the postelection government.[18] The proposal met Sihanouk's concerns by including the Khmer Rouge, although he continued to prefer a quadripartite interim government. The Hun Sen regime found a vacant UN seat attractive because it denied international legitimacy to the CGDK and the Khmer Rouge. Moreover, the Phnom Penh regime was confident it could win the election.[19] It was nearly two years, however, before the mechanisms and details could be hammered out that would allow all parties to reach a final agreement.

Evans's proposal for the United Nations to take over civil administration of Cambodia was a radical departure for the international organization, which had long ago shed itself of "trusteeship" responsibilities as relics of colonialism. By placing the running of Cambodia in the hands of the United Nations, Evans's proposal had the effect of initiating a two-track process of discussions among the Perm Five in conjunction with the Paris Conference process.

Proposal for a Supreme National Council

What finally resolved the issue of power-sharing was a proposal that emerged in late 1989 for a Supreme National Council (SNC) composed of representatives of the four factions that would nominally govern

Cambodia during the period leading to elections. Since agreement among the factions on governance issues was likely to be elusive, however, it was expected that the SNC would turn many, if not most, of its powers over to the United Nations.[20]

According to Richard Bush, then staff consultant to Congressman Solarz on the House Foreign Affairs Committee, in the wake of the disappointing 1989 Paris Conference and the presentation of the Australian proposal, informal discussions took place, particularly within the U.S. government, on how to reconcile a role for the United Nations with Cambodian sovereignty. Since the international community did not recognize the legitimacy of the Phnom Penh regime, it was unclear who had the authority to invite the United Nations to be directly involved in running the country. Because power-sharing was one of the chief causes of the deadlock at the 1989 Paris Conference, a structure for interim political arrangements had to be devised that could assume, in theory at least, the powers associated with a sovereign government, even while the United Nations took effective charge of the country's civil administration. According to Bush, the State Department's Cambodian desk officer suggested that a council representing the factions assume those functions.[21] The first public mention of such a council was in the first ever joint statement signed by Hun Sen and Sihanouk after their February 1990 meeting in Bangkok.[22]

The development of the concept of a panfactional council resolved several important problems. It settled the issue of Cambodian sovereignty by devolving onto the council the authority to invite the United Nations to undertake responsibilities associated with the Paris Accords. It also answered the more central question of the legitimacy of an interim authority during the period leading to elections. It responded to the power-sharing issue by allowing most of the international community to maintain that the Phnom Penh regime was not the legitimate government of Cambodia—thus relegating it to a factional status commensurate with the other three—met China's concerns by granting the Khmer Rouge a legitimate place at the table, and, in its final composition, reassured Vietnam and Hun Sen by giving disproportionate weight to the Phnom Penh regime over the resistance factions.

At the Jakarta Informal Meeting on Cambodia held February 26–28, 1990, Australia presented a detailed series of working papers on the bases of a settlement. There was general acceptance of a significant role for the United Nations in organizing and conducting elections, overseeing a cease-fire and cessation of outside military assistance to all parties, and verifying the withdrawal of foreign forces (specifically Vietnamese, given continuing allegations, particularly from the Khmer Rouge, that Vietnam's withdrawal had not been complete). Agreement on the framework could not be reached, however, because of the conferees' inability to define either the

UN role in the interim civil administration of Cambodia or the authority and composition of an interim Supreme National Council.[23]

As the *New York Times* noted,

> Mr. Hun Sen wants his administration to remain intact, but is willing to have the United Nations monitor its work, with veto power over any act that might affect the impartiality of elections to be organized by the United Nations. . . . The Khmer Rouge and its non-Communist allies, the followers of Prince Norodom Sihanouk and of a former prime minister, Son Sann, want a dismantling of Prime Minister Hun Sen's administration in Phnom Penh. They want the United Nations to run Cambodia "from top to bottom," as Prince Sihanouk's son, Prince Norodom Ranariddh, said today, but to be responsible to a Supreme National Council made up of the three allied factions and the Cambodian Government.[24]

Indications of how the Khmer Rouge would eventually react to the implementation of the Paris Accords first appeared at the Jakarta meeting. The Khmer Rouge's strenuous objections to labeling its activities during the years it controlled Cambodia as "genocide" was one reason the meeting broke down.[25] The Khmer Rouge succeeded in the end in getting references to genocide removed from the final settlement agreement. But this success may have led it to believe that intransigence was an effective tool.

Signs warning of the Khmer Rouge's eventual noncompliance with the Paris Accords extended to other areas as well. The non-Communist factions had initially agreed with the Khmer Rouge in wanting the complete dismantling of the administrative apparatus of the Phnom Penh regime, with responsibility ceded to the Supreme National Council and the United Nations. In the long run, however, the non-Communist factions switched sides. They recognized the futility of breaking up the only functioning public service network throughout the country. They realized that total UN control over Cambodia's civil administration was not feasible and that the Supreme National Council, in all likelihood, was seldom going to reach agreement on the most important issues. Only the Khmer Rouge never gave up on expecting the Phnom Penh regime's administration to be taken apart. It clung to that position as the rationale for its noncompliance with the Paris Accords and nonparticipation in the electoral process.

It is unclear whether the Khmer Rouge was deluding itself about what the United Nations could or would undertake in agreeing to run Cambodia in the interim period or whether, having staked out a position, it felt backed into a corner from which it could not emerge. Despite the fact that the entire international community, the United Nations, and the other three factions were arrayed against it, the Khmer Rouge never wavered from its insistence that the UN was "supposed" to dismantle the Phnom Penh regime from "top to bottom."

REGIONAL MOVES TOWARD A DEAL

In late spring and early summer 1990, the regional players, particularly Thailand, China, and Japan, began to probe for solutions independent of the stalled Perm Five process, which was predicated on the assumption that only a comprehensive settlement that included all four factions would suffice to induce China to cut off military aid to the Khmer Rouge. Both China and Thailand began jockeying that spring to find a vehicle that would result in peace but on terms that would best promote their own interests.

Thailand's first democratically elected prime minister, Chatichai Choonhavan, suggested a three-way meeting of Thailand, China, and Vietnam to seek regional accords.[26] He had long been pressing for a step-by-step rather than a comprehensive settlement, beginning with a cease-fire. Those efforts, which resulted in agreement in late May by all four factions to sign a cease-fire, were opposed by the United States, which believed that Chatichai's approach leaned too far in the direction of the Phnom Penh regime.[27] The United States also viewed Chatichai's overtures unfavorably because they appeared to be motivated in part by his willingness to recognize the "reality" of the Phnom Penh regime so the "Indochina battlefield" could be turned into a "marketplace dominated by Bangkok."[28] Assistant Secretary of State Richard Solomon was reported as stating in Bangkok that "a cease-fire is 'not likely to get people anywhere' unless progress is made on a comprehensive solution. 'We remain committed to a comprehensive solution and would not want to encourage developments that seem to go off in another direction.'"[29]

Although China also objected to a separate deal, it made overtures to both Thailand and Vietnam that spring that signaled it was getting ready to move on Cambodia. It requested that Thailand convene a meeting with China, Vietnam, Laos, and Indonesia to seek a regional settlement on Cambodia. On May 8, China presented secret proposals to Vietnamese deputy foreign minister Dinh Ngo Liem in an unusually high-level meeting in Beijing convened to discuss Cambodia. Written proposals were passed several days later to the United States, the Soviet Union, Great Britain, and France in a Cambodia-related meeting in New York.[30]

"'The Chinese want to cut a deal,' said a source close to Chatichai in evaluating the proposals from Beijing. A U.S. official said China's decision to initiate moves toward settlement of the war may reflect a desire to improve its sagging international standing as well as a belief in Beijing that

Vietnam is in a weaker position than before and may be forced to accept terms close to those which the Chinese desire."[31]

Movement toward cutting a deal also reflected Deng Xiaoping's personal stake in relations with Vietnam. As a senior U.S. government official noted, Deng was getting old. He wanted to clean the slate with Vietnam and remove any lingering slur on his years of ruling China. Specifically, Deng wanted to rectify the loss of face incurred by his humiliating defeat when China invaded Vietnam early in 1979 to "teach Vietnam a lesson" for its invasion of Cambodia.[32] (The four-week battle resulted in 50,000 deaths—20,000 Chinese and 30,000 Vietnamese—about the same as the number of Americans killed in Vietnam between 1961 and 1975.[33]) Using the Khmer Rouge as a weapon against Vietnam in Cambodia had not yet worked, nor was there any prospect of success. Only the diplomatic arena offered Deng remediation.[34] At the same time, in the wake of the June 1989 Tiananmen Square massacre, China was seeking outlets for international acceptance. A settlement in Cambodia could go a long way to restore China's image.

China's proposals focused on a two-sided Supreme National Council: one side representing the Phnom Penh regime and the other representing the three resistance factions. China proposed that Sihanouk be named head of the SNC. However, it was not clear whether he would be empowered to break tie votes or exercise real authority.[35] Beijing suggested two alternative arrangements under which the SNC could function in the interim period: it could be a strong body empowered to run Cambodia, with a weak role for the United Nations, or it could be a weak body working with a relatively strong United Nations that would organize elections.[36] Ultimately, the latter option was adopted. China's presentation of these proposals demonstrated its seriousness about finding a workable structure for interim political arrangements. In opting for a two-sided SNC, it signaled its willingness to move away from insistence on equal status for the Khmer Rouge. In doing so, China placed its own desire for a resolution to the conflict above the interests of its chief client faction.

THE TOKYO MEETING, JUNE 1990

The lack of consensus on the role and composition of the Supreme National Council continued to cause problems at a two-day meeting in Tokyo in early June. The cease-fire agreement, brokered by Thailand, had been signed by all four factions in advance of the meeting. That agreement incorporated China's proposal for the establishment of a two-sided Supreme National Council composed of six representatives of the Phnom Penh regime and six representatives of the resistance factions.[37] Sihanouk and Hun Sen agreed to this formally in two-way talks at the Tokyo meeting in spite of a Khmer Rouge boycott over being included in Sihanouk's coalition delegation rather than being accorded separate status.[38] China's role in proposing a two-sided SNC may explain the Khmer Rouge's boycott of the Tokyo meeting.

The Tokyo meeting was a major turning point in the process that culminated in the Paris Accords. The exchange of proposals preceding the meeting, which signaled that the regional players were preparing for a deal, and the meeting itself represented an attempt by the regional players to insert themselves more forcefully into the peace process. The participation of Thailand and Japan helped to catalyze negotiations that were proceeding on several tracks simultaneously. Both the Thais and the Japanese had been pressing for a more direct role in the peace process. Japan's economic might, its nonpartisan interest in a regional solution, and its active role dating from the early 1980s in trying to end the Cambodian conflict created widespread expectations that it would pay a significant share of the costs of implementing any peace agreement.

AUGUST 1990: AGREEMENT ON THE PERM FIVE'S FRAMEWORK FOR A PEACE PLAN

As the summer proceeded, however, momentum shifted away from the regional players and back to the Perm Five. On July 17, the Perm Five announced they had made progress toward agreement on an outline for a peace formula, including on interim political arrangements. While moving away from the concept of a two-sided SNC to one of individuals representing all shades of opinion, they agreed that the Supreme National Council would assume sovereign powers in the transition period and thus could delegate authority to the United Nations. This resolved the issue of how to deal with Cambodia's sovereignty during the transition period, but left open, yet again, the issue of the composition of the SNC.[39]

Over a period of eight months, the working groups that had been established to determine how to reach the goals set at the 1989 Paris Conference had held detailed talks that were based largely on the Australian working documents presented in Jakarta in February 1990 to try to craft the main elements of a comprehensive peace plan. These talks, punctuated by occasional high-level Perm Five meetings, continued in spite of regional efforts at a more piecemeal approach. On August 28, 1990, the Perm Five announced that it had reached agreement on a framework for peace.[40] It covered five areas: administration of Cambodia during the transitional period; military arrangements; UN-organized elections; human rights protection; and international guarantees relating to Cambodian sovereignty.[41] This became the basis for the eventual agreement signed in October 1991.

Particularly important, the accord framework fleshed out the Australian proposal for interim UN civil administration of Cambodia. It stipulated that the "administrative agencies, bodies and offices which could directly influence the outcome of elections"—specifically the five areas of "foreign affairs, national defence, finance, public security and information"—should be placed under "direct UN supervision or control."[42] The press interpreted this as the United Nations supervising or controlling the Phnom Penh regime's five major ministries, overlooking the fact that the mandate also covered the (admittedly minimal or inaccessible) administrative apparatus of the three resistance factions.[43] This formality was essential during the negotiating process and UNTAC's tenure to maintain evenhanded treatment of all four factions. Nonetheless, all parties understood that the United Nations' primary focus would be the extensive apparatus of the Phnom Penh authorities.

The United Nations would also verify a cease-fire, supervise disarmament, organize elections, and ensure that all Vietnamese troops had withdrawn from Cambodia. The accord framework set out conditions for disarmament of the four factions that involved regrouping the factions' forces into cantonments while turning their arms over to the United Nations.[44]

The significance of the framework document lay not merely in the spelling out of the details of UN administration of Cambodia, or in the proposal for the establishment of a Supreme National Council that broke the deadlock over power-sharing. Its importance lay in the commitment—for the first time—of the five permanent members of the Security Council to a plan for ending the Cambodian civil war. A *Washington Post* editorial noted that the agreement "marks a breakthrough on a major and heretofore divisive, explosive and intractable regional issue. It demonstrates the awesome capability of a Security Council working the way the founders of the United Nations intended."[45]

One of the interesting facets of the United Nations' experience in Cambodia was the unity that was demonstrated by the international community in reaching this comprehensive settlement, even though it took another year before all parties were prepared to sign and implement it. This unwavering commitment was apparent in how each of the extraregional powers wielded its influence over its respective client factions.

> Moscow, by cutting aid and retreating from empire, is applying pressure to its clients in Hanoi and Phnom Penh; Washington, exploiting its new Indochina policy statement of July [which involved withdrawal of recognition of the CGDK], is wielding the incentive of normalizing relations with the local Communist regimes. Beijing proclaims a serious intent to rein in the Khmer Rouge, whose arms it supplies, in the context of a regional settlement. The British and French are applying their influence. The Japanese, are, fortunately, working too.[46]

SELLING THE FRAMEWORK TO THE FACTIONS: THE JAKARTA MEETING, SEPTEMBER 9–10, 1990

After the framework for an agreement was adopted in August, the international community still had to sell it to the factions. This was done successfully at a two-day meeting in Jakarta on September 9–10, 1990. Using the Tokyo formula rather than the one proposed by the Perm Five in July, the factions agreed to establish a twelve-member Supreme National Council, with six representatives from the Phnom Penh regime and two from each resistance faction. They held open the possibility of electing a chairman, that is, Sihanouk, as a thirteenth member of the Council.[47] Leadership of the Council was, however, left unresolved for the moment.

An important ingredient in the factions' acceptance of the accord framework was an easing of tensions between China and Vietnam. Direct talks had taken place between the two antagonists in 1989 and 1990, resulting in a twenty-five-mile withdrawal of troops from each side of their common border. A decline in Soviet aid to Vietnam, estimated to run $2–$2.5 billion annually, and a concomitant demand that Hanoi start repaying 8 billion rubles in debt falling due in 1990 increased Vietnamese eagerness to resolve tensions with China.[48]

It is questionable whether the factions would have accepted the framework had it not been for a secret meeting between China and Vietnam on September 3–4 in Chengdu, China. There the focus of talks shifted away from Vietnam's continual search for improvement in economic relations and other spheres to a commitment to resolve the Cambodian conflict. The outcome was an apparent agreement that each would press its client to accept the proposed framework. "'A deal was cut between the two sides on Cambodia,' said one diplomat of the meeting between the Chinese and Vietnamese. The Vietnamese agreed to press the Hanoi-installed Hun Sen regime to accept the peace settlement, and China agreed to press the resistance coalition, diplomats and other sources said."[49]

NAILING DOWN THE DETAILS: SEPTEMBER 1990–AUGUST 1991

The first meeting of the SNC, held on September 19, 1990, broke up in disagreement over the composition of Cambodia's UN delegation and Sihanouk's role in the interim government. The UN Security Council endorsed the framework for peace on September 20 and urged the Cambodian factions to resolve their differences. The UN General Assembly's endorsement came on October 15. An expanded draft of the framework was agreed upon by the Perm Five on November 25.

During the year it took to hammer out the details of a final agreement, the SNC continued to meet, reaffirming that it could act as the repository of Cambodian sovereignty. While the framework document drawn up in 1990 was a product of the outside players, the effort in 1991 focused largely on what Hun Sen and the State of Cambodia (SOC), as the Phnom Penh regime was called after 1989,* would accept. This process fleshed out the framework with the safeguards and structure the SOC deemed necessary for it to go forward.

At the same time, there was considerable internal struggle in Vietnam about whether to go forward. It took dramatic changes in Eastern Europe and the impending dissolution of the Soviet Union to pose a sufficiently serious threat to Vietnam's survival to make it willing to press Phnom Penh to finalize a settlement. As a senior U.S. government official recounted, Vietnam came to fear that it was about to become the next Czechoslovakia. The Communist countries of Eastern Europe were catching the terminal disease of democracy rooted in pluralism. As Eastern Europe threw off communism, the Vietnamese Politburo recognized that it would not be possible to sustain state power if it had to worry about Cambodia, China, and the West.[50] It was time to cut a deal and to turn full attention to reviving Vietnam's sagging economy.

As a further incentive for Vietnam, in April 1991 the United States proposed a four-phase plan for normalization of relations. According to the American "road map," Cambodia had to be resolved first: the UN peace plan would have to be fully implemented, elections held, and a national assembly formed before relations would be normalized.[51] The road map was designed in part to compel Vietnam to pressure the Phnom Penh regime to back the UN peace plan—although the P.O.W.-M.I.A. issue, which reemerged as a serious obstacle when a falsified photograph of alleged living P.O.W.s surfaced early in the summer, interfered with the direct linkage between a Cambodia settlement and normalization.[52]

The chief issues for the SOC concerned disarmament of its military and the extent of UN control over its five most important ministries. Because it had the most to lose of the four factions, the regime balked at the framework's suggested dismantling of much of its administrative apparatus. Moreover, its fears that disarmament would make it possible for the

---

*As part of an effort to enhance its image and credibility as a government and to make it more attractive for Sihanouk to abandon his coalition with the Khmer Rouge, on May 1, 1989, the Phnom Penh regime changed the name of the country from "People's Republic of Kampuchea" to the more ideologically neutral "State of Cambodia," known subsequently by the acronym SOC. It also adopted a new national flag that incorporated the Sihanoukist colors. This did not result, however, in international recognition as the regime had hoped; instead, the regime itself became identified with the term "State of Cambodia."

Khmer Rouge to regain power were not unreasonable, given reports in early 1991 that Chinese arms had continued to flow to the Khmer Rouge despite public assurances that China had stopped military aid the previous September. It was unclear whether China had continued to supply the Khmer Rouge directly or if the arms had been in the pipeline or warehoused in Thailand.[53]

In a memorandum presented to the U.S. government in Vientiane, Laos, on April 18, 1991, the regime outlined its security concerns, which proved prescient.

> we would like to stress that the dismantling and the disarmament of the armed forces will be only realisable with our armed forces whereas with the other parties, especially the khmer rouge, it would be impossible to implement and even up to know [sic], while we have offered the possibility for a lot of un fact-finding missions to see the situation from our side, the united nations have not yet provided any information whatsoever from the polpotists, including on the refugees camps under their control. what will happen if we accept to dismantle our armed forces which so far constitute the sole force to oppose the polpotists and which is able to contain them?[54]

On May 1, 1991, the factions agreed to a voluntary cease-fire proposed by France, Indonesia, and UN secretary-general Javier Pérez de Cuéllar. This signaled a release of the deadlock over the UN peace plan. Although violations continued to occur, the level of armed conflict dropped substantially.[55]

At talks in Jakarta on June 2–4, 1991, the Phnom Penh regime proposed a series of changes to the UN framework that "included guarantees to prevent the return of past genocidal practices, a new schedule for demobilization, and a modification of the relationship between the SNC and the UN Transitional Authority in Cambodia."[56] As a *Washington Post* editorial observed shortly thereafter, "Hun Sen's evident strategy is to load up the UN plan with conditions that make it hard for the Khmer Rouge to stay aboard."[57] While there was no agreement on these proposals, Sihanouk and Hun Sen did agree that Sihanouk would head the SNC with Hun Sen as the vice-chairman. When that proved unacceptable to the Khmer Rouge, Sihanouk announced after the Jakarta meeting that he would join the SNC as an ordinary member.[58]

THE TURNING POINT: THE PATTAYA MEETING, JUNE 1991

At a meeting of the SNC in Pattaya, Thailand, on June 24–26, 1991, all parties finally agreed on the Sihanouk-Hun Sen leadership formula for the twelve- (not thirteen-) member SNC, on a continued cease-fire (though this had been rejected by the Khmer Rouge in Jakarta), and on a halt to the influx of foreign arms. The four factions also agreed to make the SNC fully operational by moving it to Phnom Penh, where each faction would have its own offices in a compound guarded by its own armed forces and protected outside by SOC troops.[59] Although as one diplomat commented, "Sihanouk is putting the squeeze on Hun Sen. . . . He knows that Hun Sen knows that you cannot have a cease-fire and cessation of arms without the UN plan," Hun Sen continued to hold out against full acceptance of the UN framework because he feared that demobilization prior to the elections would leave his regime vulnerable to any takeover attempt by Khmer Rouge forces.[60]

A subsequent meeting in Beijing of the four factions resolved the issue of Cambodia's UN seat, which had been left vacant the previous fall. This would now be occupied by a delegation headed by Prince Sihanouk. The delegation would also include two SOC delegates (Hun Sen and Foreign Minister Hor Nam Hong) and a Khmer Rouge delegate (Khieu Samphan).[61]

Several developments after the Pattaya talks facilitated progress toward a Cambodia peace agreement. One was resolution of an internal power struggle in Vietnam, which resulted in the ouster in July of Foreign Minister Nguyen Co Thach, long hostile to Beijing, in favor of those seeking economic liberalization and rapprochement with China. On August 10, China and Vietnam announced that they hoped to normalize relations and that they agreed a comprehensive political settlement in Cambodia should be based on "a framework document of the five permanent members of the United Nations Security Council."[62]

The four factions, following up on their progress by returning to Pattaya on August 26, agreed to ask the United Nations to send a contingent of peacekeeping observers to Cambodia as soon as possible. This came after a twelve-member UN survey team had been dispatched at the SNC's request in July to examine the prospects for monitoring the cease-fire and arms moratorium agreed to in June.[63]

Agreement on Troop Reductions, August 1991

The August 1990 draft of the framework agreement had called for a cease-fire, then regroupment and relocation of the factions' forces into cantonment areas under UN supervision. The forces' arms were to be stored under UN supervision in the cantonment areas. According to an operational timetable to be devised, the United Nations would then begin a phased process of "arms control and reduction." The framework had left it to future negotiations to specify the timing, the extent of the reductions, and the number and type of each faction's forces to which the reductions would apply.[64]

In August 1991, the factions largely resolved the issue of troop reductions. After rejecting first an offer by the resistance to reduce each side's forces to 6,000 troops and then Hun Sen's counteroffer to reduce forces by 40 percent, the factions agreed to a French proposal to cut each of their military forces and their weaponry by 70 percent and regroup the remaining 30 percent in UN-supervised cantonment areas.[65] Left unspecified, however, was the number of each faction's forces to which the demobilization would apply. Not only was there disagreement on how many forces each side had, but the Khmer Rouge demanded that Phnom Penh's paramilitary police be included in the forces to be reduced by 70 percent. "Phnom Penh sought to keep as much of its army intact to limit opportunities for the Khmer Rouge to seize power. The Khmer Rouge sought as much disarmament as possible—which could be monitored more easily in the case of Phnom Penh's forces—in order to prevent their opponent from consolidating its position in the capital.[66] The Khmer Rouge also believed it would be able to hide a substantial number of its forces. While Hun Sen refused to include the regime's paramilitary security force, he did agree to total demobilization of the SOC local militia, which he claimed numbered 220,000. Resolution of the issue of the size of each faction's forces did not take place until the United Nations collected information from the factions during a military survey mission in November–December 1991.

What the Phnom Penh regime achieved with the August 1991 agreement was not its first choice—cantonment with no force reductions. But it did obtain assurance that its forces would not be completely dismantled, leaving the country potentially undefended or at least heavily reliant on the United Nations against a possibly resurgent Khmer Rouge. The compromise was not a bad one for the Phnom Penh regime. Although its fears that disarmament by the Khmer Rouge would not take place later proved to be accurate, the 70/30 formula in fact preserved a substantial portion of Phnom Penh's military forces. Once it became clear that the Khmer Rouge was not going to cooperate with the disarmament process, Phnom Penh was free to press the United Nations, successfully, to suspend disarmament.

While the agreement on a formula for troop reductions was a major step toward a settlement, there was still no accord on how the electoral system for the national assembly should be structured. The United States insisted on a system of proportional representation, hoping to enhance the chances for the non-Communists, particularly Son Sann's Khmer People's National Liberation Front (KPNLF), and this was incorporated into the framework agreement. Nonetheless, Hun Sen advocated a system of traditional, single-seat constituencies apportioned by district or province. The constituency system, similar to that used in the United States, would more likely favor the established rulers of the country.[67]

Because of the costs associated with the UN plan, the Perm Five held an effective veto over any arrangement made by the factions. On August 30, they endorsed the agreements that had already been made, while urging resolution of the dispute over the electoral system and insisting that the troops subject to reductions include paramilitary as well as regular forces.

A NEW POWER EQUATION IN INDOCHINA

What took place in the summer of 1991 was the setting of conditions under which the State of Cambodia would remain intact—at least until after the elections took place. Part of the progress resulted from Sihanouk striking out on his own, apparently with China's approval and the Khmer Rouge's acquiescence. With rapprochment between China and Vietnam imminent, and diminished support from Phnom Penh's Vietnamese patron tightening the screws, "the Phnom Penh administration had to make substantial concessions in order to remain in existence."[68] It had to agree to turn over control of five critical ministries to the United Nations; it had to accept a 70 percent reduction of its armed forces and cantonment of the remainder; and it had to agree that Cambodia's sovereignty would lodge in the Supreme National Council. The price, while substantial, turned out to be far less than it appeared that summer because the United Nations proved unable to exert real control over the five ministries, disarmament was suspended, and the Supreme National Council's ineffectiveness left Phnom Penh under only minimal constraints.

Moreover, the Beijing and Pattaya meetings demonstrated that a new power equation dominated Indochina. Conflict over Cambodia was nothing new. In 1991, however, Vietnam's economic vulnerability and isolation were no longer reconcilable with preserving its hegemony over Cambodia. The Cambodian question had been detached from Soviet-American and Sino-Soviet relations as well.[69] China's goals since the Vietnamese invasion had been the end of Vietnamese military occupation and the removal of the Phnom Penh government. The former had been achieved in 1989; the latter looked likely under the UN plan.

Robert Miller talked about Vietnam's security from a historical perspective:

> Vietnam's history has been a confusing mosaic of its lust to dominate the weaker Indianized peoples to its south and west, and its own obsessive resistance to China's repeated efforts to impose its imperial will on a tributary state.
>
> . . . Throughout this turbulent 2000-year history, Vietnam's own national goals have been to achieve and preserve its independence; to expand its territory to meet the needs of a dynamic, growing population; to promote national unity; and to enhance its national security by dominating its weaker neighbors, principally Cambodia. Despite major and recurring setbacks, including the 1000 years of direct Chinese rule, the brief occupation by

Japan, and the more than 30 years of warfare against the French and then the Americans to reestablish its independence and its unity, Vietnam has pursued its goals with a singular tenacity and has achieved them to a remarkable degree. And in the process it has accumulated great potential in national power. Today Vietnam is a unified country with a homogeneous, dynamic population of well over 60 million with the fifth or sixth largest standing army in the world, and with one of the world's lowest living standards as well.[70]

The central issue from the beginning of the Cambodian conflict had been that "China and Vietnam each need to be assured that the actions of the other are not undermining its security. For both, this requires that neither is able to use Cambodia to the detriment of the other's security."[71] More than anything else, the UN plan was the result of both China and Vietnam taking risks. They gambled that the other would be denied the benefits of having Cambodia within its own sphere of influence; at the same time, the plan would buy China international respectability in the wake of the Tiananmen Square massacre and would buy Vietnam breathing space for economic reforms.

AGREEMENT ON A COMPREHENSIVE PLAN FOR PEACE

On September 19, 1991, the last obstacle to a comprehensive peace plan was overcome when the factions agreed to a system of proportional representation for the elections, with seats in the national assembly to be allotted on a province-by-province basis. In essence, the Phnom Penh regime bowed to the inevitable, concluding it could not convince the international community to alter the electoral system specified in the framework accord to its liking.

Even before the Paris Accords were signed on October 23, 1991, the Phnom Penh regime moved to improve its party's image. On October 18, the Kampuchean People's Revolutionary Party changed its name to the Cambodian People's Party (CPP). The party then abolished communism, replaced Heng Samrin with Chea Sim as party president, made Hun Sen party vice president, and embraced the concept of a multiparty system.[72]

As Chea Sim said in his closing speech to the party congress, "The CPP pursues a democratic and free political system, a multi-party system with three centers of power . . . the legislative, the executive and the tribunal, with a president and National Assembly elected by the people through universal suffrage." In a bow to the future, the Cambodian People's Party promised that after the elections "it will willingly join forces with all other political parties of all political tendencies to administer the nation well."[73]

The signing of the Paris Accords ushered in a period in which the struggle for the allegiance of Prince Sihanouk intensified. Recognizing the symbolic importance of Sihanouk as a figurehead—to say nothing of him as a power in his own right—Hun Sen urged that the Cambodian People's Party support the prince as national president.[74]

3

UNTAC's Mandate, Structure, and Implementation

The Paris Accords were signed by nineteen countries on October 23, 1991.*
The agreement consisted of three separate documents. One covered
a comprehensive political settlement. The second guaranteed Cambodia's
sovereignty, independence, and neutrality. The third committed the sign-
ers to aid Cambodia's reconstruction.[1] The Paris Accords also provided for
the establishment of the United Nations Transitional Authority in Cambodia.

On October 31, the UN Security Council expressed full support for the
agreement and requested Secretary-General Javier Pérez de Cuéllar to
draw up an implementation plan with detailed cost estimates. The Security
Council also authorized the secretary-general to designate a special representative for Cambodia.

UNAMIC—UNTAC's Advance Team

A 268-person advance contingent of UN military and civilian personnel
was then sent to Cambodia in early November to monitor the cease-fire that
went into effect when the Accords were signed and to prepare recommendations for UNTAC's eventual size. The advance contingent was called
the United Nations Advance Mission in Cambodia (UNAMIC).

In November and December 1991, military, civil administration, and
electoral survey teams traveled to Cambodia to begin to prepare plans for
UNTAC's operations.[2] The work of the electoral survey team proved to be

---

*On behalf of Cambodia, all twelve members of the Supreme National Council,
which represented all four factions, signed the Paris Accords.

exceedingly useful; that of the military and civil administration teams was less so.

UNAMIC also included a twenty-person "mine awareness" team but did not undertake mine clearance operations. Lack of emphasis on mine clearance in the early stages of the UN operation, criticized by some relief officials and human rights advocates, was to have serious repercussions for repatriation efforts later because mine clearance operations could not keep up with demand for mine-free land.[3] The task of clearing hundreds of thousands, if not millions, of mines was daunting, particularly since the factions continued to lay mines and no maps of minefields existed.

Because of the inherent difficulties of planning for and recruiting a peacekeeping force of a magnitude not seen since the Congo operation in the 1960s, the full deployment of peacekeeping troops to Cambodia was not expected until March 1992. The United Nations was blamed by Prince Sihanouk and others for excessive delay in deploying its blue-helmeted soldiers. The lag between initiation of the operation at the end of October 1991 and deployment of troops, which did not even begin until the following March, meant that the UN presence was insufficient to prevent an outbreak of violence that nearly killed Khmer Rouge leader Khieu Samphan as he attempted to return to Phnom Penh on November 27.[4]

Ironically, the lack of a strong presence in those months may ultimately have worked in the United Nations' favor. The spontaneous violence—first directed against the Khmer Rouge and then in a wave of protests in late December against official corruption and police repression of dissent—forced the postponement of the first meeting of the Supreme National Council on Cambodian soil. It also caused Sihanouk abruptly to abandon the coalition he had announced with the Phnom Penh regime upon his return to Cambodia on November 14, after a thirteen-year exile.[5] (In typical Sihanouk fashion, he had repudiated his alliance with the Khmer Rouge and even went so far as to declare in his first public speech that he favored trials for Khmer Rouge leader Pol Pot and his top aides. He had also disclosed at a November 16 press conference that he expected his followers to form a coalition government after the elections. He said it was "'inevitable' that his longtime followers, and those of Mr. Hun Sen and his associates, would take control of the government after the elections."[6]) The collapse of this Sihanouk-Hun Sen coalition in only a few short weeks reflected Sihanouk's mercurial personality, as well as his shrewd assessment that it may have been a mistake to reveal his hand so early in the process. A coalition with the Phnom Penh regime may have made sense, but it was too soon; he would lose all leverage if he cut a deal right away. He felt safer in continuing to play all sides against each other than in redrawing alignments. Moreover, he retained his deep belief that he was the father of all Cambodians, including the Khmer Rouge, and he sincerely felt that national reconciliation would only be possible if the

Khmer Rouge were included. Sihanouk's repudiation of the coalition on December 3 returned the four factions to an uneasy balance of power that made it harder for them to act in concert to oppose UN leadership.[7] A solid Sihanouk-Hun Sen coalition could have derailed the UN peace plan or, at the least, made it more difficult for the United Nations to retain control over the peace process.

The violence against the Khmer Rouge and corrupt Phnom Penh officials was an early signal of the pent-up longings of the Cambodian people and a clue to their voting intentions in the still-distant elections. The *New York Times* commented, "Something important is going on here. Cambodians are demanding a greater role in their own political future."[8]

THE IMPLEMENTATION PLAN

On February 28, 1992, the Security Council approved the plan of the new UN secretary-general, Boutros Boutros-Ghali, to implement the Cambodia peace agreement. The unanimously approved resolution authorized a total force of roughly 22,000, including 15,900 soldiers, 3,600 police monitors, and 2,400 civilian administrators. Total costs were projected at $1.9 billion for a mission lasting eighteen months.[9] The plan called for separate voluntary contributions for the rehabilitation and reconstruction of Cambodia, with early estimates of need reaching $800 million. Repatriation of the 350,000–370,000 refugees was budgeted at $116 million and also financed separately from the rest of the UNTAC operation.[10]

A dispute over the size of the factions' forces was resolved by information provided to UNAMIC. As a result, UNTAC peacekeepers were expected to disarm 70 percent of each of the following: 131,000 forces of the Phnom Penh regime, 27,000 Khmer Rouge forces, 27,800 troops under the control of the Khmer People's National Liberation Front (KPNLF), and 17,500 Sihanoukist troops. In addition to these regular forces, the United Nations was expected to disarm another 250,000 local militia associated with the four factions.[11]

The UN peacekeeping force was to consist of twelve infantry battalions of roughly 850 soldiers each, other assorted military forces including sector and headquarters staff, an engineering unit, a military observer group, a signals unit, a medical unit, a military police company, a logistics battalion, and a naval unit. It also was to have an air-support group to operate and maintain ten aircraft and twenty-six helicopters. The factions' forces were estimated to have 300,000 modern weapons and 80 million rounds of ammunition that would be subject to UN custody.[12]

Although the Security Council had approved a $200 million start-up fund for the Cambodia operation and letters had been sent requesting member countries to pay their assessed contributions, no funds had yet been received at the time the Council endorsed the secretary-general's plan.[13] The constant drumbeat for funds was to be a serious source of concern during the Cambodia mission. Many members were behind in their peacekeeping payments. Russia, obligated to pay 15 percent of the bills, was unable to pay at all, and the United States, required to contribute 31.7 percent, had been in arrears for many years. Although Washington began to pay off its multimillion-dollar arrears in 1990, the explosion of UN peacekeeping operations resulted in the United States falling behind by nearly $1 billion by October 1993.[14]

UNTAC's TASKS

The tasks assigned to UNTAC by the Paris Accords fell into six major categories:

1. **Refugee repatriation;**

2. **Cease-fire and demobilization:** monitoring, supervising, and verifying the withdrawal of all foreign forces and advisers and the cessation of outside military aid; locating and confiscating caches of weapons and military supplies; and supervising the disarmament and transfer of 70 percent of each faction's military forces into designated cantonment areas;

3. **Elections:** educating voters and organizing all aspects of free elections for a 120-person constituent assembly that would draft a new constitution, transform itself into a legislature, and then create a new Cambodian government;

4. **Human rights:** developing a human rights program and investigating abuses;

5. **Civil administration:** controlling five critical areas (defense, foreign affairs, finance, information, and public security) of the four factions' administrative structure (negligible though those may have been for all but the Phnom Penh regime) during the period leading up to the elections, in order to ensure a neutral political environment conducive for the elections; and

6. **Rehabilitation and reconstruction:** coordinating an international effort to provide relief and long-term assistance to rebuild the country.[15]

The tasks facing UNTAC were daunting. This was not to be just a peacekeeping operation separating combatants who had agreed to stop fighting. UNTAC was to run Cambodia for a period of eighteen months. It was to resettle 350,000–370,000 refugees from the Thai border areas, 170,000 "internal refugees" displaced within Cambodia, and 150,000 demobilized soldiers from the four factions' forces. It was to supervise and train the civil police forces of each faction. At the time, many thought that it was not realistic to expect that one UN operation could effectively rebuild a country from the ground up—and then conduct a Western-oriented, free, fair, and democratic election in a country that had no history of free elections or power-sharing, for that matter.

As Michael Leifer pointed out, "The Cambodian conflict eluded resolution for so long because it did not lend itself to any of three general ways of overcoming an internal war fueled by international rivalry": military defeat; one side giving up because the costs of continuing are too steep; or agreement on genuine compromise or power-sharing.[16] "There has been no decisive military victory, but a military stalemate has occurred, accompanied by a loss of will on the part of an enfeebled Vietnam.... At issue, therefore, is whether the measure of compromise reached in the political settlement of October 1991 is genuine or is merely a tactical accommodation leading to renewed confrontation."[17]

Choosing UNTAC's Leaders

One of Boutros-Ghali's first acts as the new UN secretary-general was to name Yasushi Akashi to head UNTAC. Akashi was also named the secretary-general's special representative for Cambodia. The first Japanese ever employed by the United Nations (starting in 1957), Akashi had been the organization's respected undersecretary-general for disarmament affairs and undersecretary for public information, but had no direct experience in overseeing peacekeeping operations. He was, however, a special favorite of Sihanouk's, who made known his preference for Akashi as head of UNTAC.[18]

The choice of Akashi was made not only in deference to Sihanouk but in recognition of Japan's growing importance in the region and in the United Nations. As Akashi himself said in an interview at the time of his appointment, "Japanese interest in Cambodia is extensive and genuine.... We want to show our sense of international responsibility."[19] A leading journalist remarked that "the appointment of Mr. Akashi, a 61-year-old career United Nations official and author, also illustrates the growing visibility of Japan and a new breed of Japanese internationalists in United Nations operations."[20] The UN high commissioner for refugees, Sadako Ogata, who was given primary responsibility for the Cambodian repatriation operation, was also Japanese. Akashi's selection, however, was also a not-so-discreet nudge to urge Japan to accept world responsibilities commensurate with its economic superpower status. According to Representative Stephen Solarz, chairman of the House Foreign Affairs Subcommittee on East Asia and the Pacific, "This appointment clearly signals the arrival of Japan on the international stage as a major player in the resolution of regional conflicts. . . . If this is coupled with Japan's willingness to contribute more to the peacekeeping operation, that would be a great accomplishment. . . ."[21]

In choosing Akashi, the international community hoped to increase Japan's involvement in UN peacekeeping. Akashi stated that "Cambodia is a good outlet for Japanese with humanitarian concerns. . . ."[22] Japan went further than it had in the Persian Gulf War effort, to which it contributed $13 billion but no troops.[23] In its first military deployment overseas since World War II, Japan sent eight military observers and a 600-member unit to join Cambodia's peacekeepers.[24] Although this unit, an engineering battalion, was assigned to rebuild two major highways during a six-month tour and normally remained unarmed, its deployment caused protests in the Philippines against renewed Japanese militarism. Japan also contributed seventy-five civilian police to UNTAC.

The debate in Japan on the decision to contribute peacekeeping forces had been a long and wrenching one. The deployment had been championed by Prime Minister Kiichi Miyazawa, "whose Government sees the Cambodia mission as an opportunity for Tokyo to reassert itself in foreign affairs—and a chance to end international criticism of Japan as a nation willing to write a check to maintain world peace but unwilling to put its own citizens at risk."[25] Yet the killing of a Japanese electoral volunteer on April 8, 1993, and of an unarmed Japanese civilian policeman on May 4, caused a furor in Japan, with some politicians pressing unsuccessfully for the recall of the Japanese peacekeepers.[26]

As a test case for more active Japanese diplomacy, participation in UNTAC was a success. In late April 1993, despite the death of the elections worker, Japan's cabinet authorized the dispatch of a forty-eight-person transportation unit to the UN peacekeeping operation in Mozambique—a country in an area with virtually no economic or political interests for Japan.[27] It may have been less of a success, however, for UNTAC. In the wake of the death of the Japanese police officer, under pressure from the Japanese government, UNTAC eased the risk for forty-one Japanese election monitors by stationing them in safer areas of Cambodia. Akashi refused, however, a request that the Japanese police force be recalled to the relative safety of Phnom Penh, ostensibly for discussions of security matters.[28] More than twenty Japanese police officers fled to Phnom Penh anyway. Many never returned to their stations, pleading illness. Four left the country entirely. Faced with danger, nearly a third of the Japanese civilian police had deserted their posts.[29] There was also criticism of special privileges accorded the Japanese. Their living arrangements were more luxurious than were those of other peacekeepers. They were sent to one of the safest areas of Cambodia, the southern province of Takeo, far from Khmer Rouge camps. They were also one of the first units to depart as UNTAC wound down after the May elections.[30]

As Akashi's UN assignment reflected Japan's deepening involvement in world affairs, so, too, the choice of Major General (soon-to-be Lieutenant General) John Sanderson to head UNTAC's military component was a recognition of Australia's central role in breaking the stalemate in negotiating the peace plan by proposing that the United Nations assume control over Cambodia during the transition. The choice of Sanderson came only after resolution of a dispute between the United States and France. France, which with Indonesia had chaired the Paris Conference, wanted French to be the official language of, and a French officer to head, UNTAC's military operations. The United States opposed choosing a representative of one of five permanent Security Council members, which traditionally keep a low profile in peacekeeping. Besides, a French-only military operation would be inconsistent since UNTAC's official languages were both English and French. The conflict was resolved by appointing Sanderson as head of the military command, with France's Brigadier General Michel Loridon as deputy commander.[31] In implicitly rejecting the primacy of France's colonial ties to Indochina, the United Nations underscored that Australia considered Cambodia to be in its backyard, much as the United States has viewed the Western Hemisphere.

UNTAC made special concessions to the French contingent as well. They were initially assigned to the relative safety, but comparative obscurity, of the jungles of northeastern Cambodia. After further lobbying by Paris, they were transferred to a high-profile assignment in Kampot Som province in the south, which afforded the troops access to Cambodia's beaches.[32]

Prioritizing the Tasks

The United Nations' first priority, after dispatch of UNAMIC and the choice of civilian and military heads of UNTAC, was to determine what was needed to encourage an outcome that came closest to genuine compromise or power-sharing. The heart of UNTAC's mandate was to take the structure laid out in the Paris Accords and give Cambodia a chance to establish a government that would be strong enough to prevent further civil war.

Each mandated task was designed in some way to facilitate that outcome. Get the refugees back home and reintegrate them into Cambodian society, so their camps will cease to be a staging ground for armed insurgents. Disarm the factions; the fewer guns, the fewer able to fight. Keep the troops that were not demobilized in cantonment areas so they cannot fight. Teach the Cambodians not to abuse human rights, to defuse what Elizabeth Becker called "a violence that has been a strain of the national character since at least the days of the Angkor era."[33] Develop a civilian police force to help damp down the level of violence. Build the structures of a civil society. Get the international community to undertake a massive effort to rebuild Cambodia and help it rejoin the community of nations from which it has so long been excluded; economic liberalization and investment can help thwart a return to power by the Khmer Rouge. Finally, educate Cambodians about free and fair elections; then, organize and carry them out.

It is hardly surprising, given the scope of the mandate assigned to UNTAC, that the tasks did not get carried out fully in every instance. That would have been exceedingly difficult, if not impossible. The UN peace plan was not designed to heal all of Cambodia's wounds and completely repair the wreckage of more than fifteen years of civil war. As Akashi said in August 1992, "We are not here to solve all the problems of Cambodia."[34] The UN peace plan was designed to jump-start the process, not carry it through to completion.

When the Paris Accords were drawn up, no specific priority was attached to the various tasks charged to UNTAC. But during implementation, UNTAC established a working set of priorities through both deliberate decisions and, in some cases, sheer necessity.

The highest priority was given to ensuring that the election was carried out. It can be argued that UNTAC was election-driven in its approach to its entire mandate. If it was not so initially, certainly it was near the end. In response to Khmer Rouge complaints about the United Nations not dismantling Phnom Penh's administrative structures, Akashi noted in an interview in July 1992, "The goal is to ensure a neutral political environment for the elections—nothing more and nothing less."[35]

Shortly after the United Nations technically ended its operation in Cambodia, Akashi spoke at the Johns Hopkins University School of Advanced International Studies. In that speech, the priority he accorded to carrying out the elections successfully was apparent. He attributed the elections' success to three causes: UNTAC's single-minded commitment to bringing about free and fair elections, the Cambodian people's deep desire for peace, and Sihanouk's outstanding balancing ability. As a result, he concluded, Cambodia was spared Angola's agony of having carried out free and fair elections, only to have the outcome repudiated by one side and civil war erupt anew.[36]

The single-minded focus on the elections was more a product of necessity than design. The Paris Accords had laid out a set of definable tasks, with disarmament of the factions' forces the key to everything else. When disarmament failed to take place, UNTAC should have collapsed. In fact, the chief consequence of disarmament being suspended was an increasing focus on the elections. In November 1992, Akashi and Sanderson restructured UNTAC's military tasks accordingly, to ensure conditions that would allow the elections to take place. That meant redeploying the military to protect electoral workers, political party offices, and candidates, as well as a host of other election-related tasks. This shift in emphasis increased the stakes for holding the elections, which had been looking like a doubtful prospect up to that time.

The other area accorded high priority—by design rather than by necessity—was refugee repatriation. The success of the refugee repatriation effort may have been due in part to its physical and administrative separation from UNTAC's other tasks. UNTAC's locus of operations was Phnom Penh. From there, it fanned out gradually to encompass the rest of country except for Khmer Rouge strongholds. The repatriation effort, however, was designed to move refugees across the Thai-Cambodian border. It depended to a lesser extent on UNTAC's other components. Although it coordinated where necessary with them, it operated largely independently.

Refugee repatriation was conducted jointly under the auspices of UNTAC and the UN High Commissioner for Refugees (UNHCR). This separate status helped the refugee effort to be perceived as more neutral than other UNTAC activities. Although the factions did not fully cooperate in the carrying out of UNTAC's other tasks, each one cooperated fully on the return of refugees to Cambodia.

A lower priority appears to have been assigned to UNTAC's human rights mandate. This seemed to be a result of the inherent difficulty of implementation. In addition, more vigorous pursuit of human rights goals ran the risk of upsetting the delicate political balance that was necessary if the elections were to take place. In a country with a history of human rights abuses that approached genocide, it was going to be an uphill task to educate the population, to develop indigenous human rights organizations, and most important, to develop mechanisms that would truly protect the people from human rights abuses. UNTAC had to deal with a country that "had no free press, the Buddhist church was state-controlled, and the civil police and judiciary were both rudimentary and totally politicized."[37]

For similar reasons, less emphasis seemed to be placed on UNTAC's civil administration mandate, although its efforts were critical in ensuring the neutral political environment deemed essential for free and fair elections. But with the acknowledgment that UNTAC could not dismantle the State of Cambodia administrative apparatus came a recognition as well of the magnitude of the governance task. To supervise, much less control, the administrative structures of all four factions was simply beyond UN capability—unless the United Nations had been prepared to deploy an armada of civilian administrators equaling the size of the peacekeeping force at nearly 16,000. That would have been prohibitively expensive, and there would have been little support for such an initiative—contributing countries were already grumbling at UNTAC's costs.

UNTAC's Structure and Deployment of Personnel

UNTAC was headed, as are all UN operations, by a special representative of the secretary-general. That position was filled by Yasushi Akashi, who reported directly to Secretary-General Boutros Boutros-Ghali, and to the Department of Peacekeeping Operations in New York. Chart 1 on page 40 shows UNTAC's overall organization.

UNTAC ORGANIZATIONAL CHART

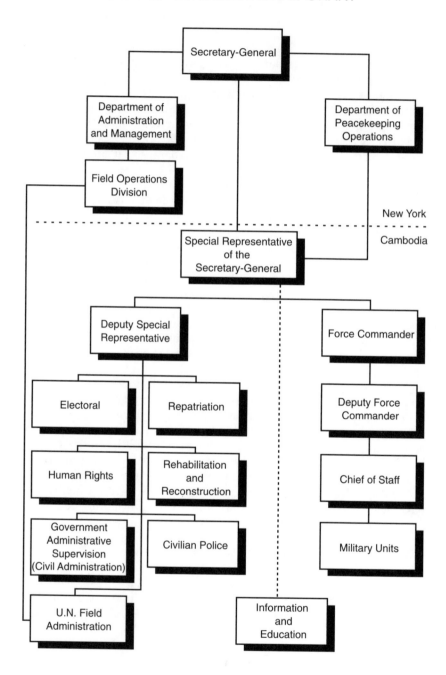

Under Akashi, UNTAC had two divisions—civilian and military operations. The civilian side was headed by the deputy special representative, Behrooz Sadry, a career UN bureaucrat. The military side was headed by Lieutenant General John Sanderson of Australia.

The deputy special representative supervised six UNTAC components responsible for carrying out Paris Accords mandates and one UN field administration office. The six were Electoral, Repatriation, Rehabilitation and Reconstruction, Human Rights, Civilian Police, and Government Administrative Supervision, better known as Civil Administration. Another subsidiary, the Information and Education division, was not originally defined as a separate component in the secretary-general's implementation plan; it functioned as a unit within the Office of the Special Representative. Its importance grew throughout UNTAC's implementation, and its work was essential to the efforts of virtually all the other offices.[38] Sanderson was in charge of UNTAC's seventh substantive component, that of the military.

UNTAC was planned to have nearly 16,000 military, 5,800 international and local civilian staff, 3,600 civil police, and 62,000 Cambodians to help with the elections.[39] It is difficult to tally accurately the number of personnel associated with each component due to slow deployment and monthly fluctuations. Rough approximations of the number of people assigned to each component tend to reflect not only the size needed to accomplish the task but the degree of priority assigned to it.

The electoral component included 400 to 470 UN Volunteers (depending on the month) in the provinces. The UN Volunteers were similar to Peace Corps workers, and received a stipend, airfare, insurance, and living expenses. They were the primary international field staff organizing the election at the local level and supervised the more than 50,000 Cambodians who helped with the elections. An additional 150 international staffers were deployed in Phnom Penh and the provinces. The international staff was augmented by 1,000 personnel seconded from foreign governments for two or three weeks in April–May 1993 to help with the elections.[40]

By contrast, civil administration consisted of only about two hundred professional staff. As will be seen, a shortage of personnel seriously hindered the civil administrators' ability to control and supervise the four factions' administrative structures, particularly the State of Cambodia, which had an estimated 140,000 civil servants in twenty-one provinces.[41]

The human rights bureau was similarly understaffed, with no personnel at first working at the provincial or lower levels. A small number were deployed to the provinces by the fall of 1992 when it became clear that the work could not be carried out without a provincial presence.

Overall, UNTAC was slow to deploy and took much longer than should have been necessary to get all its components fully operational. This owed partly to inadequate planning in some cases; in others, it was a result of procurement difficulties affecting equipment, office space, and housing for its personnel. The unique difficulty of recruiting and properly equipping contingents from many different countries was the primary cause of slow deployment by the military. The civil administration, which missed an opportunity during the summer of 1992 to exert control over the Phnom Penh regime's administrative structures, was also hampered by the late arrival of its director. Neither the civil police nor the human rights units were fully staffed by the end of 1992.

PROCUREMENT AND LOGISTICAL DIFFICULTIES

UNTAC, like other large peacekeeping missions, was bedeviled by difficulties with procurement of supplies and the logistics of getting them where they were needed in Cambodia. The abysmal state of Cambodia's infrastructure was just one problem. "Not only did UNTAC have to bring in its own vehicles, communications and military equipment, but in many cases it had to import buildings, clean water and food, spare parts, paper and typewriters, and skilled personnel."[42] A General Accounting Office report highlighted the limits on UN capacity to plan, support logistically, and deploy peacekeeping operations. It observed that the lack of UN supply depots requires the organization to purchase supplies only after each peacekeeping mission has been approved. But that kind of an "on-demand" procurement system proved to be inadequate for an operation as large as UNTAC. "[P]urchasing supplies in the quantity needed by UNTAC took much longer than expected. There were problems with identifying reliable suppliers, reviewing the bids, and ensuring delivery to Cambodia."[43]

The sheer quantity of each item needed overwhelmed suppliers' capacity. There was a shortage of the 8,000 vehicles needed in the early months. Modular offices worth $100 million ordered in April 1992 were not delivered until November. UNTAC had to search widely for the 2,500 electrical generators needed for field operations. Civilian staff lacked radios, computers, adequate housing, water, and other supplies and equipment needed in the early months. "In one province, the civilian administration staff had received its first shipment of office supplies in mid-December 1992, 10 months after the operation started, and it still did not have generators, chairs, or tables for the office."[44] Slow procurement hindered almost all aspects of UNTAC's operations.

THE POLITICS OF IMPLEMENTATION

When the Paris Accords were signed, it was widely believed that the acid test of Khmer Rouge intentions was whether it implemented the security provisions of the agreement: disarmament and cantonment of its forces. Most observers felt the linchpin of the agreement was disarmament. It was widely recognized that if the Khmer Rouge did not disarm, then neither, in all probability, would the forces of the Phnom Penh regime or the non-Communist factions.

Critics charged that UNTAC had been planned on a best-case scenario envisioning all four factions cooperating with the mandate, with no contingency plan for addressing the failure of one or more parties to cooperate in such essential areas as maintaining a cease-fire or disarming their militaries.[45] The UN Secretariat argued that to have developed "contingency plans for UNTAC to be implemented if one or more of the factions violated the peace agreement . . . would have suggested that the United Nations distrusted one or more of the parties involved. This would have been viewed as an act of bad faith by the factions and could have undermined the UN's role in implementing the agreement."[46] After all, each party had signed and agreed to uphold the Paris Accords. While detailed contingency planning probably would have been counterproductive, general contingency plans might have been useful given the high risk of obstructionism.

What the United Nations needed was a fallback strategy. A significant portion of its success in Cambodia can be attributed to the ability of the peace agreement to define implicitly the terms of political legitimacy. "The UN as a framework was critical in providing a structure that was not only neutral, but had the mandate such that for the parties to act by any other calculation, they would have been instantly frustrated by problems."[47] Participation in the elections was equated with legitimacy; refusal to participate signaled the opposite. The drafters of the Paris Accords had provided an inclusive structure for the political process, since, if the outcome of the elections was to be legitimate, all parties had to participate. At the same time, the drafters were pragmatic. They believed that unless the Khmer Rouge was included in the peace process as a legitimate player, it would act as a spoiler. Sihanouk himself insisted that it was safer to have the camel inside the tent rather than constantly trying to stick its nose under the tent flap. Lingering concerns about the Khmer Rouge, however, were mitigated by the expectation that the Khmer Rouge would do poorly in the elections.

Ironically, this strategy of inclusion worked in reverse. Having been drafted on the presumption that inclusion of all parties was essential to success, the framework proved remarkably adaptable to changed conditions. When one party, the Khmer Rouge, chose to exclude itself, the result was that it denied itself political legitimacy in the eyes of the Cambodian people, even while proclaiming it still adhered to the framework's "true" principles.

Critics of the Paris Accords deplored the plan's structure, which gave equal status to the Khmer Rouge. They argued that the Khmer Rouge's history automatically disqualified it from participation in the peace process. They believed it was not merely unwise but suicidal to include the Khmer Rouge in any interim arrangements—much less on an equal footing with the other three factions. Yet both the peace plan's final structure and its implementation demonstrated this assessment may have been in error for two reasons. First, the Paris Accords were a far cry from the quadripartite interim government first proposed by Sihanouk and favored by the United States and others. The Khmer Rouge, in fact, did not have fully equal status. The twelve-member Supreme National Council was two-sided:[48] the Phnom Penh authorities on the one hand and six representatives of the three resistance factions on the other. The Khmer Rouge's two members were easily outnumbered. In addition, the SNC was designed to operate by consensus. While that gave the Khmer Rouge a de facto veto, what it really meant was that the Council was unable to operate effectively as a decisionmaking body. That suited the Phnom Penh regime, which had little interest in ceding authority and control to a body that contained its mortal enemies. The lack of consensus was anticipated by the designers of the accords, intended to ensure that the United Nations had the real authority to make decisions while recognizing the reality that to dismantle Phnom Penh's entire administrative apparatus would cause the country to collapse. Furthering the Council's impotence was its lack of staff to concentrate on reaching or carrying out decisions.

As it worked out, there were times when the SNC was in fact able to reach consensus; at other times it could not, and decisions were then deferred to the UN special representative or to an informal working group convened by him. Akashi was always careful to defer to the SNC, even when it meant delay, which was often, since Sihanouk spent most of the interim period outside of Cambodia.

The Khmer Rouge undoubtedly miscalculated in a number of ways. Its goal was to destroy the military effectiveness of the Phnom Penh regime through disarmament, but it also expected that the effect of the agreement would be to dismantle the Phnom Penh regime's control over the country. For the Khmer Rouge, the SNC was the key. It expected the Council to supplant the Phnom Penh authorities. That it did not do so substantially revealed that Pol Pot and his followers had made a major miscalculation.

As implementation proceeded, Khmer Rouge complaints increasingly focused on the unwillingness of the United Nations to dismantle the Phnom Penh regime's governing apparatus. Akashi's position, as stated in an interview in July 1992, was that "the Paris Agreement says that existing administrative structures have to be maintained. . . . UNTAC cannot replace these structures. Otherwise, the whole country will crumble."[49] The Khmer Rouge failed to recognize that the game had changed. It had only intended to implement the Accords as it saw real reductions being made in the SOC's power. Although it was outnumbered on the SNC, it expected its influence to be equivalent to that of the SOC, and it banked on Sihanouk to side with the Khmer Rouge against the Phnom Penh authorities. That, too, was a miscalculation. Sihanouk made no move to take political power directly. After the initial period when the prince formed and then abandoned a coalition with the SOC, he retreated for the remainder of the interim period to his traditional insistence on national reconciliation and his position as father of all Cambodians. The Khmer Rouge and Prince Sihanouk had been involved for years in a mutually manipulative relationship. Sihanouk's marriage of convenience with the Khmer Rouge, forged in 1982 (but foreshadowed by earlier accommodations with it during his reign prior to 1970 and after Khmer Rouge accession to power in 1975), was more than a political alliance to oust the Vietnamese. It also reflected his psychological need to be the fount of Cambodian political legitimacy—the human personification of the Cambodian state and the figure around whom all could rally.

The Khmer Rouge also misjudged its approach to the UN presence. Yasushi Akashi assumed leadership of UNTAC with his eye fixed on the elections as the process that would define and legitimize governance in Cambodia. General Sanderson shared Akashi's approach. The Khmer Rouge completely missed the shift in emphasis from bullets to ballots. It hoped to scare, although probably not shoot, the United Nations out of Cambodia. Its campaign, first of noncompliance with disarmament and then of scattered violence throughout the country, was designed to render the UN plan moot. Given that its powerful patrons, the Chinese and the Thais, were committed to the peace plan, the Khmer Rouge knew it could not attack the UN peacekeeping forces frontally. Instead, its basic strategy was to create fear in the countryside. Khmer Rouge guerrillas threw bombs, engaged in sporadic shelling, and killed ethnic Vietnamese peasants. When they took on UN troops, they did so initially by way of hostage-taking incidents that never lasted more than a few days. This strategy backfired. The terror campaign did not chase the United Nations out of Cambodia. Instead, it simply delegitimized the Khmer Rouge as a political force.

Much of what took place politically during the implementation of the UN plan involved an edgy scrambling to redraw political alliances. What made it work, however, is that the action took place within the framework of the Paris Accords. That agreement ceded primacy in day-to-day life to the Phnom Penh regime, while reserving moral legitimacy for the non-Communist factions, particularly Sihanouk's political party, the National United Front for an Independent, Neutral, Peaceful, and Cooperative Cambodia, known by its French acronym as FUNCINPEC. This uneasy balance lasted until just after the elections, when the results were translated into a new coalition that excluded the Khmer Rouge.

While Khmer Rouge leaders had spent the entire implementation period complaining that the United Nations was denying the SNC's role as the true interim government, they were counting on Sihanouk to ensure that they were never fully locked out of power. Sihanouk, for his part, never quite expected the elections to take place. He assumed that something would happen to disrupt them, and in fact most indicators throughout the implementation process suggested that there was a good chance that he was correct. Moreover, he physically stayed away. Most official SNC meetings—those over which Sihanouk presided—took place outside Cambodia in Beijing or Thailand.

It is incorrect to conclude that it was only the Khmer Rouge that failed to comply with the UN plan. The Phnom Penh regime did everything it could get away with to keep its hands on the reins, conceding as little as possible to the United Nations, particularly control over the designated five ministries. It also systematically engaged in a campaign of violence to intimidate potential voters and its political opponents. Its political campaign was designed to emphasize the threat of a return to war and brutal misrule and persuade voters that only it was sufficiently powerful to counter the Khmer Rouge. Just as the Khmer Rouge miscalculated, so, too, did the Phnom Penh regime. Many Cambodians chose to vote against the status quo. The election was a vote for peace, against the Khmer Rouge and further civil war surely, but equally a vote against the undeniable corruption and incompetence of the Phnom Penh administration.

What the election did was break the marriage of convenience between Sihanouk and the Khmer Rouge and forge a new political alliance between FUNCINPEC and Hun Sen's Cambodian People's Party (CPP). The Phnom Penh regime understood FUNCINPEC's political appeal and had wanted alignment before the election. Sihanouk and FUNCINPEC gambled successfully on the outcome of the election, thereby winning a political alliance on their own terms. That new alliance resulted in the formation of a constituent assembly, the adoption of a constitution, and the return of Sihanouk now as king. It will take time, however, for the control of this new political alliance to permeate the bureaucracy and filter down to the provincial and district levels. The SOC's governmental apparatus, which effectively retained control of the countryside under UNTAC, will continue to do so for some time to come. This is where the real test of the new alliance will come in future years.

4

Getting Ready to Rebuild:
The Return of the Refugees and the Rehabilitation of Cambodia

The one task that was essential for UNTAC was the repatriation of the 350,000–370,000* refugees on the Thai-Cambodian border. Their upkeep since 1979 had been expensive. They had served as a recruiting ground for all four factions. Thailand wanted the refugees back in Cambodia; so, too, did the international community. Luckily for UNTAC, all four factions did as well.

Return of the refugees was viewed as necessary for preparing to rebuild Cambodia. As long as a substantial number of Cambodians were dispersed—and there were many who had fled overseas, or had sought political asylum outside of the region—it would be difficult to bring about national reconciliation. The first step was to repatriate the refugees from the border. It was hoped that the changes Cambodia would undergo during UNTAC's tenure would lure back expatriate Cambodians whose skills were desperately needed for the country's long-term reconstruction.

If return of the refugees was the first step toward rebuilding Cambodia, rehabilitation of the country's human and physical infrastructure would be the final step, though UNTAC's mandate on reconstruction was not to complete the task, but to jump-start it. The Paris Accords gave UNTAC the task of planning and coordinating an international effort to rebuild Cambodia.

---

* Estimates of the number of refugees to be repatriated varied from 350,000 to 370,000. The secretary-general used the figure of 360,000 in his implementation plan. The final total repatriated was between 365,000 and 370,000.

The intention was that the process would begin during UNTAC's tenure with projects that were designed to meet Cambodia's immediate and medium-term needs, and would be funded by international donors. UNTAC was to lay the groundwork for long-term reconstruction by mobilizing and positioning donors, defining what was necessary and setting priorities.

REFUGEE REPATRIATION

By almost any definition, refugee repatriation was a success. Consensus was reached on a written document for refugee repatriation at the first Paris International Conference on Cambodia in 1989. The text was ultimately adopted word for word in October 1991 as Annex 3 of the Comprehensive Political Settlement of the Cambodian Conflict. This remarkable unanimity of opinion is noteworthy not only by comparison with the other tasks entrusted to UNTAC, which were subject to repeated reconsideration, but because it signaled the necessity of depoliticizing humanitarian issues after nearly two decades of conflict. The consensus on the drafting of the language for repatriation presaged cooperation from the competing factions that was not seen in any of UNTAC's other mandates to the same degree. It would be going too far to say that the consensus on refugee repatriation reflected all factions' intention no longer to use civilian populations for political and military purposes. However, there is no question but that all four saw it in their interest to have the refugees return to Cambodia. Most refugees were affiliated with a specific faction and thus were seen as a basis of support that could be transferred across the border in preparation for the elections.

Although such motives worked in favor of repatriation, the logistics of transferring 350,000–370,000 refugees into the interior of Cambodia were daunting. The refugees had to pass through areas that were heavily malarial. Roads, bridges, and transportation networks were in abysmal condition.

It was surprising that so many refugees wanted to return, particularly given the length of time they had resided outside Cambodia. To contemplate hundreds of thousands leaving the relative comfort and physical security of the Thai camps to return to stricken areas of a Cambodia with an uncertain and potentially perilous political future seemed to require an enormous leap of faith. The land to which the refugees were to be returned was littered with hundreds of thousands, if not millions, of mines. Making a living would be precarious at best. Refugees who had fled a ravaged Cambodia were being offered an opportunity to return to a country that was not yet free of civil war, despite the Paris Accords. That they did so, without a single accident or deliberately disruptive incident, by April 1993 is a tribute to their courage and to the will of the four factions and the international community to bring about a smooth population readjustment.

The participation in the repatriation process of the Office of the United Nations High Commissioner for Refugees (UNHCR) helped lubricate the cross-border flow. Given the primary responsibility for refugee return, UNHCR already had a long-standing relationship with the region. This gave it a procedural and operational head start in comparison with UNTAC's other units in the country. UNHCR was far less hampered by the procurement and logistics difficulties that bedeviled all the branches of UNTAC. UNHCR had the support not only of the four factions and the international community; it also had a good relationship with the refugees themselves and their Thai minders. The same was true for the UN Border Relief Operation (UNBRO), which had initiated aid to the border refugees in the late 1970s and was favorably viewed by both the refugees and the Thais. Furthermore, UNHCR operated with a degree of institutional ambiguity that worked in its favor. UNHCR could legitimately claim a degree of independence from UNTAC when it served its interests to do so. This was particularly helpful in dealings with the Khmer Rouge. UNHCR's special envoy Sergio Vieira de Mello could quietly praise the Khmer Rouge for its cooperation with repatriation while Yasushi Akashi was criticizing Khmer Rouge leaders for their noncooperation with disarmament. On the other hand, UNHCR could emphasize its relationship to UNTAC when that furthered its purpose.

In addition to the border refugees, of which 75,000 were in Khmer Rouge-controlled camps,[1] there were another 170,000 displaced inside Cambodia by fighting and mines.[2] It was also expected that the repatriation and resettlement effort would cover the 150,000 soldiers of the four factions due to be disarmed and demobilized. The United Nations predicted that around 90 percent of the camp residents would return to Cambodia. For the most part, the refugees were not prepared for life in Cambodia. As Vieira de Mello, the head of the repatriation program, noted in an interview in April 1992, "International generosity may have gone too far in terms of the care and maintenance, even the spoon-feeding, of Cambodians in exile in the Thai border camps. . . . So we wonder if the refugees are now capable of reacquiring initiative and independence and of accepting a lowered standard of living and health care."[3] It was unclear whether the refugees had the skills necessary to adapt to a harsher life inside Cambodia. More than two-thirds had lived in the border camps beyond ten years. Most were originally farmers, but they had not been farming while in the camps. Better than 90 percent of the refugees were under the age of forty-five, with almost half under the age of fifteen. As a result, many had little memory of Cambodia. There was also a high rate of illiteracy.

UNTAC's Repatriation Mandate

The secretary-general's February 19, 1992, refugee plan for implementation by UNTAC laid out the objectives for repatriation and resettlement.

1. Repatriation of the refugees and internally displaced persons was to take place over nine months.

2. Available agricultural land was to be identified, and resettlement assistance and food for the refugees was to be provided for a year, or for up to eighteen months if necessary.

3. Resettlement assistance and food for up to twelve months was to be provided for up to 30,000 people who returned to Cambodia on their own rather than through the repatriation program.

4. Limited reintegration assistance and upgrading of essential services (such as health care, education, banking, telecommunications and other basic utilities) was to be provided for the refugees through so-called quick-impact projects in areas resettled by refugees. The United Nations Development Programme (UNDP) would undertake infrastructure improvements with funds to be raised separately from UNTAC's repatriation budget.[4]

The repatriation process was expected to take place under the UNHCR's lead in three stages. Refugees were to be moved from the border camps to staging areas in Thailand for final registration and boarding of buses and trucks. They would then cross the border to reception centers inside Cambodia, where they would stay for up to one week. Six such centers were built, with a combined capacity of up to 10,700 returnees. From there, they would travel in trucks to their final destinations.[5]

The first group of 527 refugees crossed into Cambodia on March 30, 1992, where they were met by Prince Sihanouk in Sisophon.[6] By April 8, however, only 2,574 refugees had returned to Cambodia. By then, the United Nations was already reevaluating its working hypothesis of 10,000 returnees per week and acknowledged that the plan, drawn up in July 1991, had seriously underestimated the difficulties involved.

THE PROMISE OF LAND

As originally designed, the resettlement package the refugees were supposed to receive would get them through twelve months, on average. Their building survival kit was to consist of a simple house frame, tools, mosquito nets, and a water container. They were to receive food, which was stockpiled by the World Food Program, so the refugees could eat until they harvested their first crop twelve to eighteen months later. Refugees were also to receive two hectares of land (approximately five acres) for an average family of 4.4 persons. This aid package was estimated by the *Washington Post* to be worth more than $570, nearly four times the average Cambodian family's annual income.[7] Although UN officials recognized that the aid had the potential to be a source of friction between the refugees and local villagers, they believed it was necessary to facilitate the refugees' reintegration.

The promise of land for returning refugees was one of the most problematic aspects of an otherwise uncontroversial program. Preliminary satellite surveys identifying potentially suitable, unclaimed land turned out to be seriously flawed, causing the United Nations to concede as early as April that the offer of land had been too generous. Ground surveys revealed far fewer mine-free areas than originally expected. Getting title to the land was problematic, and where there were prior claims it was usually too expensive to purchase.

The pressure to find land in the four provinces nearest the Thai border increased UNHCR's difficulties. Eighty percent of the refugees asked to be resettled in those provinces, largely because of their proximity to Thailand, even though only 60 percent had lived there before fleeing Cambodia.[8] Those provinces had also been the site of much of the fighting between the Phnom Penh regime and the resistance factions. As a result, much of the land was heavily mined.

The inability of the leaders in the capital to compel local authorities in some areas to make land available prolonged the dependence of some refugees on food assistance and put off their prospects for attaining self-sufficiency. Years of conflict had enhanced the degree of local, district, and provincial autonomy in many places. This was not a problem, however, in areas under the control of the three resistance factions.

In late May, conceding that the promise of land was no longer realistic, UNHCR offered the returnees other options, including cash, instead. While many refugees wanted land, most (88 percent) opted for cash grants of $50 per adult and $25 per child. The change in policy nonetheless triggered a violent protest at one of the Thai border camps.[9] As of mid-June, 27,000 refugees had been returned to Cambodia, but none had received the originally promised allotment of land.[10]

By September, when about 100,000 refugees had been returned, criticism from both returnees and refugee officials had intensified that UNTAC and UNHCR were not resettling refugees, but merely transporting them back into Cambodia and then leaving them to their own devices. The prospect of refugees taking the money, dashing across the border, and then dropping out of sight, alarmed UNHCR officials. The debate over how much the agency should be undertaking in order to help resettle the refugees opened a rift in the organization. On the one hand, criticism that UNHCR failed to deliver what had been promised—specifically, land—was valid. On the other hand, there was serious concern about creating social tensions between returning refugees and local villagers. Even without receiving land, the refugees

economically had been given a leg up. One *New York Times* article reported that local officials in Battambang Province said that villagers, who lived
at bare subsistence level, were resentful of the refugees who returned with
a package of aid that was far above subsistence.[11]

THE PACE OF RETURN QUICKENS

Despite the inability of UNHCR to make land available to refugees, repatriation continued throughout 1992 and early 1993. While the monthly rate
of return had been only 4,000 in April 1992, it rose to 20,000 in June, then
to 35,000 in November, and peaked at 40,000 in January and February
1993.[12] By the end of January, five of the seven Thai border camps had been
closed, including three Khmer Rouge camps. The largest border camp, Site
2, was closed on March 30, 1993. Of the 260,000 refugees who had returned
by the end of January, 55,000 were from Khmer Rouge camps.[13]

Unlike with regard to other aspects of the UNTAC program, the Khmer
Rouge placed no obstacles in the way of the repatriation effort. While it refused
to allow UNTAC military or electoral personnel access to its areas, the Khmer
Rouge cooperated with UNHCR to identify suitable land for resettlement. It
allowed UNHCR access to Khmer Rouge-controlled areas to survey it for
soil quality, mines, road and water access, and to make health assessments.
Repatriation into Khmer Rouge-controlled areas began on January 14, 1993.[14]

Most refugees returned under UNHCR auspices (the 600 who refused
to be repatriated were informed by the government of Thailand that they
would be deported),[15] but untold numbers returned on their own. Even
the onset of the rainy season did not deter them. Road, aircraft, bus, and
boat returns continued despite weather difficulties and the acute disre-
pair of Cambodia's transport systems. More than 90 percent of the
refugees returned to SOC-controlled areas rather than to those controlled by the resistance factions. Although there had been fears that
landless refugees would flood Phnom Penh, that did not happen. In all
likelihood, refugees returned to areas where they had relatives, and reintegrated themselves, assisted by UN cash grants. The cash grants gave the
refugees substantial flexibility. Many responded resourcefully, quickly resuming productive activity.

However, criticism of UNHCR never fully dissipated; instead, it shifted from a focus on failing to meet the refugees' expectations to a concern
that UNHCR was inadequately monitoring the refugees' reintegration once
back in Cambodia. Critics charged that repatriation was overfunded and thus
excessively costly. The chief error lay in budgeting for problems that did not
exist. UNHCR—unlike most of UNTAC's other components—planned for
a worst-case scenario. It wrongly expected that the refugees would have
to be moved back into areas that continued to be wracked by war. There
were other reasons as well to find fault. Sergio Vieira de Mello reflected,

"Our mistake was being too paternalistic. . . . We simply had to abandon the imbecilic notion of giving away land and telling people where to go."[16]

Largely thanks to their own determination, the refugees were successfully reintegrated into Cambodian society. Repatriation efforts focused almost exclusively on the border camp refugees largely because of the visibility and clear definition of the task. Since disarmament of the factions' forces did not take place, UNTAC did not have to reintegrate the roughly 150,000 demobilized soldiers that had been anticipated. Nor was much done about the internally displaced, who largely migrated when and to where they chose, without much assistance from UNTAC.

QUICK-IMPACT PROJECTS

UNHCR's triumph can also be partially attributed to the successful undertaking of quick-impact projects for refugees, funded by the United Nations Development Programme and nongovernmental organizations as well as by UNHCR. Although their number and funding were modest, the quick-impact projects were designed to be labor-intensive, and thus served as a source of employment. They helped to facilitate not only the refugees' reintegration but also, by pumping cash into the local economy, rallied the villagers' support for UNTAC. Some of these projects, which included the repair or construction of roads, bridges, hospitals, dispensaries, schools, and latrines, and the digging of wells and ponds, were similar to work done by other agencies of UNTAC, especially in the implementation of the military's civic action plan. The quick-impact projects were not limited to improvement of Cambodia's infrastructure. Start-up loans were offered; vegetable seeds, fishing equipment, mosquito nets, and water jars were distributed; and special assistance through nongovernmental organizations was made available to those who were particularly vulnerable, such as the elderly, female household heads, orphans, and amputees. By the end of January 1993, $3.4 million of the $9 million allotted to such projects had been spent.[17] By June, UNHCR had funded a total of eighty projects in all twenty-one provinces, including areas controlled by all factions but the Khmer Rouge.

The quick-impact projects were important for the refugees. They were equally important, if not more so, to the local villagers in areas absorbing resettlement, as a tangible means of confirming the international community's concern about Cambodia. They helped to consolidate support for UNTAC and inform the population about its mission, particularly in remote areas. Quick-impact projects also served as a bridge between relief aid and longer-term rehabilitation and reconstruction activities. This "hearts and minds" activity helped make repatriation work and provide UNTAC with a major success.

UNHCR did many things right, including initiating a training program for its Cambodian staff to carry out similar work after its own was finished.

UNHCR's activities were also well-coordinated with UNTAC's overall mission. Repatriation was included as an important component of the Paris Accords, and it was not handled in isolation from other UNTAC tasks. Cooperation between UNHCR and UNTAC's military and civil police components in particular, helped to make repatriation a success. UNHCR served as an important link between UNTAC and the UNDP and the World Food Program, which had responsibilities in the demobilization and cantonment process as well. UNHCR was also a link to other UN agencies, such as UNICEF, and nongovernmental organizations, whose work cut across UNTAC mandates.

UNHCR worked hard to establish and maintain its credibility with all parties. In that way, it was able to insist that fundamental principles be adhered to by all parties. By providing equal treatment to the populations of all factions and strictly respecting their freedom of choice, those involved in the repatriation effort had an easier time ensuring access to and movement in all factions' areas. UNHCR's protection of all refugees in the transportation process, its logistical support for those who wished to return to Khmer Rouge areas, and its protection from retaliation of those from Khmer Rouge camps who returned to SOC-controlled areas helped convince the Khmer Rouge that UNHCR was sincere about depoliticizing the repatriation process. Making certain that all factions were apprised of developments in the repatriation process, which entailed endless dialogue and negotiation, helped allay their suspicions and gain their cooperation. Even when cease-fire violations and political violence were rampant, the repatriation effort continued unhindered. Moreover, by depoliticizing repatriation, UNHCR succeeded in preventing the refugees from being viewed as interlopers or fifth columnists. While the Cambodian population recognized that return of the refugees was an important aspect of its national reconciliation (Sihanouk's personal interest in making repatriation work, as well as his influence over all factions, especially the Khmer Rouge, was critical), UNHCR had an important role to play in raising public awareness.

REHABILITATION AND RECONSTRUCTION

UNTAC's mandate for rehabilitation and reconstruction was simply to lay the groundwork for the international community to bring Cambodia out of economic isolation. Unlike the other components designed to carry out UNTAC mandates, the rehabilitation office had no implementation capability. UNTAC had several objectives in the area of rehabilitation. The first was to design a plan for Cambodia's rehabilitation and reconstruction, which included determining immediate as well as medium- and long-term needs. UNTAC was to set priorities for meeting Cambodia's many needs, which included humanitarian relief and resettlement needs, as well as improving its physical infrastructure and promoting economic development. UNTAC was also to mobilize funds and then coordinate rehabilitation activities that would be undertaken directly by international, bilateral, and nongovernmental organizations, often through existing Cambodian institutions. Thus, the most important aspect of UNTAC's rehabilitation mandate was that it would catalyze the commitment to Cambodia's reconstruction that had been made in the Paris Accords by UN member nations and the international financial community.

APPEAL FOR DONORS

In April 1992, the secretary-general issued an appeal for $595 million for Cambodian rehabilitation. Much of that figure was intended for the repatriation and resettlement of the refugees—$116 million above and beyond UNTAC's main budget for repatriation and another $82.8 million for resettlement of the border refugees, those internally displaced, and demobilized soldiers. Significantly smaller amounts were called for in other areas viewed as rehabilitation: $44.8 million for food security, seeds, and agricultural equipment; $40.6 million for health, nutrition, safe water, and sanitation; and $33.6 million for education and training. A substantial amount, $150.3 million, was requested for repair and restoration of major infrastructure such as public utilities, roads, ports, and railroads.[18]

The secretary-general also made a controversial request of $111.8 million for commodity aid and balance of payments support to help stabilize the economic and social situation in the country.[19] These funds, in essence, were to be used to prop up the Phnom Penh regime's administrative structure. This aspect of the plan was bitterly opposed by the Khmer Rouge. Over its opposition, the Supreme National Council adopted the framework outlined by the secretary-general on May 7, 1992.[20]

The Declaration on the Rehabilitation and Reconstruction of Cambodia, one of the three Paris Accords documents, stipulated that particular attention should be given in the rehabilitation phase to food security, health, housing, training, education, the transportation network, and the restoration of Cambodia's basic infrastructure and public utilities.[21] The secretary-general's February 1992 implementation plan categorized the urgent needs to be met as three types: humanitarian aid (food, health, housing, etc.), resettlement assistance—both for the refugees and for the populations in the villages where the refugees would settle—and physical infrastructure renewal and services.[22]

In defining the nature of Cambodia's infrastructure needs, however, the focus was heavily weighted toward preserving the economic stability of the Phnom Penh regime. In the foreword to an economic assessment of Cambodia's rehabilitation needs prepared jointly by the International

Monetary Fund, the United Nations Conference on Trade and Development, the World Bank, and UNTAC, Akashi defended such emphasis.

> Each of the four Cambodian parties administers the territory it controls. A future elected government must have the administrative means to govern, and will necessarily have to draw, as appropriate, on the existing administrative structures of all four parties, adapting and reforming them as necessary. It is the Phnom Penh administration, however, that has a fully articulated structure capable of formulating and executing economic policy. The structures of this administration will thus be of particular relevance in this process; hence, their present problems and the ways in which they are addressed are of special interest.[23]

The Khmer Rouge objected not only to the UN appeal for budgetary support for the Phnom Penh regime but the emphasis on the need to preserve Phnom Penh's stability and administrative apparatus. "The language of the document equates 'Cambodia' with the Phnom Penh government, fueling Khmer Rouge charges of UNTAC 'de facto recognition' of that party as the country's legitimate representative."[24]

The secretary-general's appeal for funds, particularly the request for budgetary support intended in part to pay civil servants, was not the sole cause of the Khmer Rouge refusal to cooperate with UNTAC. But it reinforced the Khmer Rouge's belief that the United Nations was biased in favor of the Phnom Penh regime. When the Khmer Rouge complained to Akashi, he waved aside their complaints and pressed forward to seek the funding the United Nations believed was necessary to keep the country from falling apart.

THE TOKYO DONORS' CONFERENCE, JUNE 1992

On June 20 and 22, 1992, Japan hosted the Ministerial Conference on Rehabilitation and Reconstruction of Cambodia (Tokyo Conference) in response to the secretary-general's appeal. The donors' commitments exceeded Boutros-Ghali's expectations with pledges totaling $880 million. The United States promised $135 million, France offered $57 million, Australia $40 million, and Sweden $38 million. The international financial institutions, including the Asian Development Bank and the World Bank, plus the UNDP and the European Community, made commitments of roughly $250 million in all. Japan, whose leaders were seeking to make "the Cambodia peace process into a test of their ability to take the political lead in an Asian crisis," pledged between $150 and $200 million.[25] While aid was granted with unforeseen enthusiasm, in their final statement the donors expressed serious concern about "the difficulties UNTAC is encountering in the implementation of the Agreements, in particular over the refusal of one party to allow the necessary deployment of UNTAC. . . ."[26]

In May, an SNC/UNTAC Technical Advisory Committee on Rehabilitation, under the chairmanship of the UNTAC director of rehabilitation, had been established to review, with all four factions, all proposals and programs for rehabilitation projects. This Technical Advisory Committee would then recommend to the Supreme National Council projects for approval. The Khmer Rouge refused to cooperate with the Technical Advisory Committee on the grounds that many of the proposed projects tended to support the Phnom Penh regime.[27] The donors' conference welcomed the establishment of a procedure for clearance of rehabilitation projects because while it left approval in the hands of the SNC, it put UNTAC in charge of coordinating the delivery of aid. It also established a Donors' Consultative Group, composed of diplomats from the donor countries, that met monthly in Phnom Penh for updates on the general aid situation and to share information on the donors' bilateral aid activities.

The UN attempted to reassure the Khmer Rouge that it would be evenhanded in delivering rehabilitation aid. The working paper for the donors' conference stated:

> It is a fundamental principle that multilateral assistance and budget support activities coordinated through UNTAC during the rehabilitation period shall be designated to the Supreme National Council and shall be disbursed when UNTAC can supervise the delivery or expenditure of money. In any United Nations documents referring to assistance or budget support for 'Cambodia' or for 'the Cambodian authorities', it is clearly understood that these terms refer to the whole territory of Cambodia or to the administrations of all Cambodian parties. It is also clearly understood that budgetary support to pay or subsidize the salaries of teachers, administrators, officials, health workers, etc., in 'Cambodia' is applicable according to need of the territory or administration controlled by each Cambodian Party.[28]

Akashi pledged on June 22 that "he would insure that funds were distributed 'in an equitable manner' to areas controlled by each of the four factions."[29] But he also sent a signal that unless UNTAC was able to deliver the assistance freely, the Khmer Rouge was not going to receive it. "The Khmer Rouge has not allowed any freedom of movement for United Nations military or civilians in areas they control. . . . And it is very hard for us to distribute aid and assistance [until] we determine needs in those areas."[30]

APPROVAL OF REHABILITATION PROJECTS

Although the secretary-general indicated in September 1992 that Khmer Rouge cooperation increased after the donors' conference, it still posed obstacles to the approval of projects. At the July 16 meeting of the SNC, UNTAC presented ten projects, worth more than $187 million, for SNC approval. The four factions agreed to nine of the ten, but the Khmer Rouge blocked approval of a proposal for a $74.4 million Asian Development Bank soft loan for projects in transport, power, agriculture, and education. It opposed borrowing from an international financial institution until the role and powers of the SNC were resolved—which they never were to the Khmer Rouge's satisfaction. Consequently, Sihanouk, in a rare exercise of his authority as president of the Supreme National Council, approved all ten projects.[31] The SNC approved an additional seven programs with a combined value in excess of $15 million on August 24, and six more totaling $27 million on September 10, 1992.[32]

By mid-September, the UNTAC director for rehabilitation reported that $408 million had been committed for specific activities, with an additional $338 million pledged for the transition period. Despite those commitments and pledges, essential services at the rural level in health, water supply, sanitation, education, and agriculture, especially in the northeastern provinces, remained underfunded. So, too, were programs in repairing ports, railways, and other public works.[33]

Six months after UNTAC had begun operations in Cambodia, however, virtually none of these proposals had been translated into activity on the ground. Most remained at the proposal stage, pending completion of further studies. The slow rate at which actual work was undertaken resulted in criticism of UNTAC for insufficient progress on reconstructing Cambodia's physical infrastructure. That criticism reflected a lack of understanding about UNTAC's role in the rehabilitation process, which gave it responsibility for coordinating reconstruction but no mandate for initiating or undertaking projects itself. Moreover, even the criticism focused on the planning rather than implementation stages was misdirected. The lion's share of the blame for slow progress belonged elsewhere.

Although it was represented on the Technical Advisory Committee, the Khmer Rouge largely blocked its effective use, causing the director of rehabilitation to fall back on a process of individual discussions with each faction about rehabilitation proposals. That process created problems, causing donors to circumvent the formal procedures, often appealing directly to Sihanouk for project approval, believing that his signature would suffice in place of SNC approval. UNESCO used that procedure until it ran into problems with implementing projects and then turned to the Technical Advisory Committee for assistance.[34]

UNTAC was further hampered in its coordination of rehabilitation activities because there was less than full cooperation on the part of donors. Some donors requested approval of projects only after they had already signed agreements with Phnom Penh, thus depriving the Technical Advisory Committee of any real chance of amending the projects. Two such examples, uncovered by the General Accounting Office, were French rehabilitation of the Pasteur Institute in Calmette Hospital and a survey of the water supply network in the capital.[35]

There were numerous examples of bilateral aid projects that for political reasons were never even submitted to the Technical Advisory Committee for approval. The Thai government rebuilt roads in the border area to facilitate its own logging interests. Other projects that were not submitted included the rehabilitation of roads, schools, and health facilities in the FUNCINPEC zone by the United States. This effort was the continuation of an aid program designed to bolster the non-Communist resistance. Similarly, the Japanese government undertook reconstruction of the bridge of Chrui Changvar as a gesture of goodwill to the Hun Sen administration.[36] In other instances, governments claimed that so-called "projects" were initiated by the private sector, over which they had no control, even though the companies involved presented them as development or assistance projects. The GAO noted several U.S. private-sector projects that fell into this category.[37]

As the formal mechanisms for approving projects did not work well, neither did the informal process of UNTAC consultation with the factions separately. Most of the assistance was negotiated by donor agencies directly and exclusively with the Phnom Penh administration, leaving out the other three factions. Donors essentially went their own way, arguing that since it was their money, they should control how it was spent. The result was that, of the $880 million pledged, donors directed $85 million to activities that were not identified by the United Nations as priority needs or were not intended to begin until after the elections were held.[38]

SLOW DISBURSEMENT OF DONOR FUNDS

A more serious problem, however, was that disbursement of assistance by the donors proceeded exceedingly slowly. At the same time, the list of approved projects grew ever longer. In addition to those given the go-ahead by mid-September 1992, the SNC approved four projects totaling $11.7 million at meetings on September 22 and October 20, and another nine worth more than $100 million on December 8. In all, thirty-five projects worth $340 million had been adopted by the Supreme National Council by the end of 1992. On January 28, 1993, seven more projects worth $24 million were approved.[39] At the end of January 1993, although $540 million of the $880 million pledged had been committed for specific rehabilitation activities, only $95 million had actually been disbursed.[40] By March, that figure had risen to only $100 million.[41]

Slow commitment of donor funds was one concern that prompted a technical-level meeting of the donors on February 25, 1993. The background document for the meeting described the nature of the problem.

> [A] quick response to these specific priority needs has thus far been limited. The generous pledges made at the Tokyo Conference, by and large, have not been translated into funded rehabilitation activities in Cambodia. Certainly they have not been implemented as speedily as was originally anticipated. Pledges have only in part been turned into commitments and commitments have only to some extent been converted into disbursements. Overall financial constraints on aid budgets undoubtedly are a factor at work, but other causes lie closer to the heart of the problem.[42]

Aid disbursement was hampered by a variety of considerations including donors' greater interest in long-term projects, which were often conditioned on additional studies, than in meeting immediate needs and national rehabilitation. Donor countries preferred larger-scale rehabilitation projects, "possibly for reasons of profile as well as of development philosophy."[43] By contrast the nongovernmental organizations initiated a large number of projects, many of which were small and simple but effective in the Cambodian context. Donor governments also had difficulty adapting to Cambodia's actual requirements, particularly at the community level, finding it hard to respond with projects that met small-scale needs or that cut across different aid functions.

The United States, the largest donor at the Tokyo Conference, had only come up with $14 million of the amount it had pledged. The second-largest donor, Japan, had only made available $9 million. Japan blamed the time-consuming scrutiny of all foreign assistance projects by its own foreign ministry; the United States placed the blame on false expectations about what could physically be done in Cambodia in a postwar environment.[44] Underpinning much of the hesitation, however, was a fundamental unwillingness to embark on large-scale aid commitments with the country's political future so uncertain. Political violence had been rising during the fall, peaking in December 1992. In the early months of 1993, it appeared uncertain whether the election would be held at all, despite a remarkably successful voter registration drive that was completed by February 1993. UNTAC's rehabilitation director, Roger Lawrence, expressed concern that donor nations had been slow to make good on their pledges for fear the peace process would fall apart. "We are in a vicious circle here in which the peace process founders in part because the economic component isn't working—and the economic part is not working because the peace process is perceived as foundering. . . . It's disturbing. Whole regions of Cambodia haven't seen any tangible evidence of reconstruction."[45]

Rehabilitation was also hindered by other problems, including donors' tendency to neglect the rural areas in favor of projects to benefit Phnom Penh city dwellers. Five of Japan's nine projects were for Phnom Penh residents, even though 90 percent of Cambodia's population lived in rural areas.[46] The background paper for the February donors' review meeting observed that the donors' concentration on Phnom Penh and the northwestern provinces, where the bulk of the refugees were expected to settle, was leading to an uneven distribution of projects that could adversely affect Cambodia's reconstruction. The lack of clear focus on rural rehabilitation had resulted in the particular neglect of the remote northeastern provinces. It also contravened the objectives of the Paris Accords, which stipulated that "economic aid should benefit all areas of Cambodia, especially the more disadvantaged, and reach all levels of society."[47]

Donors tended to fund their commitments associated with repatriation and resettlement, but not their pledges related to training and the maintenance of essential social services. In fact, 77 percent of disbursements through mid-December 1992 had gone to repatriation and resettlement-related activities, with only 5 percent to infrastructure support, 5.8 percent to general education and training, and 6.6 percent to health and sanitation.[48] Nor did disbursements mirror overall pledges since only one-third of the total funds committed were for resettlement activities. Although 34 percent of donor commitments had been directed toward improvement of Cambodia's public utilities and infrastructure, no substantial disbursements had been made for that purpose by February 1993, not even the $43 million that donors had specifically identified for road repair and construction.[49] What activity there was in road building was being directed by the military unit of UNTAC in civil action projects.

Although the February donors' review meeting resulted in the reaffirmation of pledge commitments and a stated willingness to speed up disbursements, the pace did not significantly pick up until after the May elections. The success of quick-impact projects as part of the repatriation and resettlement activities was recognized and incorporated into the development strategy. "Donor response to the Rehabilitation Component's initiative to implement small-scale quick-impact projects was relatively positive after the election had taken place, while in the period leading up to the election, donors generally expressed great reluctance to support implementation of rehabilitation activities."[50] By July 1993, donors pledged $600,000 toward more than 150 labor-intensive projects that were estimated to cost $1.7 million to repair and maintain rural public utilities and education and health facilities in northern and eastern Cambodia.

Donor commitment was once more reaffirmed at the first meeting of the International Committee on the Reconstruction of Cambodia (ICORC) of September 8–9, 1993, in Paris. The establishment of ICORC had been agreed upon at the 1992 Tokyo Conference, but it was not intended to become operational until after the formation of a new Cambodian government. It was to serve as an international mechanism for coordinating, together with the new government, medium- and long-term assistance for Cambodia's reconstruction.[51] By the first meeting of ICORC, donors' efforts had as a matter of course shifted from rehabilitation to reconstruction, with a recognition of the need for urgent financial assistance to the newly elected government to provide effective administration throughout the country.[52] A subsequent ICORC meeting in March 1994 reaffirmed the international community's commitment to the reconstruction of Cambodia, as well as increased pledges from contributing countries.

Budgetary support for the new government was supposed to come from the international financial institutions as well as from direct bilateral aid. Assistance from the multilateral lending institutions had been previously blocked by failure of the four factions to agree on terms for loans. The formation of the new government enabled the start of loan negotiations between Cambodia and the World Bank, which included a provision for retroactive financing in order to speed disbursement of World Bank aid.[53] In October 1993, the managing director of the International Monetary Fund visited Cambodia as part of an Asian tour.[54]

UNTAC'S PROTECTION OF CAMBODIA'S NATURAL RESOURCES

UNTAC early on recognized the serious threat posed to Cambodia's environment and its economic future by overexploitation of natural resources, particularly the rapid depletion of timber stocks and gem mines. On May 7, 1992, UNTAC suggested that the Supreme National Council consider establishing a mechanism for reviewing the contractual arrangements relating to extraction of natural resources. On July 23, the SNC decided to set up a second Technical Advisory Committee, also chaired by UNTAC's rehabilitation director, to recommend specific measures to deal with the problem. That work, which included the review of the prospects for a countrywide moratorium on the export of logs from Cambodia, principally into Thailand, laid the groundwork for measures taken against the Khmer Rouge later that year.[55]

On September 22, 1992, the SNC, acting at UNTAC's recommendation, adopted a moratorium on the export of unprocessed logs beginning December 31. When the UN Security Council adopted measures on November 30, designed to force Khmer Rouge compliance with the peace plan, it included the moratorium on the export of logs from Cambodia "to protect Cambodia's natural resources," as well as a ban on oil sales to Khmer Rouge areas.[56] Neither the Thai government, nor its military, nor Thai businessmen had any interest, however, in abiding by the logging provisions of the UN embargo, which jeopardized their lucrative trade with the Khmer Rouge. A moratorium on the export of minerals and gems from Cambodia was adopted by the SNC on February 10, 1993, over Khmer Rouge objections, but this was also bound to be ignored by the Thais.[57]

UNTAC's EFFECT ON FOREIGN INVESTMENT

Donor governments' reluctance to disburse funds was not shared by the private sector. There was a remarkable growth in indigenous trade and entrepreneurship, spurred by UNTAC's expenditures as well as foreign private investment, which fostered a general sense of confidence in Cambodia's future. Although this was limited largely to Phnom Penh, nonetheless, it had a notable effect on Cambodia's economy. By December 1992, UNTAC's Economic Adviser's Office reported nearly two hundred companies, from more than twenty countries, were investing in more than three hundred projects. Much of the foreign investment was directed toward serving UNTAC itself through growth in transport, communications, and business service links between Cambodia and the outside world. Some, however, was involved in natural resource exploration, beer and beverage production, and facilities for the manufacture of steel and cement products.[58]

To the extent that UNTAC catalyzed foreign investment, it accomplished what some of the Paris Accords' drafters had intended. While their motives ranged from the pure to the somewhat less so, many believed that the only way to defuse the Khmer Rouge threat was to reintegrate Cambodia into the international community. Ending Cambodia's diplomatic isolation was important; rebuilding Cambodia economically was equally so. The Khmer Rouge's appeal, they believed, would be rendered less attractive if Cambodians were to see the economic benefits that could flow from Western-style commerce. Thailand's and Japan's backing for such an approach was hardly disinterested. Both moved in quickly (and in Thailand's case, rapaciously, for Cambodia historically had been a source for economic exploitation).

LAYING THE GROUNDWORK FOR REBUILDING CAMBODIA

Unlike repatriation, which was a virtually unqualified success, rehabilitation and reconstruction had a somewhat less favorable outcome. This was not UNTAC's fault. Donors were less forthcoming with their pocketbooks than they were with rhetoric. Their hesitation to commit funds when the outcome of the political process was in doubt was unhelpful, if understandable. Moreover, the need to keep the aid flows neutral had an inhibiting effect on development. "UNTAC must ensure that its development support is not used for the primary benefit of any one political party. Political considerations of this nature, over and above problems of absorptive capacity, have probably had the effect of slowing down potential disbursements. Bilateral and multilateral infrastructure investment and project development has also been somewhat constrained until such time as a democratically elected government is in place."[59]

Like most of UNTAC's other components, the rehabilitation and reconstruction office was not truly neutral in how it carried out its work. While it attempted to keep aid flows distributed fairly, it was not capable of controlling foreign investment, nor was it possible to prevent donors from directing their aid to support their political clients. Undoubtedly, the preponderance of assistance to urban areas skewed rehabilitation work in the Phnom Penh authorities' favor. Khmer Rouge objections were vehement, but to no avail. By denying UNTAC access to the areas it controlled, the Khmer Rouge handed UNTAC its most powerful lever: money. While funds flowed, to a greater or lesser extent, into the areas controlled by all three other factions, the Khmer Rouge-controlled areas were denied the economic benefits of both official donor rehabilitation assistance and private foreign investment. While the Khmer Rouge leaders must have chewed their nails in frustration, they never backed down, undoubtedly fearing that exposure to Western commerce and ideas could erode their political support if they opened their areas even the slightest bit.

Yet for all its problems, the UNTAC rehabilitation unit laid the groundwork for Cambodia's eventual reconstruction. It developed a plan, set priorities, established mechanisms for coordinating international assistance, both during UNTAC's tenure and after the formation of the new government, and sustained donors' interest in rebuilding Cambodia. It will be up to the Cambodians to keep the process going.

5

WORKING TOWARD A NEUTRAL POLITICAL ENVIRONMENT: THE MILITARY, CIVIL POLICE, AND CIVIL ADMINISTRATION UNDER UNTAC

The Paris Accords stipulated that there be a neutral political environment in which Cambodian elections could take place. Although the work of most of UNTAC's component bodies was structured to contribute to accomplishing this mission, three of them were viewed as central: the military, the civil police, and civil administration. The military was to disarm the factions and control Cambodia's guns; the civil police were to provide law enforcement; and civil administration was to oversee all four factions' (primarily Phnom Penh's) administrative structures. The tasks assigned to the military component were considered key not only to ensuring a neutral political environment but to UNTAC's overall success. Without disarmament, confiscation of weapons, and cantonment of the factions' forces, fighting was expected to continue, putting all plans for the country's recovery into danger.

It did not work out the way the drafters of the Paris Accords had intended. In contrast to the successful repatriation of 365,000 refugees and the free and fair elections of May 1993, neither the military, the civil police, nor the civil administration components fully accomplished their missions. The factions were not disarmed, their forces were not confined to cantonment areas, and their guns were not confiscated. Fighting continued, albeit at a much reduced level over previous years. The civil police were not effective at providing law enforcement. Civil administration was never able to assert the degree of control over the factions' administrative apparatus the drafters had desired. When the elections took place, there was no truly neutral political environment.

In retrospect, it is clear that all three units were initially assigned unrealistic missions. The civil police and civil administration components also were given inadequate resources. The civil police were particularly hampered by seriously undertrained and, in many cases, unqualified, staff. While they were unarmed and did not have arrest powers (except toward the end of UNTAC's tenure), they were expected to monitor the police forces of each faction to ensure that law and order prevailed and that abuses were curtailed. Civil administration, whose efforts were intended in large part to neutralize—insofar as possible—the inherent advantage of incumbency by controlling the administrative apparatus of the State of Cambodia, was badly understaffed. The military tasks were predicated on the full cooperation of all four factions, and UNTAC had neither a mandate to enforce compliance nor contingency plans in case of obstruction by any faction.

But it turned out that a truly neutral environment was *not* essential to free and fair elections. Somehow, Cambodians managed to overcome the setbacks and participate in an electoral process that resulted in a legitimate new government for the country. In that sense, each of the political and security units contributed to achieving the most important of UNTAC's missions. Each also accomplished a number of other tasks that assisted in the process of building peace in Cambodia.

THE MILITARY COMPONENT

There is no question but that the military component failed to accomplish the tasks laid out in the Paris Accords. While UNTAC did not bring about a complete cessation of hostilities, though, neither did the country disintegrate into conflict, as many had feared. The level of conflict during UNTAC's tenure was lower than it had been for years.

PEACEKEEPING; NOT PEACE ENFORCEMENT

UNTAC was authorized by the Security Council under Chapter VI of the UN Charter. The vast majority of UN peacekeeping missions are authorized under Chapter VI. These are the traditional "peacekeeping" operations, in which neutral UN military personnel separate parties that have agreed to stop fighting. By contrast, missions authorized under Chapter VII of the Charter permit the use of force to accomplish their goals and are generally regarded as "peace enforcement" operations. Although the Korean War and the Congo operation met the criteria for peace enforcement missions, authorization under Chapter VII was never undertaken until recently. It has been used during the 1991 Persian Gulf War, and afterward to keep Iraqi troops in check, and in support of the U.S.-led intervention in Somalia.

The mission in the former Yugoslav republics was ultimately upgraded from a Chapter VI to a Chapter VII operation. The U.S.-led intervention in Haiti in September 1994 was authorized under Chapter VII.

UNTAC, while authorized under Chapter VI, has been termed a "Chapter VI and three-quarters operation" because its military duties exceeded the generally acknowledged scope of peacekeeping. The "three-quarters" acknowledges the ambiguity regarding how far UNTAC was authorized to go in enforcing its Paris Accords mandates. As a Senate Foreign Relations Committee report on peacekeeping operations noted,

> Cambodia and Yugoslavia represent operations more robust than the traditional peacekeeping mission but still short of the heavily armed military involvement characteristic of an operation such as Somalia.... [They] were conceived as Chapter VI operations—traditional peacekeeping operations but with an expanded force structure.... Parts of the Cambodian peace settlement, however, broke down. Sporadic fighting re-emerged, including attacks on U.N. personnel, which endangered the entire settlement. Field commanders found that they had to reinterpret their mandate in order to ensure the success of their operation's overall objective—holding national elections.... 'Mission creep' has now become a major problem as forces inserted into conflict areas with limited military capabilities have now had to enforce an enlarged mandate.[1]

That UNTAC ultimately stayed within the parameters of a Chapter VI mission and did not "creep" into Chapter VII enforcement actions was due largely to the insistence of John Sanderson and Yasushi Akashi not to resort to force to disarm the factions, as many had urged. UNTAC was, a UN official declared, "diplomatically aggressive, militarily passive."[2] Akashi sought at every opportunity to negotiate a solution to UNTAC's impasse with the Khmer Rouge—and was criticized extensively by those who wanted to compel the Khmer Rouge to disarm. Sanderson believed that the United Nations was better suited for peacekeeping missions and that peace enforcement should be left to the major powers. UNTAC would have required a new mandate to engage in peace enforcement. It would also have required a totally different command structure.[3] Sanderson, who had served in Vietnam, also knew that it did not make sense to go into the jungle to try to make people do what they don't want to do.

Even if the Security Council had authorized additional troops to force Khmer Rouge compliance, their use would have jeopardized the United Nation's neutrality. It would also have created difficulties for the troop-contributing countries. Some contingents were not trained for, and may not have been capable of, peace enforcement activities. In other cases, even with Security Council authorization, some governments might have objected to the use of their troops for peace enforcement rather than peacekeeping.

THE MILITARY MANDATE

According to the secretary-general's February 19, 1992, implementation plan for UNTAC, "The objectives of the military arrangements during the transitional period are to stabilize the security situation and build confidence among the parties to the conflict. The achievement of these objectives is a necessary precursor to the successful conduct of the functions of the other components and, in particular, the repatriation programme."[4] Following the Paris Accords, the implementation plan laid out four main tasks for UNTAC's military wing:

a. Verification of the withdrawal and non-return of all categories of foreign forces and their arms and equipment;

b. Supervision of the cease-fire and related measures, including regroupment, cantonment, disarming and demobilization;

c. Weapons control, including monitoring the cessation of outside military assistance, locating and confiscating caches of weapons and military supplies throughout Cambodia, and storing of the arms and equipment of the cantoned and the demobilized military forces;

d. Assisting with mine-clearance, including training programs and mine awareness programmes.[5]

The military component was also charged with several other tasks including investigating complaints about noncompliance with the Paris Accords' military provisions, facilitating the release of prisoners of war, and assisting in the repatriation of refugees and displaced persons.[6] As originally conceived, the military unit was not intended to assist in registration of voters, or protection of political party offices, or of UNTAC civilian workers, patrolling for bandits, provision of security for polling places, or initiation of civic action projects. All of these duties it eventually undertook as the mission evolved.

SLOW DEPLOYMENT

The first UNTAC troops joined the UNAMIC force of 300 on March 16, 1992. The initial contingent of 200 Indonesian soldiers grew to a total force of roughly 16,000, with peacekeepers from 32 countries.[7] The troops included 12 infantry battalions from 11 countries,[8] United Nations Military Observers (including a naval unit to patrol the Mekong River), five engineering units, communications, air support, mine clearing, medical and logistical units.[9] UNTAC had 10,200 infantry troops in battalions and between 5,000 and 6,000 in support units.[10]

The 830-person military logistics battalion was small (less than half the size of what would normally support a force of UNTAC's size) and deployed late. Recruitment of logistics forces for UNTAC was hampered because of the high demand by other UN missions for the same specialists. For maximum efficiency, logistics personnel should be deployed prior to the main force; in Cambodia, four of five logistics companies arrived in July 1992, after all twelve infantry battalions had been deployed.[11]

Recruitment of forces for UNTAC would have been a slow process under any circumstances. But it was further impeded by the simultaneous recruitment for UN operations in the former Yugoslav republics. Formal requests for troops could not be made until UNTAC was officially established on February 28, 1992. Deployment was delayed by domestic political debates in the contributing countries over whether and what type of troops to send. It was also slowed by problems in UN logistics planning and support, as mentioned. Sanderson told the GAO that he made "the 'perilous decision' to begin [disarmament] on June 13 with only 8 1/2 infantry battalions."[12] It took until the end of June—half a month after the disarmament process had begun—for all military battalions to be on the ground in Cambodia.[13]

VERIFICATION OF WITHDRAWAL OF FOREIGN FORCES

"Strategic investigation teams" made up of UN military observers were given the responsibility for investigating reports of the presence of foreign (that is, Vietnamese) forces still in Cambodia beyond the deadline for withdrawal. Between mid-July and November 1992, they investigated ten such reports and found no evidence of foreign military personnel operating in Cambodia. In early December, UNTAC set up two quick-reaction strategic investigation teams to address the continuing concerns of the Khmer Rouge and other factions about the Vietnamese presence.[14] Nevertheless, the secretary-general reported that "UNTAC has not so far found evidence of any formed units of foreign forces in areas of Cambodia to which it has access."[15] Although all factions were asked to provide additional information to support claims that such forces existed in Cambodia, none did so. That does not mean there was a total absence of individual Vietnamese soldiers. However, the small number eventually identified had neither strategic nor tactical significance. The question of foreign forces in Cambodia became a major point of contention, especially by the Khmer Rouge, which used such charges to justify its noncompliance with the Paris Accords. Anti-Vietnamese sentiment was rampant in the Cambodian population and was whipped up by all three resistance factions to deflect attention from other matters.

On March 1, 1993, UNTAC announced that it had determined that three persons under investigation fit the definition of foreign forces that was approved by the Supreme National Council (SNC) the previous October; four more were so identified by May 1. The first three were married to Cambodian women and had children, and although two were serving with the Phnom Penh regime's armed forces, there was no indication that they were in any way under the control of Vietnamese authorities.[16]

INVESTIGATIONS OF CEASE-FIRE VIOLATIONS

UNTAC's mandate contained no mechanism to enforce the cease-fire agreement. As a result, when disarmament did not take place, cease-fire violations increased. UNTAC was able only to investigate, report to the factions, and attempt to negotiate further cease-fire agreements.

The number of cease-fire violations rose from June through September 1992. Casualties, mostly civilian, increased due to shelling and attacks on villages. An increase in banditry resulted in the UN military detachment being assigned to protect UNTAC's civilian personnel, especially electoral workers during the registration process. Until the imposition of a selective trade embargo on the Khmer Rouge on November 30, however, UNTAC personnel did not appear to be targets. Hostage incidents, including those involving UNTAC military personnel, increased markedly in December, but all were resolved without casualties. From June through early December, UNTAC confirmed 610 of the 1,200 violations reported.[17] Most took place in Kompong Thom, Siem Reap, and Battambang provinces in central and northwestern Cambodia.

The security situation deteriorated in 1993, partly because the Phnom Penh regime launched military attacks on the Khmer Rouge in an attempt to regain territory lost during the rainy season. More civilians were displaced and suffered casualties from these attacks than during the previous year. Attacks on UNTAC personnel also increased, particularly during the period leading up to the elections. On March 27, a Bangladeshi soldier was killed in the first deliberate attack on UNTAC personnel. By May 3, eleven UNTAC civilian and military workers had been killed. Security measures were increased accordingly. The lack of contingency planning in the event of a failure to disarm likely increased UNTAC casualties.

DISARMAMENT, DEMOBILIZATION, AND CANTONMENT

UNTAC ran into difficulties with the Khmer Rouge almost immediately. In response to the deployment of multinational troops, the Khmer Rouge denied UNTAC access to its areas that it needed to survey for cantonment sites. UNTAC had hoped to start disarmament, cantonment, and demobilization on June 1, 1992, but lack of cooperation compelled a two-week delay.[18] Even so, the process of getting troops into Cambodia was held up, and Sanderson had to proceed with disarmament before all of UNTAC's infantry battalions had arrived.

The military mandate, under Chapter VI, was premised on the idea that all four factions would willingly participate in the disarmament, demobilization, and cantonment process: "Thus, the peace agreement and implementation plan gave the military the responsibility of monitoring, supervising, and verifying the parties' adherence to the agreement, rather than enforcing the military aspects of the agreement."[19] Charging that the United Nations had not implemented other aspects of the Paris Accords—in particular, that it had neither verified the withdrawal of all foreign forces nor dismantled the Phnom Penh regime—the Khmer Rouge refused to disarm, demobilize, and regroup its forces into cantonment areas. The lack of an enforcement mechanism ultimately meant that UNTAC either had to acquiesce and halt the disarmament process or alter its mission to use force to compel Khmer Rouge compliance.

Akashi and Sanderson were unwilling to use force. Lengthy negotiations took place, one round during the summer of 1992, the other in the fall. Neither succeeded in securing Khmer Rouge compliance. As a result, only 50,000 troops, mostly those of the Phnom Penh authorities, had been cantoned by September 10.[20] Only 50,000 weapons, many of which were not serviceable, had been taken into UN custody. According to UNTAC's chief of operations, Colonel Aris Salim, the regime used cantonment to reorganize and rid its army of undesirable soldiers and weapons, thus increasing its efficiency and effectiveness.[21] Eventually the United Nations allowed the factions to remove their weapons from storage for self-defense and released the cantoned soldiers for "agricultural leave" until December 15. GAO investigators noted that, to their knowledge, "no formerly cantoned soldiers returned to their cantonment sites on that date, nor did UNTAC notify them to do so."[22]

Although UNTAC did not accomplish the objective of disarming and demobilizing the factions' forces, blaming it would not be warranted by the situation as it developed. Yasushi Akashi defended his organization vigorously:

> I think it is crucial to recall that that objective was set by the four Cambodian factions, who then committed themselves to it by signing the Paris Agreements. The same goes for the cease-fire provisions. UNTAC . . . was not a signatory to the Agreements but was created as a result of them. To imply . . . that the failure to disarm was in some way UNTAC's responsibility seems to me to miss the whole point about peacekeeping as opposed to peace

enforcement. . . . [O]ne of the parties reneged on its signed agreement to commit its forces to cantonment and demobilization. Responsibility for the failure to carry out those operations should therefore be laid squarely at the door of the Party of Democratic Kampuchea [Khmer Rouge]. To do otherwise is to imply that UNTAC somehow had the right to compel cantonment and disarmament by force, which . . . is incorrect. Nor did UNTAC have sufficient military force to accomplish such an undertaking; blithe proponents of "enforcement" seem to overlook the fact that the Vietnamese occupied Cambodia for a decade with 200,000 troops without managing to bring the country fully under their control.[23]

MINE CLEARANCE

The slow pace of clearing mines dogged UNTAC and the repatriation effort from start to finish. Mines were everywhere. They had been laid, and were still being laid, by all factions, as well as by some villagers, and no maps of the minefields existed. It was reported that mines had maimed 1 out of every 236 Cambodians by September 1992, giving Cambodia the highest proportion of amputees in the world.[24]

Although the Security Council expanded UNAMIC's mandate on January 8, 1992, to include training in mine clearance for Cambodians and the initiation of a mine-clearing program,[25] the task was never given priority attention, adequate funding and personnel, or a defined line of authority under UNTAC. The $14.7 million program was mired in legal wrangling over liability, the extent of the UN mandate, and questions about how to disburse the funds. Until the Cambodian Mine Action Centre became operational, responsibility for mine clearance was uncertain. For most of 1992 and 1993, the only groups regularly engaged in mine-clearance operations were three nongovernmental organizations: McGrath's Mines Advisory Group and the HALO Trust, both from Great Britain, and Norwegian People's Aid.[26] UNTAC initially planned to train 5,000 mine clearers by the end of 1992. By September, fewer than 800 had been trained and only 100 had begun work under the auspices of the nongovernmental organizations.[27]

The slow start and limited progress on mine clearance was the result of several uncertainties. The United Nations initially had difficulty specifying its own mine-clearing mandate. It first had to determine whether to undertake mine clearance with UNTAC personnel or to contract with others to clear mines. In early to mid-1992, UNHCR channeled money to the nongovernmental organization Handicap International to clear mines along repatriation routes. Handicap International then subcontracted with deminers. Not until August and September did UNTAC personnel themselves, including the engineering branch's Mine Clearance Training Unit, start clearing mines. By December 1992, only 43 hectares had been cleared by UNTAC.[28] The United Nations also had serious difficulty recruiting national troop contingents to undertake mine-clearance operations. UNTAC's force engineer, Colonel Neil Bradley, pointed out that "plenty were prepared to supervise but none to actually do mineclearing."[29] Ultimately, only eight of the national contingents in UNTAC had personnel engaged even in training Cambodians in mine-clearance techniques.[30]

Mine clearance is tedious, hazardous, and costly. UNTAC estimated that a de-mining team cleared about 1,300 square meters each week at a cost of about $2,000.[31] The cost of clearing one mine, including the training of de-miners, was estimated at three hundred to one thousand dollars each.[32] Although UNTAC explored different methods of speeding up the process, Force Engineer Bradley told GAO that there was no magic technology for defeating Cambodia's mine problem.[33]

The Cambodian Mine Action Centre (CMAC) originated as an element of UNAMIC on February 21, 1992. It was reestablished later that spring by the Supreme National Council as a Cambodian rather than an UNTAC organization to institutionalize and "Cambodianize" mine-clearance operations, as well as to provide a channel for international donations toward demining.[34] UNTAC transferred responsibility for the coordination of information about mine locations to the Cambodian Mine Action Centre, with UNTAC repatriation director Sergio Vieira de Mello serving as CMAC's interim director. The Cambodian Mine Action Centre did not actually take over mine-clearance operations until mid-1993.[35]

The pace of mine clearance picked up in 1993, though the difficulty of coordinating information from the four factions about mine locations with villagers' recollections did not diminish. It was not surprising that as of May 1993, only 15,000 mines and other pieces of unexploded ordnance out of an estimated 2–4 million—or nearly one mine for every two Cambodians—had been cleared.[36] Progress was made over the summer, nevertheless, and the secretary-general could report on August 26 that more than 4 million square meters had been cleared of mines, about 37,000 mines and other unexploded devices had been destroyed, and that 2,330 Cambodians had been trained in mine-clearance techniques, of whom about 1,400 were employed for that purpose.[37]

The termination of UNTAC's mission on September 26, 1993, made CMAC's future appear uncertain. In October 1993, it was announced that all foreign employees of CMAC would be withdrawn by November, although this deadline was extended another month. However, by March 1994 the situation had stabilized. CMAC had become a wholly Cambodian organization with an ongoing relationship with UNDP. Further funding had been pledged at the International Committee on the Reconstruction of

Cambodia meeting in March, and foreign military supervisory staff offered assistance to the organization.[38]

MILITARY-CIVILIAN COORDINATION

It was widely believed that without general disarmament the other UNTAC units could not succeed at their tasks. Yet the military's work was not coordinated with that of the other components. "In Cambodia, both military and civilian components reported to the Special Representative, but there was no joint military-civilian staff initially to help coordinate their activities. There were weekly coordination meetings involving all components, but according to UNTAC military officers, this was initially at a policy level, and not at the working level. A joint working staff from the beginning would have facilitated the planning and implementation of UNTAC operations."[39] This lack of coordination caused duplication and overlap of tasks.

> The military had little input into the planning for civilian activities even in areas where similar tasks were planned. . . . UNTAC's civilian components planned several projects, such as road building and water sanitation, with private voluntary organizations working in Cambodia. Due to the lack of coordination, some of these projects, which were intended to provide income and skills to the local population, were preempted and completed by the military as part of its civic action campaign. According to the Force Commander, providing security and proceeding with the civic action campaign were crucial to the success of the mission and could not be delayed until the civilians were in place to begin planning and coordinating rehabilitation.[40]

The absence of joint planning between the civilian and military sides of UNTAC also left electoral workers in some provinces fearful for their safety as banditry became an increasing problem and political violence escalated in late 1992. In other provinces this was not a problem. Despite the lack of a formal coordination mechanism, some civilian administrators and military commanders had good working relationships based on respect for each other's professional competence. In cases where the working relationship was less favorable, having no formal coordination proved to be a serious hindrance. The GAO reported that

> in one province, the U.N. civilian director complained about the lack of cooperation he was getting from the military in protecting U.N. staff. He said some electoral workers had requested protection from the local U.N. military unit. When they did not receive protection, they postponed operations. An UNTAC military observer

told us that the electoral workers had not coordinated their activities and the military could not immediately reassign troops from already planned commitments. Another U.N. civilian director said banditry was a problem because, after the factions refused to disarm and demobilize, many Cambodian troops turned to banditry to survive. He had asked the military for help and was told the UNTAC police would provide protection. After the UNTAC police could not provide protection, the military began to patrol for bandits.[41]

The absence of a single designated head of all civilian and military operations in each province was part of the problem. The Malaysian sector commander told GAO that a civilian administrator should have been named as the top provincial official in the chain of command.[42]

Problems with UNTAC Troops

Problems that typically arise in any peacekeeping mission appeared in UNTAC as well. UNTAC troops were not of uniform caliber. Some contingents did not arrive with the required basic equipment; some were inadequately trained. Language difficulties got in the way of effective coordination. UNTAC did have standing rules of engagement that emphasized the peacekeeping nature of the operation. However, each national contingent differed in its interpretation of the following language from standing operating procedures: "The use of force is authorized either in self-defence or in resisting attempts by forceful means to prevent UNTAC from accomplishing its mission."[43] The well-equipped and well-armed, specialized Dutch battalion stationed in northwestern Cambodia had a reputation for rapid and decisive action in defense of its soldiers and civilians. The Malaysians, in western Cambodia, also had a tough reputation. Many of their soldiers learned the Khmer language and attempted to develop a working relationship with Khmer Rouge in the region. By contrast, the Indonesians and Uruguayans were more passive when threatened. In one incident, thirty Indonesians were asked by the Khmer Rouge to give up their weapons and to come to its provincial headquarters. They were then held prisoner for five days.[44] An assessment of the overall caliber of UNTAC's national contingents was offered by FUNCINPEC's head of security, as reported by the General Accounting Office:

> [S]ome of the UNTAC contingents had no teeth. Some military units simply camped out, did not protect Cambodians, and did not fire back even when the Khmer Rouge fired upon them. . . . Some troops, however, were to be respected. The Dutch and Malaysians were to be feared. The Bulgarians he [FUNCINPEC's head of security] had no respect for. The Uruguans [sic]

were simply after money and artifacts. The Khmer Rouge and all forces knew which troops were weak and not to be respected, and which could be taken advantage of. All the factions also knew which troops to avoid and not to anger.[45]

Disciplinary problems were the cause of much of the criticism UNTAC's troops received. The *Washington Post* reported at the end of UNTAC's mission that "military contingents and civilians of many nationalities served with distinction in Cambodia. But the behavior of others tarnished the U.N.'s reputation here. . . . [C]omplaints against U.N. soldiers and police have centered on weapons smuggling, sexual harassment, non-performance of duties and numerous Cambodian fatalities from reck-lessly driven U.N. vehicles. . . ." The Bulgarian battalion caused the great-est number of unpleasant incidents.[46]

The problems with UNTAC troops and civilian police were not mere-ly disciplinary. According to the General Accounting Office summary of an interview with the local director of the American Red Cross,

UNTAC troops were not culturally aware of the Cambodian peo-ple, nor respectful of them. UNTAC soldiers frequently abused Cambodians, swore at them, and were rude. When driving, UNTAC troops virtually ran over school children, who until recently had almost never seen trucks and cars before. . . . [S]ome troops were first rate, including the Malaysians and Thais, but most were rude, even to international staff.[47]

The lack of cultural sensitivity was not merely an annoyance. It reduced the respect that Cambodians had for UNTAC and made it easier for oppo-nents to discredit the operation. A director of one of the nongovernmental organizations in Phnom Penh had seen an UNTAC Bulgarian soldier put a gun to the head of a Cambodian worker to intimidate him. A GAO investi-gator viewed records indicating that the soldier in question was repatriated.[48]

But the United Nations was also faced with a problem: It had no author-ity to discipline those who served in its name. It could investigate incidents, request that the offender be sent home, or garnishee wages. Between July and November 1992, UNTAC repatriated eighty-one military personnel for dis-ciplinary reasons, including fifty-six Bulgarians.[49] But, a UN spokesman said, although the Bulgarians "behave in a manner that makes all of us blush," they could not be sent home en masse. "It would be a terrible insult."[50]

THE MILITARY COMPONENT'S REDEFINED MISSION

The military's greatest successes largely lay in the tasks it undertook that were either not part of the original implementation plan, such as civic-action programs, or were part of the redefined mandate after demobilization and disarmament fell apart, namely, providing security for the elections. When it became clear the Khmer Rouge was not going to cooperate with disarmament and cantonment, and that the negotiations designed to induce compliance had been unsuccessful, Akashi recommended to Secretary-General Boutros Boutros-Ghali and the Security Council that UNTAC proceed with its mission with an enhanced focus on the elections. The Security Council had warned the Khmer Rouge in a resolution adopted unanimously on October 13, 1992, to join the peace process by November 15 or face punitive action.[51] At the recommendation of Akashi, Sanderson, and the secretary-general, the Security Council adopted another resolution on November 30, 1992, that reconfirmed the intent to move forward with the elections, with or without Khmer Rouge participation. This resolution also imposed a selective trade embargo on the Khmer Rouge,[52] which was to be enforced by UNTAC troops. This involved establishment of border checkpoints and UNTAC monitoring of petroleum shipments into Cambodia and exports of logs, gems, and other minerals from Cambodia. The Khmer Rouge refused to allow UNTAC to establish nine additional checkpoints in areas it controlled along the Thai border. UNTAC was unable, therefore, to monitor log exports—a major source of Khmer Rouge income—to Thailand from those areas.

With this action, UNTAC's mission was reoriented to emphasize the May elections as its priority. Although the redefined mission appeared to be a radical alteration in the peacekeepers' role, it was consistent with the objectives laid out in the Paris Accords. Article 11 of the Paris agreement stipulated that the military objectives were to "stabilize the security situation and build confidence among the parties to the conflict, so as to reinforce the purpose of this agreement and to prevent the risks of a return to warfare."[53] The new focus affected the work of many UNTAC units in Cambodia, but none more so than the military. UNTAC had originally expected to reduce its force level substantially by the end of 1992 on the assumption that disarmament would be completed. Instead, the secretary-general now proposed that the current deployment be maintained through the elections.[54] The Security Council agreed to that recommendation on November 30.

One of the most visible changes resulting from the shift in mission was a redeployment of forces in support of the electoral process. Effective December 31, 1992, battalion boundaries were realigned to coincide with provincial boundaries—the basis for civilian components' work. UNTAC also established an Electoral Coordination Center at headquarters in Phnom Penh and joint coordination centers in each province to provide twenty-four-hour combined military and civilian command posts during registration and the election. Military observers accompanied electoral teams in order to negotiate, where necessary, with local authorities or officials who tried to obstruct voter registration.

Orders were issued for troops to undertake more active patrolling to control banditry, shield electoral workers, and protect party offices and candidates. UNTAC troops also continued to provide security for the repatriation process. Although these measures helped to improve the security situation for the registration process, begun in September and completed early in 1993, it also brought UNTAC troops under increasing attack as they entered areas controlled by the Khmer Rouge.

The redeployment of forces was essential in ensuring that the elections were held. It is questionable whether UNTAC's electoral team could have carried out its massive registration effort without the increased protection provided by the military forces. Although a few civilian workers, mostly electoral staff, came under attack as the elections drew nearer, the presence of UNTAC soldiers helped to provide confidence in the electoral process. UNTAC's military presence protected the integrity of the election and the security of the ballot boxes, thus helping to guarantee a reasonably free and fair election.

Just as the repatriation process was enhanced by the quick-impact programs, the military's civic action projects reinforced UNTAC's commitment to the Cambodian people. Its "hearts and minds" campaign was a new foray for UN peacekeeping troops. UNTAC's troops provided free medical care in the countryside. They built roads, bridges, and schools, and repaired airports. They taught languages and instructed Cambodians in how to purify water and treat intestinal disorders. They sponsored sports and cultural activities, and showed UNTAC videos and films at cantonment sites and other locations. UNTAC military units dug wells and constructed toilets for villages. They even carried out some projects in Khmer Rouge-controlled areas.[55] These activities were paid for by individual governments; UNTAC's budget did not include funds to cover them. India, for example, supplied the Indian field hospitals with medicines to be provided free of charge to Cambodians.[56]

In addition to its contribution to the holding of elections, UNTAC's military component kept down the level of conflict and helped to prevent an escalation of ethnic, particularly anti-Vietnamese, violence. While the military did not accomplish its primary disarmament mission, nonetheless, it achieved the unwritten goal of many signatories of the Paris Accords: it helped keep the Khmer Rouge out of power.

The Civil Police Component (CIVPOL)

The civil police mandated by the Paris Accords was modeled on the United Nations' successful Namibia operation. Civil police there faced numerous obstacles, particularly from the South West African police, who did not want to cooperate and resented having UN personnel monitor their operations. The UN police dealt with complaints of election-related intimidation and violence. In doing so, they instilled confidence in the population about the election process, which was central to the Namibian mission's outcome.[57]

While the use of civilian police in Namibia broke new ground for UN peacekeeping, in Cambodia, the civil police component (CIVPOL) was probably UNTAC's least successful. The civil police were charged with ensuring that law and order was maintained effectively and impartially, and that human rights and fundamental freedoms were fully protected. It quickly became apparent that this was an impossible task given the small number of police officers available.

Unable to fulfill its initial assignment, CIVPOL's mission then devolved into monitoring the SOC police forces. Although charged with supervising all four factions' police, only the Phnom Penh regime had anything approximating a regular police force. The United Nations initially estimated that SOC police numbered 47,000. However, these were poorly equipped, had few cars, were largely untrained, had no standardized procedures, and often went unpaid. The Khmer Rouge police reportedly numbered over 9,000, although they were scarcely distinguishable from Khmer Rouge military forces. The non-Communist factions had only token forces: 150 FUNCINPEC police and 400 KPNLF police.[58] UNTAC's work with the two non-Communist factions focused on instruction in the use of a civilian police force, rather than soldiers, to maintain law and order. As in other areas, Khmer Rouge cooperation was not forthcoming.

After disarmament was halted, the work of the civil police was redirected toward support of the elections through an enhanced focus on creating a neutral political environment. Even so, this reduced mandate was probably still unrealistic. As the civilian police commissioner told the General Accounting Office, it was difficult to implement because it involved changing the hearts and minds of the Phnom Penh regime's police and the Cambodian people.[59] While the peacekeepers in many places were able to create goodwill toward UNTAC among the Cambodian people, CIVPOL's efforts were directed toward the largely untrained and ill-equipped SOC police, who more often than not were tied politically to the SOC political structure. To have recast such a police force in a Western mold during UNTAC's tenure would have necessitated far greater commitment of resources, as well as a massive education program targeting the civilian population.

DEFICIENCIES IN CIVPOL PERSONNEL AND AUTHORITY

It took the United Nations even longer to recruit civilian police than peacekeeping troops or staff for other civilian operations. Only 200 police were in Cambodia in April 1992 and 800 in May. By September 21, when disarmament was supposed to have been completed, only 2,500 of the expected 3,600 civil police had been deployed. The component was still not fully staffed as late as December.[60]

The factions' failure to disarm not only made the civil police's tasks more difficult; it also made CIVPOL's weaknesses more apparent. The ability to carry out its mandate was hampered not only by slow deployment, but by insufficient staff, uneven caliber of its personnel, questions about the extent of their authority, and the lack of a common frame of reference to guide investigations of human rights abuses. Deficiencies in equipment did not make the situation any easier. Even as late as December 1992, the police chief of staff did not have a system that allowed him to communicate directly with the provincial offices.[61]

While a force of 3,600 may have appeared to be large, once police were dispersed to the provincial and district levels their numbers were inadequate to cover all the assigned tasks. Battambang province was assigned 162 UNTAC police from sixteen nations. Of those, only 20–22 were available to monitor 1,500 local police. The others were expected to investigate human rights complaints (as many as sixty in one three-month period), to protect—in teams of three—each of the forty to fifty voter registration sites, and to guard all of the political party offices in the province. Insufficient personnel also meant that CIVPOL was unable to do the independent patrols needed to monitor properly the activities of the local police.[62]

All of UNTAC had staff that were insufficiently trained or unsuited for their duties, but the civilian police had a higher proportion. A significant number did not possess the minimum requirements for the force: many spoke neither English nor French (UNTAC's two official languages), nor possessed a driver's license, nor had the required six years of police experience.[63] Some had no police training at all. Recognizing the problem, on November 27, 1992, Boutros-Ghali notified contributing countries that he wanted them to test all replacement recruits before they left their home countries to ensure they met UN requirements. Driving and language tests were then conducted by UN personnel or experts engaged by the organization.[64]

Not all of CIVPOL's units were of low caliber. A unit of Singaporean police in Battambang province exemplified an effectively trained civilian police force utilized for the best results. The UN electoral workers in Battambang told the General Accounting Office that the Singaporean police were the most effective in UNTAC and that registration could not have been completed without their help.[65] The Singaporeans' effectiveness was due in part to careful screening and training. They were part of a national contingent of about seventy-five who were specially groomed for UNTAC. Before coming to Cambodia, they had been checked for a minimum of ten years' police experience, as well as the ability to speak English and to drive. They took a special eight-week training course focused on mental stress awareness, physical conditioning, intercultural communication, and leadership. Professors from the National Singapore University also gave sessions on Cambodian history and culture.[66]

Singapore's multifaceted approach is a model for training police for future UN missions.

UNTAC's police were expected to function as regular police, particularly in investigating criminal activity, but they did not have police authority or enforcement capability. Although the civilian police in Namibia had been unarmed, the decision to have an unarmed force in Cambodia was probably detrimental to the accomplishment of UNTAC's policing tasks, given the security situation and the factions' failure to disarm. That decision was not popular with officers from countries where police carry weapons, although many other officers were from countries with unarmed police.[67] Since they did not carry guns, it was difficult for the civil police to provide real security for refugee convoys and refugee reception centers. Unarmed (and sometimes careless) police proved incapable of doing so in Battambang province, through which many refugees had to transit. After a convoy came under fire, the nongovernmental organization CARE requested that peacekeeping troops, rather than the civil police, provide protection along all routes.[68]

The civil police also had no power of arrest. As a result, they had no ability to follow through on their human rights investigations. Their only recourse was to refer cases to the SOC police, who did nothing. Consequently, UNTAC police were given arrest power in January 1993—too late to be effective.

Many of the civilian police proved to be ill-suited for investigating human rights abuses. They came from thirty-two countries, not all of which have either a capable, established police force or one that upholds civil liberties while it maintains law and order. Without such experience, UNTAC's civil police could not realistically be expected to show Cambodian police how to operate in a democratic system.[69] As a result, despite having standard operating procedures for human rights violations, UNTAC's police did not have a common understanding of what constituted a human rights problem.[70] Some police were hesitant or unwilling to prevent, investigate, or take remedial action against abuses. That made the human rights officers' work more difficult.

Insufficient Coordination and Overlapping Mandates

Lack of coordination among UNTAC's component parts handicapped the civilian police. Because the police were unarmed and understaffed, their tasks became limited largely to investigating human rights complaints, inspecting prisons, providing security for returning refugees, and monitoring the local SOC police. While UNTAC civilian staff in the provinces looked to the civil police for protection, the police had neither the staff nor the time for the job. This created friction, particularly as the security situation deteriorated and banditry increased. Eventually, the military unit was directed to protect UNTAC civilian staff. Since it reduced

CIVPOL's ability to monitor local police, the responsibility to protect political party offices was also shifted to the military.

Civil police work also overlapped with that of the civil administration. Specifically, the civil police were assigned oversight of the activities of the SOC Ministry of National Security, whose administrative apparatus stretched countrywide. Although internal security was one of the five areas over which UNTAC planned to exert control during the transition period, the number of staff assigned (three) was wholly inadequate to the task.[71] Efforts to reduce police intimidation of political opponents and the civilian population were largely unsuccessful. In part, this was because UNTAC's civilian police were overly absorbed with their monitoring mission and neglected their responsibility to press human rights investigations.[72] One UNTAC official told the General Accounting Office that "some UNTAC police were unfamiliar with fair investigative procedures and also became too close to their Cambodian counterparts to effectively monitor them."[73] Critics charge that what UNTAC should have done was take over the factions' police forces, not just supervise them. But to have done that, UNTAC's police would have had to have been armed, far greater in number, better equipped (their mobility was hampered in many areas by lack of equipment), and been much more willing to take casualties resulting from likely local police resistance to the more aggressive approach.

TRAINING OF CAMBODIAN POLICE

As one senior police official observed, it would have been more realistic, and more beneficial in the long run, if a major effort had been made to train new police officers for the postelection government. Although training had not been identified as a priority for the UNTAC police, once in the field, they could clearly see the value of training the local police and the judiciary. Few resources, however, were available for it.

Some civil police undertook makeshift training using their own training manuals when they were able to scrounge resources from their national contingents.[74] Civil police trained small numbers from each faction, including Khmer Rouge police in one area near Thailand. The courses covered such topics as the traffic law implemented August 6, 1992, criminal law, basic police procedures, and the role of a police officer in a judicial system. This last concept was difficult to teach Cambodian police since the country's court system was primitive.[75]

TOUGH CONDITIONS; MARGINAL SUCCESS

It would have been nearly impossible for UNTAC's civilian police to succeed as thoroughly as did those in Namibia. Its police chief of staff had also been involved with the Namibia police mission. He told the General Accounting Office that he had hoped that the experience in Namibia would be directly transferable to Cambodia. It was not. The two operations took place in different political environments. All parties in Namibia had been committed to holding a free and fair election. That was not the case in Cambodia. At the beginning of their missions, UNTAC and the UN mission in Namibia had different levels of administrative and logistical support. Namibia was a far more developed country than Cambodia, where the physical infrastructure was nonexistent.[76] UNTAC's civil police were asked to do too much, and given too few resources with which to do it. As a result, their ability to contribute to creating a neutral political environment was limited.

THE CIVIL ADMINISTRATION COMPONENT

UNTAC's most striking departure from previous peacekeeping missions was in its insistence on exerting control over five essential areas of each faction's administrative structures: defense, foreign affairs, finance, public security, and information. When the Paris Accords were signed, there was a widespread perception that this meant that the United Nations would actually run Cambodia. "Real authority is to be wielded by a United Nations administration that will manage virtually all civilian and military affairs until free elections can be held."[77]

UNTAC was careful to define its mandate in terms of overseeing "existing administrative structures," referring "not to the administrative structures of one of the parties, such as the State of Cambodia, but all 4 parties."[78] But while the intent was to oversee all four factions, it was tacitly understood from the beginning that the Phnom Penh regime's administrative apparatus was the primary target. The Khmer Rouge never permitted the United Nations to have access to its areas, and neither non-Communist faction had governance structures of any significance. Thus, the five major "fields of scrutiny" were largely translated into the five relevant SOC ministries.

To a large extent, what the United Nations wanted to do was to level the playing field and neutralize, as much as possible, the advantages in an election that would naturally accrue to the incumbent power. The military component's chief task in creating a neutral political environment was to disarm the factions. Once that did not take place, the civil administration's efforts became even more important. But UNTAC's civil administration was not prepared to shoulder such a large share of the burden.

CIVIL ADMINISTRATION'S MANDATE

Critics have charged that UNTAC was insufficiently aggressive in exercising control over the country. This gap in perception was due in part to outsiders' failure to recognize UNTAC's narrower interpretation of the Paris Accords. The civil administrators did not see themselves as having a mandate to *govern* Cambodia or to be in charge of managing the country's day-to-day affairs. Nor did they see their task as changing the existing administrative structures.

In an internal UNTAC document, the civil administration unit laid out its philosophy for the conduct of its work.

> UNTAC is not in Cambodia as a legislative entity and it is not empowered to act as legislator (save for . . . codes of conduct). Acting as a legislative entity would under the circumstances be in conflict with the strict neutrality as requested by UNTAC in the Peace Accord.
>
> It is, however, within UNTAC's power and explicit mandate to detect administrative practices which may cause social unrest and thus be a threat to national unity, peace, reconciliation and free and fair elections.[79]

By the time the secretary-general's implementation plan was written, it was recognized that the ability of the United Nations to "run" Cambodia was going to be limited. The plan accordingly reiterated the necessity for flexibility. Consistent with the Paris Accords, it outlined three levels of UN interaction with existing administrative structures. The first level was "direct control," which was to be exercised "as necessary to ensure strict neutrality" over the five "fields of scrutiny."[80] Areas identified for the second level of "optional control" were ones that had propaganda value, or in which public or humanitarian funds could be used for electoral purposes, or that could promote discrimination through the improper use of government funds.[81] On May 26, 1992, the Supreme National Council agreed to UNTAC's proposal for authority for optional control over the areas of education, agriculture, fishing, transport, energy, tourism, mines, and general administration.[82] The third and lowest level covered all remaining administrative entities. These were generally supposed to function without UNTAC supervision or specific monitoring mechanisms. They were expected to continue to provide services in an equitable and nondiscriminatory manner.[83]

Civil administration did not have sole responsibility for implementing its mandate. It examined issues at the policy level, while others verified whether those policies were being carried out.[84] The civil administrators collaborated with the military unit in supervising national defense. In the area of public security, they relied on UNTAC's civilian police and human rights workers. UNTAC's information and education division, formally part of the Office of the Special Representative, was responsible for monitoring and countering propaganda by all factions. Thus, the two areas over which the civil administrators assumed direct responsibility themselves were foreign affairs and finance.

SLOW DEPLOYMENT; MISSED OPPORTUNITIES

As with other UNTAC units, civil administration was instituted slowly. Although it should have been at full complement by August 1, 1992, full deployment was not achieved until mid-October, more than one-third of the way into UNTAC's eighteen-month mission.[85] By July 1, UNTAC had begun oversight of Phnom Penh's five key ministries. By July 15, civil administration offices had been established in all twenty-one provinces. In late August, civil administrators began to tackle the two non-Communist factions but never were granted access to Khmer Rouge-controlled territory. By mid-September, 200 international and 600 locally recruited staff had been deployed. Most focused their efforts on Phnom Penh regime structures.[86]

Although UNTAC did not intend to "run" Cambodia on a daily basis, the civil administrators did want sufficient control over the Phnom Penh authorities to prevent them from using their incumbent position to gain unfair advantage over the other factions. This was particularly true in the areas of internal security, where the potential for political intimidation was nearly unlimited, and information—more aptly termed propaganda. Thus, as a result of the slow deployment, UNTAC largely missed an opportunity in summer 1992, when concerted efforts might have made significant inroads into Phnom Penh's administrative apparatus. "During early June, there would have been a chance to establish some control because SOC officials were waiting for UNTAC to come in and take over. The officials were basically compliant and thought UNTAC would exert authority. However, during July and August, while UNTAC was planning the details, the SOC public officials took a harder line."[87]

Slow deployment and inadequate planning seriously eroded UNTAC's ability to control the Phnom Penh authorities' defense establishment as well. GAO noted, in its record of a meeting with UNTAC officials charged with overseeing defense, that

> they were to control the Ministry of Defense in Phnom Penh in June and July, [h]owever, they did not arrive until August. The initial months, September–October were spent in mapping out the organization of the defense ministry and understanding its relationship with the provincial forces. They were also supposed to approve all memos and directives, but they could not get Cambodian translators until August. . . . They thus lost critical time drawing up operational plans when they could have been establishing some control over the defense area during initial phases of the operation. They believe that the SOC was more compliant

early and if they had been in a position to establish initial control, it might have worked. But by the time they had determined what to do and how to implement the plans, the SOC had become intransigent.[88]

Throughout the summer of 1992, Phnom Penh was testing UNTAC's seriousness, as was the Khmer Rouge. By fall, when UNTAC had its full staff in place, it became clear that UNTAC was not going to be granted any access by the Khmer Rouge. As a result, the Phnom Penh authorities took a harder line against UNTAC control over its ministries. The Battambang provincial director for UNTAC stated that, despite constant fighting and armed camps, "the problem was in controlling the local SOC government. No real control was possible because the provincial governor had issued orders not to obey UNTAC edicts. Originally it had been possible to work with the civil administration in the province, but recently they kept asking when UNTAC would control the Khmer Rouge. If UNTAC could not control the Khmer Rouge, they would not allow UNTAC to supervise SOC operations either."[89]

Consistent with its interpretation of its mandate, UNTAC did more supervision and monitoring than direct control. The secretary-general's implementation plan repeatedly used the term "scrutiny" to describe the tasks and activities of the civil administration component. In large part, that was because UNTAC did not allocate the resources to civil administration that would have been necessary for more direct control of the Phnom Penh authorities' administrative apparatus. UNTAC allotted only some 200 professionals—95 in Phnom Penh and 123 in the provinces—to cover the activities of 140,000 civil servants.[90] The civil administration's minimal presence in each province, at least in the early months, generally amounted to only five international staff and seven local staff per province.[91]

TOOLS AND PROCEDURES

The civil administrators' general strategy was first to evaluate the administrative mechanisms in place and then to insist on examining the various factions' decisionmaking before and after the fact. As UNTAC's staff became more effective at this, Phnom Penh's bureaucrats in particular resorted to utilizing back channels and informal networks for communicating with each other. Civil Administration director Gerard Pourcell reported that while civil administrators examined all the instructions and guidance issued by the ministries, often decisions were transmitted informally without UNTAC's knowledge. Sometimes they were deliberately hidden. The Public Security Ministry, over which UNTAC was supposed to have control, transferred a particularly notorious unit, used to harass political opponents, from one ministry to another in order to elude UNTAC. It ended up in the culture ministry, over which UNTAC had no authority.[92]

The tools UNTAC had available to control the existing administrative structures included "codes of conduct and guidelines for management, especially regarding ethical conduct, measures to counter corruption, measures to ensure non-discrimination and other principles of accountability."[93] UNTAC also had the right to install its own personnel in the administrative apparatus of all four Cambodian factions, and it was supposed to have unrestricted access to all administrative operations and information.[94] The ability to burrow into the factions' power centers offered the United Nations its greatest potential leverage—especially over the Phnom Penh authorities, though its effectiveness was limited by insufficient personnel.

In addition, UNTAC had two tools it could use to keep the factions in line. It could issue binding directives on an ad hoc basis, and it could reassign or remove personnel from the bodies it was overseeing. However, Akashi's insistence on cooperation and consensus with the factions limited the use of binding directives. Akashi preferred what he called the Asian give-and-take method of negotiation, even if it slowed down the process. He was backed in that approach by Secretary-General Boutros-Ghali, who told journalists on his trip to Cambodia to open the election campaign, "The mission in Cambodia is a peacekeeping mission. It is not a mission of enforcement. . . . So the only way to solve the problem is through dialogue, negotiation, persuasion, and diplomacy."[95] Though the Paris Accords permitted UNTAC to take "corrective action, as appropriate," UNTAC rarely tried to reassign or remove personnel, even in the most egregious cases. It worked with existing personnel and tried to reform from within. Too direct an attack, particularly on those members of the regime who were trying to undermine the neutrality of the peace process, could have caused the SOC to refuse to cooperate at all. That might have been fatal for UNTAC.

Civil administration was charged with investigating complaints about authorities misusing their power. UNTAC issued a public statement on June 26, 1992, instructing the Cambodian people about their right to complain to the director of UNTAC's Civil Administration office in their province, to UNTAC police at the provincial level, or to UNTAC police or electoral personnel at the district level.[96] While UNTAC was not able to remedy all abuses, the open-door policy toward complaints from the Cambodian people had the unintended benefit of providing a ready flow of information about the factions' doings. It also helped UNTAC to keep its finger on the pulse of the Cambodian people throughout its tenure.

The civil administration unit was able to have greater impact in Phnom Penh than in the countryside. Some Cambodian provincial administrators were too closely connected politically with senior SOC leaders. It was also easier in the countryside to avoid leaving a paper trail that could be monitored by UNTAC. The small number of regional UNTAC staff simply were unable to exert much authority over provincial officials. One provincial director admitted that UNTAC did not have control over the Cambodian provincial officials. Although it tried to monitor some official correspondence, the governor (who was Hun Sen's brother) circumvented UNTAC by giving verbal orders that were carried out by his department heads.[97]

THE PHNOM PENH REGIME AND POLITICAL VIOLENCE

UNTAC's inability to exert control over the SOC ministry of defense could not be attributed entirely to the continuing military threat from the Khmer Rouge. The United Nations quickly discovered a high level of political activity by the Cambodian People's Party within the armed forces.[98] UNTAC was never able to quell the regime's use of the military or security forces for political purposes. Violence against political opponents largely was conducted by military and security units in the villages and communes, whereas UNTAC did not have much power outside of Phnom Penh.[99]

The *Washington Post* revealed after the election that police and military units in the provinces had organized "reaction forces" to engage in a wide-scale, violent campaign of intimidation and sabotage of the regime's political opponents. In reporting on these forces, the *Post* pointed out that "while the 'reaction forces' carried out political violence, a much more organized and centrally run network of A-groups infiltrated opposition parties and disrupted their activities in a 'structured sabotage effort.'"[100]

While UNTAC knew about the campaign for months, it was long unable to document the existence of these undercover squads. In January 1993, recognizing that its regular supervision was inadequate at the local level, UNTAC established a control team to conduct operations that eventually produced evidence of the organized campaign of violence in four raids on Cambodian police and military provincial offices on the eve of the election.[101] These raids "finally put the Phnom Penh government on notice that UNTAC was serious about asserting control under its mandate."[102] From the standpoint of human rights critics, however, UNTAC's actions were too little, too late.

ACCOMPLISHMENTS

While the UNTAC civil administration never exerted real control over the Phnom Penh regime's apparatus, it did lay the groundwork for a more modern and efficient government that should enhance the prospects for national reconciliation. It set up six offices to oversee the five ministries. The sixth, the Service of Specialized Control, covered those areas that had been added to UNTAC's mandate by the SNC, including Cambodia's cultural heritage, health, transportation, and forest sectors.

The office overseeing foreign affairs substantially simplified passport procedures and relaxed the Phnom Penh regime's tight control over movement in and out of Cambodia. The Foreign Affairs Service maintained a presence six days a week in the regime's passport section. It abolished entry and exit visas for Cambodians holding SOC-issued visas, ended the policy of the authorities keeping Cambodians' passports upon their return from abroad, and streamlined immigration procedures. To prevent officials from lining their pockets, the office overseeing defense required approvals for any sale, rental, or exchange of land by the ministry of defense, monitored the transfer and reorganizing of two ammunition dumps, and conducted a partial inventory of the defense ministry's fixed assets. To bring some semblance of law enforcement and a more mature judicial system, the Public Security Service approved an interim penal code, ran a training program for magistrates and police, organized a working group to deal with the problem of increasing banditry, set up a working group to draft a traffic code, and conducted prison inspections. The Finance Service controlled revenue, monitored currency production, and helped prepare the regime's 1993 budget. The Information and Education office monitored media institutions, prepared media guidelines, established a working group of Cambodian journalists, and arranged briefings. The Service of Specialized Control set up a Ports Authority, health and forestry working groups, and focused on protecting Cambodia's cultural heritage.[103]

Not wanting to usurp any faction's autonomy, UNTAC did not resort to complete control of revenue collection and distribution. Instead, it attempted to hold the purse strings. It monitored the Central Bank's issuance of currency, to which the regime resorted to meet its budgetary needs as inflation spiraled out of control, and pressured the authorities to reduce excessive printing of currency. "Procedures were established to check government outlays. Every government request to reimburse government agencies or provincial officials for expenses had to be cleared by the UN. Four customs officers were recruited to control exports."[104] UNTAC's civil administrators controlled key entry ports and were largely successful in their efforts at customs control. They also tried to control the PhnomPenh authorities' revenue by insisting on approving all decisions relating to the sale or rental of properties. This became particularly important after the election as the regime attempted to sell off state assets to line its officials' pockets before the newly elected government took over.

In attempting to reshape Cambodia, the civil administration division tried to bring the ways of the West to a Cambodia with no tradition or history of a free and independent judiciary, respect for human rights, or an independent media. UNTAC's civil administrators did the best they could with limited resources. They helped to identify abuses and served as a conduit for Cambodians' complaints, though they could not ensure action or restitution. They helped to codify legal, penal, traffic, and media codes. They helped to preserve and protect Cambodia's natural resources

and cultural heritage. They attempted to guide the handling of the economy in order both to deal with the inflationary pressures due directly to
UNTAC's presence and spending and to counter the deteriorating financial situation.

Their most important function, however, was to combat the most egregious of discriminatory actions and instances of corruption by the Phnom
Penh authorities. While they were more successful in some areas than
others, their efforts were far from wasted. Had civil administration not been
part of UNTAC's mandate, there is little doubt that there would have been
no check at all on the regime's harassment and intimidation of its political opponents. Just by forcing the regime to be circuitous and to resort to
back channels, as its formal decisionmaking process became more tightly monitored, the civil administrators probably contributed to creating as
benign an atmosphere for electoral progress as was possible.

There is no disagreement that UNTAC failed to create a truly neutral
political environment. Akashi often felt frustrated in his attempts to do so,
and declared that failure his Achilles' heel. UNTAC did, however, succeed
in creating something that Akashi defined as "an approximation" of fair-
ness.[105] In that sense, both the military and civil police were critical. By protecting voters seeking to register, candidates, party offices, and Cambodians
who attended rallies at which candidates from all parties were able to
speak freely, UNTAC peacekeeepers and civil police helped to maintain what
UNTAC's electoral director, Reginald Austin, called "neutral political
acreages."[106] The importance of these activities to the success of the electoral effort should not be underestimated. Similarly, the military and
police protection of the ballot boxes and polling places gave Cambodians
a sense of security that they could vote without retaliation. They did so, in
overwhelming numbers, and there were no reported incidents of violence
subsequently. Perhaps virtual neutrality was all thats Cambodia needed to
guarantee free elections.

6

BUILDING A FUTURE FOR CAMBODIA: UNTAC's HUMAN RIGHTS AND ELECTORAL COMPONENTS

Whereas UNTAC's military, civil police, and civil administration units attempted to create a neutral political environment in which elections could take place, the human rights and electoral components were designed to create a new Cambodia. The human rights component's mission was to reject Cambodia's recent past based on the violence of the Khmer Rouge and Communist eras and instill in the Cambodian people a respect for the rights and welfare of the individual. The electoral division's mission was to organize and conduct a free and fair election that would allow Cambodia to rejoin the international community with a government that represented the views of the people.

Whether the human rights effort succeeded in changing the attitudes of the Cambodian people toward their own rights is a question that will not be answered for many years to come. While critics charge that UNTAC devoted insufficient attention, resources, and personnel to the work of its human rights component, at least the organization prepared the ground from which a new interest in fundamental liberties may spring.

The work of the electoral component was successful—remarkably so—in bringing about an election deemed free and fair by the world. More than 90 percent of Cambodia's registered voters cast their ballots in secret. Yet, here again, the long-term benefit is uncertain. It takes obviously more than one election to make a democracy.

THE HUMAN RIGHTS COMPONENT

The provisions of the Paris Accords pertaining to human rights investigation and education, written by the United States, were incorporated into
the agreement in part to assuage a lingering sense of global responsibility for the lack of intervention against earlier Khmer Rouge excesses.
Reflecting concern about the prospects for a return to Cambodia's savage
misrule that characterized the 1970s, the secretary-general's implementation
plan described human rights first, before any other aspect of the peace process. The elliptical wording in his plan in regard to concern for human rights
("Cambodian authorities must ensure respect for and observance of
human rights and fundamental freedoms, including . . . effective measures
to ensure no return to the policies and practices of the past. . . ."[1]) expressed
the United Nations' need to keep China on board.

Although an intense debate over charging the Khmer Rouge with
genocidal practices had concluded with no stronger reference than to
"policies and practices of the past," there was widespread agreement that
one way to make a Khmer Rouge return to power less likely was to foster
an environment of less acquiescence in and tolerance for human rights abuses. By sensitizing the Cambodian people to the concept of human rights,
UNTAC hoped to make them better able to organize and run a society in
which there was respect for the rule of law. While recognizing that the impe-
tus for the concern about human rights was largely the record of the
Khmer Rouge in power, the United Nations knew its focus during the
transition period had to be on the Phnom Penh authorities, which had the
most at stake in the election process.

MANDATE, PERSONNEL, AND DEPLOYMENT

UNTAC had the responsibility for "fostering an environment in
which respect for human rights is ensured."[2] To achieve that goal, there
were three primary tasks to carry out. It had to educate people about
their human rights, exercise general administrative oversight with an eye
on how each faction's activities impinged on basic freedoms, and investigate allegations of abuses that occurred during the transition period. As
originally conceived, UNTAC would not have the power to prosecute.
The implementation plan specified that "UNTAC would naturally retain
the right to order or to take corrective action, as appropriate," but then dilut-
ed the force of that statement by noting, "In this connection, UNTAC
may choose to associate the Supreme National Council with its pro-
ceedings, if necessary, in order to promote effective redress."[3] Since the
SNC operated by consensus, it was highly unlikely that it was going to side
with the United Nations on any instance of human rights violation per-
petrated by any of its factions.

From the first, Yasushi Akashi was at odds with his human rights staff on what could practically be accomplished in Cambodia. In his view, UNTAC could plant the seeds of democracy and human rights, but only Cambodians could ensure that those seeds would grow. In a speech given after UNTAC's mission ended, Akashi said that he had not followed some of the recommendations of the staff for stronger guarantees and safeguards on human rights, believing that they were out of sync with the reality of the situation in Cambodia. The human rights component—and human rights advocacy organizations—set standards that were too high for Cambodia at that time.[4]

Not surprisingly, that attitude left the UNTAC human rights staff, and its director, Dennis McNamara, frustrated. They believed that aggressive pursuit of human rights objectives was essential not only to UNTAC's success but to Cambodia's future. The link between human rights and the elections was not explicitly made in the implementation plan; nevertheless, as a Senate Foreign Relations Committee report indicated, "The emphasis on human rights was viewed as a means to level the political playing field by reducing the ability of the State of Cambodia and the Khmer Rouge to intimidate the people."[5] Yet even the committee report acknowledged that "the component was originally intended to be only an educational unit with ten staff."[6] Initially, no provision was made for human rights professionals to be located in the provinces. Even though the staff was beefed up to thirty-three when work began with the first investigation in March 1992, this proved insufficient, and the unit remained understaffed for the duration of UNTAC's mandate. The human rights component was slow in staffing both its headquarters in Phnom Penh and branches in the provinces. By September, six months after UNTAC's work began, officers had been deployed to only fifteen of the twenty-one provinces and to the zones of the two non-Communist resistance factions (not to the Khmer Rouge zones, where they were denied access).[7]

An inherent contradiction in mission separated the human rights and the civil administration components. "There is little communication between human rights officers and civil administrators because, as one human rights monitor observed, the civil administrator is trying to work with the existing government while the human rights officer 'tries to tear it down.'"[8] The inability to coordinate was critical since the lack of a clear division of tasks meant that the human rights component, the also understaffed civil administration, and the civil police were compelled uneasily to share responsibility for investigating human rights complaints and pursuing the perpetrators.

IMPLEMENTATION

In one of the early steps of the human rights program, on April 20, 1992, all members of the Supreme National Council (including the Khmer Rouge) ratified two international human rights instruments: the International

Covenant on Civil and Political Rights and the International Covenant on Economic, Social and Cultural Rights. Five more instruments pertaining to women, children, refugees, and torture were signed on September 10. On the same day, the SNC adopted a new penal code based on these international agreements. UNTAC's review of prison conditions and treatment of offenders was based on their provisions as well.[9]

The human rights component placed an early emphasis on the development of a human rights civic education program. By September, training seminars had been held for several hundred education officials. Preparation of a human rights curriculum for primary and secondary school levels was undertaken, and human rights courses were introduced at the university level. These activities were supplemented by a mass information campaign. By September, four TV and radio dialogues on human rights and seventeen radio spots had been prepared and used. UNTAC distributed 5,000 copies, expected to reach 500,000 people, of a basic human rights leaflet.[10]

The human rights unit also trained the staff of UNTAC's other component parts. By September, it had held thirty seminars for fourteen hundred civilian police and five seminars for more than four hundred district election supervisors.[11] It also developed a human rights protocol for use as part of UNTAC's standard operating procedures.[12] It provided support for indigenous human rights organizations as well. It offered a number of seminars for Cambodian human rights groups and hosted an international conference on human rights in late November in Phnom Penh. It also held a one-day seminar for more than four hundred senior SOC police officials.

Cambodia's prison system was primitive and therefore received special attention from the human rights component. Prisoners were detained by Phnom Penh authorities for up to ten years without trial, sometimes for political allegiance rather than criminal actions. UNTAC devoted substantial time to investigating prisons and all cases of possible political detention. By the end of August, 258 prisoners who had been detained without trial had been released. Human rights workers also monitored health conditions in prisons. The United Nations never succeeded in getting the State of Cambodia to build a badly needed new prison, but prison conditions did improve during UNTAC's tenure.[13]

Although the lack of enforcement capability bedeviled the human rights division from start to finish, it was aggressive in investigating complaints. From March to December 1992, it investigated 339 cases of human rights abuses, primarily harassment, land disputes, and unlawful imprisonment. By November, as fighting increased between Phnom Penh's troops and the Khmer Rouge, the abuses became more violent and politically motivated. Abuses continued to escalate the closer it got to the election; so, too, did deaths and injuries. From March to mid-May 1993, UNTAC investigations confirmed 200 deaths, 338 injuries, and 114 abductions. UNTAC attributed the vast majority of the killings (131) in those months to the Khmer Rouge (only 15 to the Phnom Penh regime).[14] The Khmer Rouge was largely responsible for the killings of Vietnamese-speaking persons. However, the great majority of nonfatal attacks on political party offices and members, which peaked in December 1992, were attributed to soldiers, police, or supporters of the State of Cambodia. Most of these victims were members of FUNCINPEC, reflecting the regime's hope that it could diminish FUNCINPEC's electoral threat through intimidation and political violence.[15]

UNTAC AND ITS CRITICS

The most controversial aspect of UNTAC's operations in Cambodia was how it handled human rights matters. Given the West's strong interest in counteracting Cambodia's tragic past, it is likely that UNTAC would have been criticized no matter how much attention it devoted to rights. While UNTAC did not place lesser emphasis on this area of its mandate than on others, its lack of enforcement powers seriously impeded its ability to pursue cases through to conclusion.

UNTAC interpreted its human rights mandate narrowly. While the Paris Accords allowed it unspecified latitude for "corrective action," the prevailing view inside UNTAC was that its authority rested on the factions' cooperation. It chose to focus greater effort on gradual institutional reform than it did on penalizing abusers. It emphasized the teaching of human rights standards over documenting and exposing abuses.

Taking that approach left UNTAC vulnerable to critics' charges that it was insufficiently aggressive in pursuing human rights cases. In May 1993, Asia Watch issued a report on UNTAC's handling of human rights. Its harsh assessment was summarized in a subsequent report in September.

> The peace-keeping period was marked by major human rights violations, among them the slaughter of ethnic Vietnamese residents of Cambodia, abuse of prisoners, and incidents of politically-motivated murder, assault and intimidation that accelerated in the months leading up to the May 1993 elections. . . .
> The performance of the United Nations in upholding accountability for gross abuses in Cambodia was the focus of a May 1993 report by Asia Watch. . . . The report detailed grave human rights violations committed by the Cambodian parties to the conflict and the actions of the United Nations Transition [sic] Authority in Cambodia (UNTAC) in response to those violations. It concluded that human rights protection had too often taken a back seat to peace-making, and that UNTAC's failure to

effectively penalize abuses offered a poor model to the post-UNTAC government and encouraged continuing grave abuses in the future.[16]

UNTAC countered that the May report was unbalanced; it did not take into account UNTAC's many achievements, particularly in human rights education and the assistance it provided in the formation of indigenous human rights organizations. While conceding that the human rights situation remained far from satisfactory, "bearing in mind the Cambodian context of the peace process, considerable progress in the area of human rights has been made and should not be overlooked. . . . While some of that progress may be attributed to UNTAC's activities themselves, it may also be attributed to the peace process as a whole, and the presence of a large peacekeeping operation. In Cambodia today, there exists very visibly much broader economic and social freedom throughout the country. . . . [Moreover], the unprecedented growth of contacts with foreigners and the huge increase in the availability of new information and ideas . . . have worked to undermine to some degree the social and political controls which previously existed."[17]

By the time Asia Watch issued the September 1993 report, it acknowledged that there were two sides to the story.

UNTAC promoted human rights on all these various fronts. It provided education and training in human rights to the general public and to special groups such as human rights activists, judges, criminal defenders, and civil police. It drafted and promulgated new criminal law and media guidelines, and persuaded Cambodia's sovereign authority to accede to seven international human rights instruments. UNTAC facilitated the formation of new political parties and newspapers. It provided the protection necessary for the fragile beginnings of a civil society, with professional associations and non-governmental organizations. In the realm of human rights protection, UNTAC, and especially its Human Rights Component, performed creditably in monitoring prison conditions and supervising the release of hundreds of prisoners, even while abuse of prisoners remained an intractable problem. The Human Rights and Civil Police components investigated literally hundreds of serious human rights abuses which were committed as the date of elections approached.[18]

But Asia Watch was unwilling to retreat from its stance that UNTAC failed to take corrective action in cases where it had the authority to do so; that actions it did take came too late to be effective; and that, overall, it ought to have taken a more aggressive approach toward the noncooperation of the Cambodian parties. Asia Watch recognized that "UNTAC was neither empowered to enforce peace through use of arms nor authorized to withdraw its forces or delay elections," but it argued that the underlying problem was political. "These [UNTAC] efforts . . . were too often compromised by reluctance at the highest levels to follow through with 'corrective action' as mandated by the peace plan. 'Corrective action' encompassed a wide array of measures, from arresting and prosecuting perpetrators, to dismissing abusive or obstructive officials, to publicly exposing and stigmatizing wrongdoers. The public condemnation of individuals responsible for abuse was often seen as inimical to the ongoing diplomacy required in both peace-making and peace-keeping." It further charged that the long-term effectiveness of UNTAC's human rights efforts in the areas of education and attitudinal reform would be seriously undermined by its absence of will to hold abusers accountable.[19]

ESTABLISHMENT OF A SPECIAL PROSECUTOR'S OFFICE

UNTAC faced a serious obstacle in any effort that required pursuit through legal channels because Cambodia lacked even the rudiments of a credible justice system. Lawyers had, for the most part, been killed by the Khmer Rouge. Those who functioned in the capacity of judges were often illiterate and owed their position to regime favor. With the Khmer Rouge essentially off-limits to prosecution, the abusers that UNTAC identified for which it had even a chance of pursuit were largely those associated with the Phnom Penh authorities. The lack of an independent judiciary rendered the notion of bringing them to account difficult, if not nonsensical. "Nor would [UNTAC] provide the salaries and security that were necessary to make judges independent of political authorities."[20] It failed to establish either a witness protection program or a course for training judges. UNTAC did draft a new code on criminal law and procedure for Cambodia, but it decided that it was not feasible to retrain the judiciary before UNTAC's mission ended.

In November 1992, the human rights component did an internal study to assess whether its investigations had resulted in corrective action being taken. It concluded that no corrective action had been taken by Phnom Penh authorities against any offenders identified by UNTAC. There were many contributors to this failure: the generally nonfunctional court system, subordinated to the police, which wielded the real power in enforcement;[21] the unwillingness of Cambodian prosecutors to pursue cases against their colleagues in administration; UNTAC's reluctance to hand over its case files to SOC authorities out of fear for witnesses' safety. The study resulted in a proposal that UNTAC establish a Special Prosecutor's Office to prosecute cases in the Cambodian court system itself rather than rely on the authorities to do so. It also recommended giving UNTAC's civil and military police arrest powers and having its military unit protect safe houses and detention centers.[22] After an extensive debate about UNTAC's authority to undertake such measures, it implemented the proposal's recommendations and established the Special Prosecutor's Office with two prosecutors on January 6, 1993.[23]

Its own human rights branch continued to press for UNTAC to take stronger measures to counteract abuses. One human rights officer, according to report, "said that UNTAC's mandate is clear. It is to take direct control and supervision of the existing civilian administration and take corrective action when appropriate. He sees absolutely no ambiguity. . . . Even if UNTAC is authorized under Chapter VI, there are clear precedents for acting when human rights are violated and lives are endangered."[24] Yet UNTAC's mandate was ambiguous. On the one hand, the Paris Accords granted it the authority to take corrective action. At the same time, the agreement left primary responsibility for maintaining law and order, and administering justice, with the four factions. Faced with conflicting signals, Akashi resisted pressure for stronger action, relying on persuasion, education, and the beneficial effects of the general opening of the country to outside ideas.

Relying on the factions to police themselves, however, did not work. As UNTAC's human rights director admitted, "One party has refused all cooperation with UNTAC and makes no pretense to respect the rights of the population. Two other parties, FUNCINPEC and KPNLF, have no civil systems or legal structures in place in their zones, which remain lawless. The State of Cambodia has made minimal efforts to apprehend those responsible for political attacks since,[sic] UNTAC has been in the country. Nor have the Phnom Penh military authorities taken effective corrective action, despite the many cases in which CPAF [Cambodian People's Armed Forces, or SOC] troops have been implicated in politically-motivated crimes."[25]

In October 1993, Asia Watch concluded that UNTAC had been ineffective in holding perpetrators accountable through either administrative discipline or the judicial process.

> UNTAC conducted dozens of investigations into grave human rights violations, in some cases identifying the perpetrators and amassing evidence enough for indictments, but the full results of these investigations were seldom publicized. Dismissals of abusive officials were requested sparingly and sparingly granted. UNTAC could not obtain the removal of a policeman who, in front of a large crowd, brutalized a criminal suspect, much less the removal of the governor of Battambang province, who reportedly had organized hit squads against the opposition parties. UNTAC also took on direct powers to arrest, detain and prosecute serious human rights offenders, but this effort foundered once the Phnom Penh

government barred such cases from its courts. Altogether, UNTAC managed to apprehend only four offenders; one died of a heart ailment in U.N. custody, one was released on bail pending trial by the new government, and the two others, abusive officials under the Phnom Penh regime, await trial now in the T-3 jail of Phnom Penh.[26]

ACCOMPLISHMENTS

Despite obstacles, UNTAC's human rights accomplishments were considerable. The four factions' agreed to and signed all the major international human rights instruments. The SNC adopted a revised penal and judicial code, which UNTAC was instrumental in preparing, that contained more far-reaching human rights provisions than comparable legislation anywhere else in Asia. UNTAC gained unrestricted access to prisons throughout Cambodia. If it did not significantly improve conditions in all of them, the combined effects of UNTAC and the International Red Cross at least gained the release of all known political detainees. At UNTAC's request, the United Nations Human Rights Commission agreed to the appointment of a special representative of the secretary-general on human rights in Cambodia. It also agreed to have the UN Centre on Human Rights establish an operational presence in Cambodia to continue UNTAC's activities—the Centre's first such presence outside of Geneva.[27]

Of greater significance for Cambodia's future, however, was UNTAC's nationwide program of human rights education, training, and information. This was one of the central elements in UNTAC's efforts to rebuild Cambodia, involving an attempt to change the whole mind-set of Cambodia's people. Whether it succeeds will not be known for many years.

While UNTAC chose to emphasize the teaching of human rights standards, it did not do so at the expense of documenting abuses. What it was unable to do effectively was to insist on accountability for those violations. Asia Watch is undoubtedly correct that "accountability is no luxury, to be deferred to a more stable, peaceful moment."[28] But UNTAC's greater focus on gradual institutional reform was not because it did not want to see abusers held accountable; to the contrary, its Special Prosecutor's Office was set up for that very purpose. It simply had "no legal or political authority to undertake such punishment, or to establish tribunals to deal with violators."[29]

Even after the establishment of the Special Prosecutor's Office, however, senior UNTAC officials did at times prevent cases from being carried to conclusion. One of the special prosecutors recounted that, before going to trial, he had to clear individual cases with UNTAC's Action Committee, which represented all the components. On occasion, for political reasons, the Action Committee refused to permit a case to proceed to trial. The Committee, the special prosecutor said, was concerned about the effect on the elections if a State of Cambodia official were to be found guilty of violating human rights.[30]

With such an extensive mandate and formidable obstacles, it is hardly surprising that thirty-one professional human rights officers—ten in Phnom Penh and one in each of twenty-one provinces—were not able to accomplish miracles. But if the United Nations deemed that nearly 16,000 peacekeeping troops were necessary, it should certainly have allotted more staff to rights compliance. One of the lessons that can be drawn from UNTAC is that the United Nations should not stint on civilian staff in areas it deems critical to a peace-building effort.

The *New York Times* commented in a May 19, 1993, editorial: "Cambodia has been a sobering experience for those who imagined that the UN had magical powers to create a dramatically better world. But a more modest success is still worth working for."[31] Despite weaknesses, UNTAC achieved much on human rights with minimal resources. It was a modest success that, perhaps with a less sweeping mandate and lower expectations, might have seemed more impressive.

THE ELECTORAL COMPONENT

When the Paris Accords were being negotiated, the focus was more on the disarmament of the factions' military forces than it was on the election of a new constituent assembly. The key to a new Cambodia was a cessation of fighting and a removal of guns. Elections, while important, were viewed as possible only if the factions had been disarmed and demobilized. By the time the secretary-general's implementation plan was drawn up, however, "the election [was] the focal point of the comprehensive settlement."[32]

Yet the factions were not disarmed and the soldiers were not demobilized. Fighting, at varying levels of intensity, continued throughout much of UNTAC's tenure. Politically motivated violence, and violence toward UNTAC civilian and military forces, escalated in the months preceding the elections.

Despite what should have been overwhelming obstacles, elections were held. They were not disrupted by the Khmer Rouge, as had been widely expected, and they were deemed free and fair. Much of the responsibility for that success lies with UNTAC; unexpectedly, even more credit is due the Cambodian people, who badly wanted an end to the fighting and saw the elections as a way to bring about peace.

MANDATE AND PLANNING

Consistent with the Paris Accords, the secretary-general's implementation plan laid out five major tasks for UNTAC's electoral component.

1. In conjunction with the Supreme National Council, UNTAC was to draft an electoral law and regulations to govern the election.

2. UNTAC was to provide a framework for the formation of political parties and rights of parties and their candidates. Parties were expected to undergo a period of provisional or temporary registration before they were officially registered, having met all criteria specified by the United Nations. UNTAC was to ensure that the system would give all registered parties fair access to the media.

3. Then, for three months, UNTAC was to register voters over the age of eighteen who were born in Cambodia or were children of a person born in Cambodia.

4. UNTAC's Information and Education unit was to carry out a program of civic education and training.

5. UNTAC was to conduct an election for a constituent assembly in late April or early May 1993 over a period of no longer than three days. Voting was to be by secret ballot, for parties only, although the list of party candidates for each province was to be widely publicized. Voters' eligibility was to be subject to verification, including the use of indelible ink on voters' fingers, and polls were to be safeguarded.[33]

The magnitude of the effort associated with the holding of elections is reflected in the number of civilian personnel who were involved in carrying out the process. More than 150 international staffers were stationed in Phnom Penh and the provinces; 470 UN Volunteers supervised the work at the district and provincial levels. The Volunteers arrived at the end of May 1992, received two months of intensive language training in Phnom Penh, and left for the provinces by the end of August. Locally recruited staff, small in number initially, grew to involve more than fifty thousand people during the election itself.[34]

Key to the success of the electoral effort was the development of a comprehensive action plan for the election process. The benefit of detailed advance planning, time lines, and up-to-date information was clearly demonstrated. In November 1991, one of the first survey missions sent to Cambodia was the eighteen-member UN Survey Mission on Elections, which was headed by Ron Gould, the highly regarded assistant chief electoral officer of Elections Canada. The survey mission produced a preliminary electoral plan, in twelve chapters, that laid out electoral activities in detail and provided a blueprint that was in fact followed fairly closely. Once it had been deployed, UNTAC's electoral division then produced a detailed operational plan of twenty-six volumes.[35]

The availability of a detailed plan gave the electoral unit a substantial advantage over most of UNTAC's other offices. The UN Secretariat's small

Department of Peacekeeping Operations was both stretched thin and lacked experience in planning missions as large and complex as UNTAC. The department's staff shortage was compounded by a lack of specialists who could plan the tasks required by a peace-building mission. The dearth of specialists experienced in the areas of human rights, democracy building, oversight of government activities, and use of civil police made it more difficult for UNTAC's police, human rights, and civil administration components to organize themselves. Only the military and electoral components had detailed implementation plans, with timetables for accomplishment of specific tasks.[36]

The lack of detailed planning for the others resulted in their failure to coordinate fully with the electoral process. Even a precise plan, though, was no guarantee of coordination; the military's activities did not mesh well with those of the electoral component. This meant, among other things, there was a lack of military input into civilian plans that might require security assistance. The duties of the civil police in monitoring Cambodian police were not coordinated with election dates. Nor were target dates for UN control of key government ministries tied to the electoral timetable.[37]

The Paris Accords mandated that the United Nations organize and run the elections. The UN Survey Mission on Elections opted for an election organized by the United Nations but conducted to a large extent by Cambodians who were employed by UNTAC. This was a departure for the United Nations, which had never paid local people to conduct their own elections.[38] It differed from the system used in Namibia, where the United Nations signed off on each step of the electoral process as planned and carried out by the ruling South African government. Namibia, unlike Cambodia, had a single governing authority, for which careful UN oversight was sufficient to ensure a fair election. At the same time, conducting the Cambodian election solely with international personnel would have inflated the costs astronomically. Moreover, since one of UNTAC's chief objectives was to leave an enduring electoral legacy, it designed a cost-effective system that was heavily dependent on the use of Cambodian citizens and resources, with the benefit of involving Cambodians as much as possible in every phase of the elections and increasing their vested interest in its outcome.

The survey team initially thought the election could be held on a single day but after touring the country realized that this was not feasible. Instead, the elections were held over a period of six days. The team also concluded that UN Volunteers should help conduct the elections. The Volunteers proved to be both excellent election organizers and supervisors. Their use was also cost-effective for UNTAC, since these Peace Corps-type workers drew salaries from the regular UN Volunteers' budget, not from UNTAC's limited funds for nonmilitary activities.

The survey team's plan covered all aspects of the election, from drafting the electoral law, to procedures for registering voters, to setting eligibility criteria for registration of political parties, to the organization (though not location) of polling stations, to the voting and vote-counting operations. The plan also set specifications for computerization of voter registration records and for the mass information and civic education campaigns to be undertaken. Each stage of the electoral process was mapped out on a time line.

The first step was promulgation of the electoral law. Voter registration was to last for three to four months (tentatively set for mid-October through December 1992). In order to ensure their nationwide character and to discourage an excessive number, the political parties were required to field candidates for all 120 constituent assembly seats, with at least 5,000 supporters necessary for official recognition. This decision was important because it ensured that the primary competitors would remain the focal point of the election and would not have their support whittled away by a plethora of small parties.[39] In the initial time frame, the elections were scheduled for sometime between the third week of April and the first week of May 1993, after the conclusion of the rainy season.[40]

For the vote itself, the plan estimated that eight thousand polling stations would be needed. Cambodians were to present a valid voter registration card and to dip a finger into indelible ink after voting to ensure against fraud.

IMPLEMENTATION AND THE FIRST STEPS

Despite the comprehensiveness of the survey team's plan, the UNTAC electoral component's work got off to a slow start, suffering from the same procurement and logistics delays that hamstrung the other components in Cambodia. Its director, Reginald Austin, told the General Accounting Office that when the initial team arrived, there were no offices, desks, tables, chairs, telephones, computers, photocopiers, paper, pencils, or other basic materials. It took until December 1992 to establish a fully operational headquarters. This was much too late: 60 percent of the allotted time for the electoral process had already passed. It would have been better, said Austin, if the team had not been deployed until the groundwork had been laid. Less time would have been wasted, and the operation would have been more effective.[41]

Drafting an electoral law for adoption by the Supreme National Council was expected to be a relatively quick process, given that the Paris Accords had spelled out many of the parameters. The first draft was presented to the SNC by Yasushi Akashi on April 1. It took four months, however, for the final version to be adopted. After intense discussions and modifications to clarify the definition of "Cambodian persons," the SNC adopted the electoral law on August 5.

The electoral regulations, issued by UNTAC on September 12, were never agreed to by all factions. The difficulties UNTAC was encountering at this time with Khmer Rouge noncooperation on disarmament spread to the electoral process. Under the initial definition of eligibility, the Khmer Rouge was concerned that Vietnamese settlers could qualify to vote and affect the elections' outcome. To meet those concerns, UNTAC had amended the original draft to restrict the franchise either to a person born in Cambodia, with at least one parent who was born there, or to a person, if born outside of Cambodia, with at least one parent and grandparent who were born in Cambodia.[42]

The Khmer Rouge was not pacified by either this compromise or the procedures to verify eligibility. As Akashi said at a press conference on October 6,

> We felt that that was the only way to get agreement, if not of all four Cambodian factions, at least of three factions. And three factions have accepted. . . . but DK [Democratic Kampuchea; the Khmer Rouge] remains very adamantly opposed to it, saying that even this restricted approach allows Vietnamese in Cambodia to vote. . . . [I]n Cambodia, because of wars and fighting since 1970, many people do not have necessary papers or birth certificates or anything of that kind. So in these events, if two registered voters come forward as witnesses for the veracity of a third person, that . . . he or she is indeed a Cambodian person in the definition of the electoral law, then we will agree to register that third person. . . . [T]hese provisions . . . have satisfied three factions, but not the fourth one.[43]

Provisional registration of political parties began August 15, with fourteen parties expressing interest. While the number of parties provisionally registered eventually grew to twenty-two, the Khmer Rouge was not among them. In September, Akashi reported to the Security Council that uncertainty about Khmer Rouge plans was having an adverse effect on electoral planning. Khmer Rouge refusal to allow UN access to its zones posed difficulties not only for disarmament but for voter registration and education and for access of the other political parties to Khmer Rouge-held areas, which UNTAC was obligated to ensure.

By November, disarmament was abandoned, and intricate negotiations had failed to persuade the Khmer Rouge to comply with the Paris Accords. As the crisis came to a head, the United Nations was forced to consider whether it should postpone or abandon the elections altogether, or even withdraw UNTAC completely.

In his report to the Security Council on the matter, the secretary-general laid out the options and concluded that he concurred with the recommendation of Akashi and others who had attempted to resolve the impasse with the Khmer Rouge that the United Nations should forge ahead nonetheless.

The alternatives would be either to put the process on hold until, by one means or another, PDK's [the Party of Democratic Kampuchea] cooperation was obtained or to conclude that it was not possible to pursue the operation under present conditions and that UNTAC should therefore be withdrawn. The latter course is clearly unacceptable after so much has been achieved and so many hopes raised that Cambodia will at last achieve peace and democracy. The idea of putting the process on hold must also be rejected. Neither the political nor the economic situation in Cambodia would sustain a prolonged transitional period. In addition, it would require the international community to maintain indefinitely a large and very costly operation, whose recurrent costs are now running at almost $100 million per month.

I therefore concur with the Co-Chairmen of the Paris Conference that the implementation of the peace process must continue and that the timetable, leading to the holding of free and fair elections no later than May 1993, must be maintained. But it is necessary to spell out what this will entail if—as I still hope will not be the case—PDK maintains its non-cooperation with UNTAC. The election will take place while a substantial part of the forces of the Cambodian parties remains under arms. Few of these troops will have been cantoned and the Paris Agreements' requirement that at least 70 per cent of them should have been demobilized will not have been met. This does not by itself mean that a free and fair election cannot be held; but it will add to UNTAC's difficulties both in organizing the election and in ensuring, as best it can, the security of candidates, voters and electoral officials throughout the electoral process. It also has to be observed that if UNTAC continues to be denied access to PDK-controlled areas, the people living in those areas are likely to be deprived of the opportunity to exercise their right to register and to vote.[44]

This was a major turning point for UNTAC. Continuing toward the elections implied the effective abandonment of the basic four-faction structure of the Paris Accords. By forging ahead without Khmer Rouge compliance, the United Nations was risking the physical safety of its civilian staff and its peacekeeping troops. It was gambling that it could still hold elections despite the likelihood that the Khmer Rouge would try to forcibly disrupt them. Cognizant of the dangers, Akashi and Secretary-General Boutros Boutros-Ghali nevertheless decided to proceed with the mission, "preparing for the worst, but hoping for the best."[45] In its first exercise in the complex process of peace-building, the United Nations had much at stake in Cambodia.

On November 30, the Security Council imposed a selective trade embargo on the Khmer Rouge. The recommendation to proceed with the election without the Khmer Rouge could have threatened to divide the Council, which had until then fully backed Akashi and the secretary-general. In fact, China's abstention on the resolution cracked that unity only slightly. At no other time did China, or any other member of the Security Council, fail to back UNTAC's actions completely.

FORGING AHEAD

The United Nations' decision to continue the mission had immediate consequences. During December, UNTAC troops were taken hostage by Khmer Rouge units on four separate occasions, although all were released unharmed. The decision also appeared to unleash, or at least coincide with, a wave of SOC violence against its political opponents, and harassment of opposition candidates and political party offices. A Phnom Penh-based Western diplomat observed, "Officials in this government are just waking up to the fact that . . . they're unpopular—and may even be voted out of office. . . . So now, they're fighting for their survival, and fighting dirty."[46] The regime's systematic campaign against its political opponents, chiefly Sihanouk's FUNCINPEC and the KPNLF's Buddhist Liberal Party, included the use of organized "reaction forces" composed of civilians recruited and directed by the security hierarchy to carry out attacks on party members and offices.[47] UNTAC's response to the deteriorating security situation was to institute patrols by its military forces and civil police and to guard offices of the various political parties. The enhanced security measures did not completely quell the violence, but the regime's tactics shifted in January 1993 to lower-level intimidation. This was merely disruptive until the election neared. Then the violence escalated sharply.

The Phnom Penh regime also undertook a propaganda campaign against UNTAC through television, radio, and the party newspaper. It was designed to convey the message that only the SOC could defend the country against the Khmer Rouge; UNTAC could not be trusted to protect the Cambodian people. UNTAC responded by deploying its peacekeeping troops to 270 locations throughout the country, stepping up patrols against bandits, and taking additional measures to protect party offices and candidates. Its military unit also increased its civic action programs to reinforce UNTAC's commitment to the Cambodian people.[48]

Although it was never publicized, UNTAC's concern that regime harassment would cause the withdrawal of the two non-Communist factions led it to become even more deeply involved in the political process. In a manner typifying Akashi's leadership style, UNTAC searched for a way to deal with the threat to the elections without having to assert its authority directly by arresting Hun Sen, as head of the State of Cambodia, or arresting or reassigning the four provincial governors most deeply implicated in the campaign of intimidation and harassment. Instead, UNTAC sponsored forums, to which all political parties were invited, that allowed voters to hear directly from them. These voter forums had a deterrent effect on the regime. Obliged to participate, it could not disrupt them. Recognizing the near impossibility of ensuring a neutral political environment, UNTAC's electoral director called this strategy an attempt to create "neutral political acreages."[49]

Despite Khmer Rouge nonparticipation in the electoral process, a deteriorating security situation, and an SOC-sponsored campaign of political harassment, voter registration was surprisingly successful. The electoral component registered 4,640,000 voters in a campaign that was extended to January 31, 1993.[50] This was estimated to be 96 percent of all persons eligible.[51] UNTAC even managed to get access to some Khmer Rouge areas. In an early signal of the election's success, the secretary-general reported that "many electoral teams operating in or around zones where [the Khmer Rouge] is present have been permitted to register applicants and have reported high levels of interest in and commitment to the electoral process among the population of those zones."[52]

On January 27, twenty of the twenty-two provisionally registered political parties had applied for official party registration.[53] The Khmer Rouge had announced the formation of a political party at the end of November 1992 but did not apply for official party registration—thus ensuring that it would not be represented on the ballot. The Hun Sen regime registered as the Cambodian People's Party (CPP). FUNCINPEC, headed by Sihanouk's son Prince Norodom Ranariddh, represented one non-Communist faction. The Buddhist Liberal Democratic Party (BLDP) represented the other, the KPNLF.

UNTAC announced at a February 10 meeting of the Supreme National Council that a six-week period for political campaigning would begin April 7 and conclude on May 19. There would then be a four-day cooling-off period before the voting began. Throughout the winter, UNTAC continued to make revisions to the electoral law. These included a ban on public meetings before the campaign opened, a ban on public opinion polls that might have an intimidating effect on the populace, a ban on placing party seals on ballot boxes, and certain changes to the provisions for the removal of names from the lists of candidates for failure to meet the eligibility qualifications or for a breach of the electoral law. On March 11, Akashi met with the leaders of the twenty official parties to inform them of their responsibilities under the electoral law.

BOGGING DOWN IN VIOLENCE

Although UNTAC's military force had been redeployed to support the electoral effort, it was unable to prevent a wave of violence that accompanied the opening of the campaign. The organization was too slow in responding firmly and upgrading its security measures. The violence, which for the most part had not directly touched UNTAC's civilian international staff previously, now spilled over onto the foreigners. A Japanese district electoral supervisor and his Cambodian interpreter were killed on April 8, 1993. These killings, and the death of a Japanese civil police officer in early May, created a crisis for the Japanese government. In all, seven UN workers were killed during a two-week period. To a remarkable degree, the campaign period was not marked by violence directed against political candidates, although the civilian population still took casualties. Still, in March and April, the threat to the holding of elections was a serious one. There were widespread predictions that the Khmer Rouge intended to disrupt the vote and that the peace process was on the verge of collapse.

UN Volunteers, who had been critical of Akashi for not pushing harder to ensure that disarmament was completed and for not cracking down harder on the regime, demanded that they be given increased security or they would leave Cambodia. They also challenged his assumption that free and fair elections could take place in an atmosphere of armed violence. In response, Akashi and Boutros-Ghali recommitted UNTAC to holding the May elections. Deflecting the challenge from the Volunteers, Akashi argued that UNTAC was sowing the seeds of democracy that the Cambodian people had to nurture after UNTAC's departure. Sixty Volunteers left Cambodia. The remainder returned to their posts after a week of intensive security training and consultation, with enhanced safety procedures for the polling process. In ten provinces, electoral staff were instructed not to travel out of district capitals without an armed UN escort. In some provinces, they were relocated from the countryside into safer areas.[54] The contribution by the United States of protective gear (6,500 flak jackets, 10,000 helmets, first-aid kits, and flares) and six Black Hawk helicopters, as well as 100 additional troops by Australia and extra air support from Malaysia, gave UNTAC troops a psychological boost in the wake of casualties and helped stiffen the back of the multinational force.[55]

What kept the Khmer Rouge from escalating the violence even further, aside from Akashi and Boutros-Ghali's insistence that the process move forward, was the unwavering commitment of the factions' patrons to the elections. Both the Chinese and the Thais were obsessed with keeping the door open to the Khmer Rouge—which the United Nations did. In return, however, it expected China and Thailand to ensure that the Khmer Rouge would not sabotage the process. Their leaders would be allowed to boycott it, but not to actively disrupt it.

For some time, the Khmer Rouge did not realize the extent of its vulnerability. While it had strongholds, particularly around Pailin and in Siem Reap and Preah Vihear provinces, many of its other areas of control were in fact being penetrated and contested. The opening of Cambodia subtly threatened Khmer Rouge political dominance at the grass roots. At some point, the Khmer Rouge evidently became aware that its hold on the countryside was being challenged by UNTAC. The first signs of this were hostage-taking incidents in December 1992. When that did not scare the United Nations out of Cambodia, the Khmer Rouge tried to create fear in the countryside by throwing bombs at restaurants and polling places, followed by shooting at UNTAC personnel. In short, the Khmer Rouge gave every impression that it was scrambling, on the defensive, and seeking strategic advantage where none was to be had.

Despite Khmer Rouge intransigence and truculence, Akashi directly confronted Pol Pot's followers only once in his entire tenure in Cambodia. At an SNC meeting on April 10, 1993, after the killing of the two electoral workers, Akashi warned the Khmer Rouge that it "risks stripping itself of the legitimacy it regained by signing the peace agreement, and has taken a dangerous step toward outlaw status. . . . The world will not forgive the Party of Democratic Kampuchea for disrupting the Cambodian elections. There will be no more sanctuaries for that party, and no more chances."[56] The Khmer Rouge leader, Khieu Samphan, while appearing startled at Akashi's strong words, still refused to support an SNC resolution condemning further preelection violence and departed Phnom Penh on April 13. This contrasted with the episode the previous year when Akashi had been prevented from entering a Khmer Rouge-controlled area around Pailin by a bamboo pole placed across the road. That incident had been seen as indicative of UNTAC's weakness in the face of Khmer Rouge obstreperousness, yet Akashi's forbearance ultimately paid off.

THE INFORMATION AND EDUCATION UNIT

It was during the campaign period that UNTAC's investment in its information and education division paid off. The secretary-general's implementation plan recognized that a massive information and education campaign was central to UNTAC's efforts. Accordingly, the plan called for a centralized information unit, instead of leaving the matter to each component. The public awareness initiative was not to be limited to the election. It was intended to educate Cambodians about UNTAC's purposes, activities, and goals, as well as to undertake a massive civic instruction program in human rights, mine avoidance, and other matters relating to safety and citizenship.[57]

Given Cambodia's limited broadcasting facilities (even the radio broadcast range was limited to only half of the country because of antiquated and deteriorating equipment), UNTAC expected to run a massive campaign of "production and distribution/dissemination of radio and television programming, video cassettes, magazines, posters, fliers, textbooks and other educational materials, the staging of cultural events and simulations and the deployment of mobile information units (loudspeakers, video monitors, etc.) . . . in order to ensure that the message reaches Cambodians at all levels of society and in all parts of the country."[58] The materials for dissemination were to be translated into Khmer by the information and education unit.

Despite the well-thought-out strategy for the information and education campaign, progress was slow. Part of the delay in getting the information and education programs under way was attributable to the same logistics and procurement difficulties that afflicted other arms of UNTAC. More important, however, was a shortage of properly qualified translators.

Radio was an essential tool for getting out UNTAC's message. By September 1992, three of the four factions were cooperating with UNTAC in broadcasting information on the peace process and the United Nations' role. Only the Khmer Rouge refused to do so. UNTAC's own broadcasts, which did not begin until November 9, 1992, were over a Phnom-Penh based transmitter loaned by the regime for UNTAC's exclusive use. UNTAC broadcast unbiased information on voter registration and the electoral process, as well as on human rights and other aspects of its mandate.[59] The Phnom Penh transmitter, however, was not powerful enough to cover the entire country, making relay stations necessary for the provinces. Those were not installed until February 1993, three to five months behind schedule. In the interim, UNTAC relied on an arrangement with the Thai Foreign Ministry and Voice of America (VOA) to broadcast UNTAC programs twice daily at prime time from a VOA transmitter in Thailand.[60]

Recognizing that it was not sufficient merely to broadcast information, UNTAC distributed radios contributed by a Japanese nongovernmental organization and a Japanese political party. Forty-three thousand radios were distributed by January 1993, with an additional hundred thousand subsequently made available.[61] The radios proved to be so popular that Cambodians began stealing radios out of UNTAC vehicles.[62]

UNTAC utilized video parlors extensively to show its own Khmer-language information videos. It also produced weekly television news-magazine programs on UNTAC activities and public awareness dramas using Cambodian actors to present information on cantonment, the exercise of UNTAC's direct control functions, human rights, voter registration, and political party activity.[63]

The information division, headed by U.S. diplomat Timothy Carney, published media guidelines that had been drafted by the Media Working

Group it had set up. UNTAC also helped launch a Cambodian Media Association for all Cambodian journalists.

Guaranteeing fair access to the media for all registered political parties became an essential element of UNTAC's strategy as the election neared. Accordingly, Radio UNTAC broadcast daily electoral programs and offered every registered party weekly spots to broadcast its political material. It allowed political parties the "right of response" to what they believed was an unfair attack on or a misrepresentation of their public statements. UNTAC secured the SOC's agreement to have its Phnom Penh television station broadcast election-related material from the United Nations and from the other political parties for one hour every day.[64] Meanwhile Radio UNTAC stepped up its broadcasting to fifteen hours a day. Even Khmer Rouge members were listening to Radio UNTAC.

The information and education division had another, less publicized function. It collected information as well as disseminated it. It served in part as UNTAC's eyes and ears. With the 500 UN military observers, it helped to collate information from the multitude of Cambodians who wanted to tell UNTAC what they knew. This was useful for the military component; it was also useful for keeping a finger on Cambodia's pulse. The division conducted regular opinion surveys among Cambodians in Phnom Penh and the countryside to assess the impact of UNTAC's information program and to monitor attitudes toward UNTAC.[65] For example, although Akashi had banned public opinion polls in the preelection period, in order to prevent their use as intimidation, UNTAC had fairly good indications that the rank-and-file Khmer Rouge were unhappy with their leadership's decision to disrupt the election.

THE ELECTION

Secretary-General Boutros-Ghali visited Cambodia at the start of the electoral campaign on April 7 and 8, 1993. In addressing the Supreme National Council, he reminded those present that the international community expected them to uphold their responsibilities under the Paris Accords and to help UNTAC. He also told them that, in view of the measures UNTAC had taken to improve the security situation, it was his judgment that "the basic acceptable conditions for the conduct of an electoral campaign did exist."[66]

The campaign itself proceeded relatively peacefully, despite the atmosphere of tension. While there were continuing attacks, these were not directed specifically at the campaign. Scores of political meetings and rallies were held daily with the participation of tens of thousands of Cambodians. UNTAC also organized multiparty meetings for voters to hear the parties' messages.

More than a thousand international workers descended on Cambodia to help run the election. That number included 900 international polling station officers recruited from forty-four countries and the Inter-Parliamentary Union,* and 130 from the United Nations Secretariat. Another 370 were detailed from within UNTAC. Each of the 1,400 fixed polling stations and 200 mobile teams (some of which had been converted from fixed stations as voting continued throughout the week) were headed by one Cambodian presiding officer, paired with one international polling station officer to provide support and assist the presiding officer.

On the eve of the election, Akashi conceded that a genuinely neutral atmosphere was unattainable. "What we are trying to achieve now is the minimum acceptable condition for free and fair elections in Cambodia."[67] The *New York Times* observed, "Those words mark an important concession," since the Paris Accords explicitly stated that the elections would be held in a neutral political environment.[68] The Phnom Penh regime appeared willing to allow the elections to take place, but through political intimidation it did what it could to guarantee that the election would not be a fair one. As the election neared, Khmer Rouge violence—including its first attack on Chinese peacekeeping forces—played into the hands of the regime, whose campaign rhetoric was aimed at convincing voters that only the SOC was sufficiently strong militarily to combat the guerrillas. In addition, the SOC sought to convince voters that their ballots would not be secret and that they might lose their jobs and their homes if they voted against it.[69] Civil servants throughout the country were ordered to leave work to campaign for the SOC and to warn people against voting for opposition political parties.[70] According to UNTAC's human rights director, Dennis McNamara, "Coercion is the word for what is happening."[71]

Akashi warned that he expected violence before and during the election period, with possible attacks on as-yet untouched Phnom Penh.[72] Nonetheless, the Supreme National Council met in Beijing on May 6 and agreed to hold the election as scheduled.[73] The special representative turned out to be wrong. The Khmer Rouge, it appears, made a tactical alteration of course. When the balloting began on May 23, 1993, it was largely unmarred by violence, although there were scattered attacks on polling places. Probably no one will ever know precisely why the Khmer Rouge chose not to disrupt the election. UNTAC picked up rumors a week before the election that the Khmer Rouge had decided not to disrupt it; instead, the Khmer Rouge would throw its support to FUNCINPEC.

On the first day of balloting, 46 percent of all registered Cambodians voted. Voters flocked to polling stations hours before they opened, despite drenching early monsoon rains.[74] By the end of the second day,

---

* The Inter-Parliamentary Union is an organization of member states designed to strengthen parliamentary institutions, particularly by supporting the objectives of the United Nations.

nearly two-thirds had voted.[75] To UNTAC's surprise, voting attracted guerrillas and other Cambodians from Khmer-Rouge controlled areas. Some walked long distances to reach polling stations, since none were located in Khmer Rouge-controlled areas.[76] "I thought that the voting would be much more violent," commented a high-ranking Asian diplomat. "The Khmer Rouge may have felt they were simply outgunned at present by the U.N. forces and the Cambodian Army. Or perhaps they felt that Funcinpec will win the election, and that they have a chance of obtaining power in the new government."[77]

When the balloting concluded on May 28, an astonishing 90 percent of all registered voters had cast their ballots.[78] On May 29, at a meeting of the Supreme National Council, Akashi declared on behalf of the United Nations that "in view of the very high turnout throughout the country, the absence of violence or disruption during the polling, the success of the technical conduct of the poll and the calm and peaceful atmosphere that reigned throughout the polling period, the conduct of the poll had been free and fair."[79]

FUNCINPEC won the election with 45.47 percent of the vote, to 38.23 percent for the Phnom Penh regime's Cambodian People's Party (CPP). The KPNLF's Buddhist Liberal Democratic Party received 3.81 percent of the vote, and the other seventeen parties received 12.56 percent of the vote between them. FUNCINPEC won fifty-eight assembly seats, the CPP won fifty-one seats, and the BLDP won ten. One assembly seat went to the party of Molinaka and Nakataorsou Khmere for Freedom.[80]

As the established regime had expected all along to win the election, its initial response was to refuse to accept the results. It charged that seals on the ballot boxes had been broken and that the indelible ink used on voters' fingers to prevent fraudulent voting was erasable. "What we're seeing is panic by a group of men who have never before had their power challenged and who are shocked to discover that their hold over the people doesn't extend to the voting booth, . . ." said a senior UN official.[81] After Sihanouk's son Prince Ranariddh issued a message of reconciliation at Akashi's suggestion, the regime backed down.

It was a good thing the Phnom Penh administration expected to win. If it had not, it could have derailed the electoral process by stepping up its campaign of harassment and intimidation against opposition candidates. It might also have refused to cooperate with UNTAC, which could have caused the collapse of the peace process.

The Khmer Rouge also did not accept the outcome of the election. In a letter to Prince Sihanouk, Khieu Samphan charged that there was "no other choice" but to scrap the election and form a national reconciliation government that included the Khmer Rouge.[82] Sihanouk refused.

Although there were a number of motivations coming into play, FUNCINPEC won largely because the Cambodian people voted against the status quo. Sick and tired of SOC corruption, fed up with the brutality of some officials, voters did not buy the regime's argument that only it could contain the Khmer Rouge. The populace opted for change, hoping that it would bring peace. At the same time, the vote was not a repudiation of Hun Sen and his cohorts. The relative closeness of the vote can be interpreted as a message from the Cambodian people that reconciliation between the two chief competitors was the preferred path to peace.

FUNCINPEC's royalist connections held an undeniable appeal for the populace, reflected in Sihanouk's elevation to king in September 1993. In newspaper interviews with Cambodians after the vote, "many admitted that they did not really understand the concept of a secret ballot or political parties or democracy. They said they wanted to vote simply because they knew that this was their chance to demonstrate loyalty to Samdech—the King [Sihanouk]."[83]

Other considerations were at work as well. As one election watcher noted, "Although political observers in Phnom Penh may have worried about FUNCINPEC's associations with the KR [Khmer Rouge], that message did not make it into the rural areas. Instead, rural voters saw, in particular, two things. The first was SOC corruption. Those with first hand experience with FUNCINPEC know it is also corrupt, but its relatively weak presence in the rural areas, and the fact that it is out of power, meant rural people did not see that. SOC corruption was impossible to miss. . . ."[84]

In one regard, UN conduct of the elections in peacekeeping/peace-building missions came in to question: was UNTAC biased in favor of the non-Communist resistance, and FUNCINPEC in particular? One election observer thought so.

> UNTAC favored FUNCINPEC. It gave FUNCINPEC a radio station; it provided vehicles for political rallies, and so on. From a political perspective, this is problematic. From a strictly electoral perspective, however, these activities are sanctioned by the electoral ethos of countries such as the United States, Canada, and Australia, which have a commitment to levelling the playing field, to ensure that the incumbent party doesn't hog the show. The net result . . . was an association between UNTAC and FUNCINPEC. Voters who wanted to vote for "other" (that is, "anything but the mess we have now") would have logically picked FUNCINPEC, even in areas where UNTAC had out-stayed its welcome.[85]

Whether UNTAC violated the UN commitment to neutrality through political support for the non-Communist resistance is a fair question. Whether it was warranted for the sake of balance is another issue entirely. The non-Communist resistance and the Khmer Rouge charged all during UNTAC's tenure that it was biased in favor of the regime in place.

Human rights critics legitimately criticized UNTAC for not taking harsher measures against Phnom Penh for harassment and intimidation of its political opponents. Even dismissing the Khmer Rouge's unrealistic expectations that UNTAC would completely dismantle the SOC's administrative apparatus, efforts to control the Phnom Penh regime fell short of what was envisioned in the Paris Accords.

The various bias charges notwithstanding, the successful conduct of the election vindicated UNTAC's strategy. It transformed the Cambodian political landscape by forcing the competitors for power—for the first time in Cambodia's history—to curry favor with the Cambodian people. The people spoke, and spoke for change. For making that possible, UNTAC deserves the lion's share of the credit.

A ROARING SUCCESS

While this one election cannot by itself bring full-fledged democracy to Cambodia, it did transform the country in a relatively peaceful manner from a Communist, single-party state to a multiparty system. It also broke the marriage of convenience between the Khmer Rouge and Sihanouk and effectively restructured political alliances.

Sihanouk saw the Khmer Rouge committing suicide by its noncooperation with UNTAC and its election boycott. He knew the election was going to force him to throw his fate in with some alliance among the factions. Backing away from early moves to align himself with the Phnom Penh regime after the signing of the Paris Accords, Sihanouk decided that he could better hedge his bets by waiting.

By the same token, the SOC understood FUNCINPEC's political appeal. It wanted alignment before the election. Failing this, during the campaign it sought to intimidate FUNCINPEC by harassing its candidates and by killing its supporters. FUNCINPEC wanted alignment *after* the election. It was able to hold out because of UNTAC's efforts to level the playing field. In that sense, UNTAC's "bias" helped to ensure that it was the Cambodian people—not the drafters of the Paris Accords—who determined the elections' outcome.

It will probably never be clear why the Khmer Rouge chose to boycott the elections. "By not participating in the elections, the Khmer Rouge avoided an embarrassing, public rejection, while remaining a recognized player in the political process."[86] But in doing so, the Khmer Rouge made a grievous error. "By the end of the first day of polling, everyone knew that FUNCINPEC was ahead of SOC. Polling officials knew; voters knew; the KR knew."[87] No one will ever know how many Khmer Rouge members or supporters actually voted, or whether the Khmer Rouge helped increase the turnout for FUNCINPEC. A senior Asian diplomat in Phnom Penh remarked after the first day's vote, "We thought maybe the Khmer Rouge would use bullets rather than ballots in this election. . . . Maybe they've decided to use both."[88] By throwing its tacit support to FUNCINPEC, the Khmer Rouge gambled that Sihanouk would preserve its political power by ensuring the Khmer Rouge a role in the new government. It was wrong.

While the information and education division's work was essential to the election's success, it was not widely recognized during most of UNTAC's tenure as being critically important. There was simply no way to measure its effectiveness until the election. Given the massive propaganda campaigns by the Khmer Rouge and the SOC in particular, it is questionable, however, whether free and fair elections could have taken place without the unbiased Khmer-language information provided by the division throughout the entire country.

The work of the information and education division was UNTAC's most unqualified success. UNTAC had to convince Cambodians of three things: that their vote would be secret, that it would matter, and that the organization could deliver a vote-count free from fraud. In doing so, the information and education division accomplished its chief goal of schooling the Cambodian people in one of the most fundamental tenets of democracy— the right to free elections and their own participation in them. Similar information and education units should be considered essential elements of all UN peace missions—not just those engaged in peace-building but peacekeeping as well. "An information system to communicate why the United Nations is in a country and what is happening while the U.N. is there should be an immediate priority of every operation. In societies torn by conflict, truth is first shredded. . . . An effective public relations system can help the U.N. explain to the local population the U.N.'s mandate and to rebut propaganda."[89]

7

Lessons from a Venture into Peace-building

Although subsequent missions have undertaken activities similar to UNTAC's and others have exceeded it in size, Cambodia remains a unique experiment for the United Nations. No previous or subsequent UN mission has matched UNTAC for its scope of responsibilities, multidimensional mandate, complex administration, and unprecedented authority over a country.

The Cambodian conflict itself was unique. Unlike most of the post-cold war conflicts that have erupted in the developing world, neither ethnic nor tribal hatreds drove it. Rather, it was a simple struggle for political power by different factions. The basic issues revolved around who should rule, and through what form of government. External powers had fueled Cambodia's conflict. Their withdrawal and subsequent commitment to a political solution, coupled with the exhaustion of the contending factions and the Cambodian people, made political resolution feasible.

UNTAC must generally be considered a success. It clearly achieved its prime objective of effecting a peaceful transfer of power through the conduct of a "fair" election. William Shawcross wrote that Cambodia's nightmare is over and that the credit belongs to the United Nations. "Let there be no doubt about it. Success is the right word."[1]

UNTAC was not, however, an unqualified success. Given Cambodia's extensive problems and the length of time that will be needed to rebuild the country and reintegrate it into the mainstream community of nations, a final verdict cannot be reached for many years. A military threat still exists from the Khmer Rouge, albeit a diminished one. It will take time to assess whether the FUNCINPEC-SOC coalition will survive and how long it will remain a progressive force for change. It is also unclear how well that coalition will cope with the enormity of Cambodia's problems.

117

It is most useful to assess UNTAC in terms of what can be drawn from it to improve UN peacekeeping efforts for the future. Some of UNTAC's methods and procedures are transferable to many, if not most, UN peacekeeping efforts. Others are more useful for missions specifically engaged in peace building. UNTAC's experiences illuminated issues that warrant further exploration by the United Nations as it undertakes future operations, particularly those involving peace-building activities. U.S. policy toward such missions should also draw lessons from the Cambodian story.

LESSONS FOR PEACE-BUILDING

Peace-building is a major departure for the United Nations. In a sense, it is far more of a departure from routine peacekeeping than are the peace-enforcement exercises represented in recent years by the Persian Gulf War and the U.S.-led Somalia mission. Peace-enforcement entails UN intervention in situations where the international community has determined that a threat to the international order is so compelling or a wartime humanitarian crisis is so grave that the involved parties must be forcibly required to cease hostilities. In contrast, peacekeeping missions generally do not entail a substantial use of force. They are premised on the consent of the parties involved and are positioned to serve as a confidence-building mechanism for disputants that have decided to stop fighting.

Peace-building is what comes after. It can accompany a peacekeeping mission, as it did in Cambodia, or it can follow a peace-enforcement or a peacekeeping mission. Peace-building entails the rebuilding of the institutions of a civil society. It can help to reconstruct a failed state by strengthening institutions that have been shattered by conflict. (While the countries of Eastern Europe and the former Soviet republics are engaged in a similar process of reconstructing—or constructing—the institutions of a civil society after decades under communism, they did not have to endure the kind of fighting that has ruptured societies elsewhere to the point where UN intervention was requested.)

ELECTIONS

As the international community tentatively engages in peace-building efforts, it has tended to rely on elections to determine a legitimate political authority as the first premise for reordering the affected society. In Cambodia, the United Nations' electoral efforts were remarkably successful in bringing about national reconciliation and a government dedicated to reform. In Angola, they were not. But the Angolan case demonstrates that the mere holding of an election guarantees nothing.

Cambodia's election was an extremely important accomplishment. Its significance lies less in the coalition outcome than in its serving as a vehicle for the Cambodian people to take back a measure of political power from the leaders who for so long had manipulated and controlled them. The coalition was probably inevitable, particularly after Sihanouk's earlier, abortive attempt at an alliance with the Vietnamese-backed Communists. Had this first attempt at political realignment held, the Cambodian people could easily have concluded that the international community had predetermined Cambodia's fate. Instead, the next two years gave the Cambodian people breathing room, under the aegis of the United Nations, to make their own determination about the country's political future. The Paris Accords had structured an interim political arrangement that granted all contenders a place at the table. When the election took place, however, the Khmer Rouge forfeited its place at the table.

Elections, however free and fair, are no panacea. They can create or restructure political alliances, and they can provide a mechanism for validating a political platform via popular mandate. Thus, if the results are respected, they can put in place a legitimate governing authority. They cannot, however, reconstitute the institutions of a civil society in a failed state or a country shattered by warfare. For that, a far broader reconstruction effort is needed.

In Cambodia's case, the United Nations struggled to provide the framework for rebuilding the country's physical infrastructure with fundraising and coordination of construction and rehabilitation projects for the long term. UNTAC also undertook to provide Cambodia with the tools for social regeneration. It helped draft penal and traffic codes; it attempted to educate the populace about human rights; and it tried to get the country on a firmer financial footing by assisting the Phnom Penh administrative apparatus in budget and revenue planning. It was less successful in such efforts than in the electoral sphere for a variety of reasons, not least of which was inadequate funding and personnel. Efforts like these, however, are what the United Nations may increasingly be called upon to undertake if it moves more deeply into peace-building activities.

ALLOCATION OF RESOURCES

Because peace-building is not cheap, the United Nations should undertake it selectively in order to ensure ample resources and personnel for those activities. The United Nations' lack of experience with peace-building activities caused it to stint on resources for the civilian side of UNTAC. In fact, from their inception in the late 1940s, peacekeeping missions' focus has been on military operations. This has been so whether the chief task was to observe a cease-fire, act as a buffer force between contending parties, or ensure a secure environment for providing humanitarian aid to a starving population. Organizing and running elections, writing traffic and penal codes, investigating prison conditions, and overseeing a country's administrative apparatus are activities far removed from traditional peacekeeping operations. It is not surprising, therefore, that in designing UNTAC, the United Nations vastly underestimated the needs of most civilian functions.

The repatriation effort, on the other hand, was probably overfunded. Inaccurate assumptions about the refugees' needs for a new life in Cambodia resulted in a call for greater resources than may have been necessary. In contrast, limited financing for UNTAC's civilian components, particularly civil administration, civil police, and human rights, seriously impaired their ability to operate in Cambodia. Together, the civil administration and human rights branches were authorized a total of only 224 specialists and 84 international support staff, in contrast to the 15,900 peacekeepers charged with disarming the factions' forces.[2] It was nonsense to think that 200 international administrative staff could control the activities of 140,000 Cambodian bureaucrats. They were stretched so thinly that they did not reach the village and commune level, where the SOC's military and police presence was most pervasive. The human rights officers had insufficient resources to do the extensive training Cambodia needed. The Special Prosecutor's Office never received the funds it had requested for training programs for judges or for a witness protection program. There were also too few civil police to provide true law enforcement for Cambodia, or even to monitor the activities of the factions' police. In the eyes of many critics, UNTAC may have started the process of reconstruction, but failed to transform Cambodia in the ways necessary to make the peace settlement durable in the long run.

Forays into the unfamiliar terrain of peace-building should be undertaken cautiously, since success carries such a high price tag. Although the United Nations lacks expertise in the field, with its operations in Namibia, Cambodia, El Salvador, and Mozambique, it is slowly gaining the experience it badly needs. However, as Alvaro de Soto and Graciana del Castillo point out, although the obstacles to peace-building in El Salvador are of a different variety from those in Cambodia, what remains constant is that the undertaking is extensive, costly, and strains the United Nations' already overstretched capabilities.[3]

INFORMATION AND EDUCATION

Two particular aspects of UNTAC's work should be highlighted because they were essential in helping to win the hearts and minds of the Cambodian people: the information and education unit and the civilian quick-impact projects coupled with the military's civic action program. UNTAC's experience suggests that the United Nations should incorporate an information and education unit as an essential element of all future missions, particularly those involved in peace-building. Such efforts should not bog down in trying to procure the highest level of technology possible. They should use methods, as in Cambodia with Radio UNTAC, that best meet the country's needs. The United Nations should also retain the high priority it placed on translation of all information and education materials into the local (Khmer) language.

UNTAC's information and education unit was a model for informing the population about UN objectives and progress. It conducted a successful massive civic education campaign in human rights awareness, mine precautions, and electoral matters. Most important, it did a superb job of mass instruction in some of the basic tenets of democracy. The election's strong turnout does not mean that each Cambodian who voted did so because he or she supported a democratic system of government for Cambodia. But the information and education unit persuaded Cambodians that the election was important, that their individual voice mattered, that the vote would be secret, and that UNTAC could deliver a vote-count free of fraud. Given Cambodia's tormented history and a background in which violence still flourished, the achievement was remarkable.

QUICK-IMPACT PROJECTS AND CIVIC ACTION PROGRAMS

Based on their success as a part of its mission in Cambodia, the United Nations should also leaven the civilian side of future missions with quick-impact projects and ensure that its peacekeeping forces have the responsibility to undertake civic action programs whenever compatible with their other missions. While the information and education unit focused on the Cambodian people's political development, UNTAC's civilian quick-impact projects and the military's civic action programs targeted their physical well-being.

The larger and separate UNTAC rehabilitation and reconstruction component focused principally on Cambodia's long-term rebuilding—even though as originally conceived, it was to coordinate short, medium, and long-term projects. Reluctance to commit funds in an uncertain political climate meant that donors deferred most reconstruction projects until after the elections had taken place. The average Cambodian, particularly in rural areas, thus saw little tangible economic benefit from this grandiose effort heralded by the United Nations and by international donors.

It was, however, the average Cambodian for whom the quick-impact projects and civic action programs made a real difference. These projects were not designed to repair Cambodia's ports or to build large, modern hospitals. They were undertaken without extensive planning or expensive studies by consultants and were completed quickly. Their costs were low. Some were funded by military contingents that scrounged money from their home governments. The projects were largely nickel-and-dime operations. For example, the Malaysian battalion's civic action program for sector 8, in western Cambodia, was budgeted at only $6,650, for vocational and language training, public health teaching materials, dental care, construction of toilets, road fixing, basic tools for villagers, and minor repairs to community facilities.[4] Wells were dug, bridges repaired, children immunized. Clinics brought medical care to rural areas. Villagers received start-up loans, vegetable seeds, and fishing equipment.

These projects had two major effects. They made a tangible economic impact on the lives of Cambodian villagers. In so doing, they conveyed to the Cambodian people a sense that the United Nations and the international community cared about them. Winning the hearts and minds of the people also saved peacekeepers' lives. General John Sanderson noted that civic action "is necessary for an established 'hearts and minds' dimension to the military budget to both facilitate the acceptance of the military in the countryside and to provide an immediate dimension of humanitarian action deep in the countryside where the military, but few civilian elements, can establish a presence."[5]

Quick-impact projects cannot substitute for the longer-term reconstruction effort that is desperately needed to secure the peace. The benefits of reconstruction, however, are only felt long after the United Nations has departed. Quick-impact projects, on the other hand, can smooth the way for the UN mission while it is still in operation. In future peace-building operations, quick-impact projects should be mandatory. The United Nations should also consider undertaking them in other types of missions if circumstances permit.

LESSONS FOR UN PEACEKEEPING

THE RIGHT LEADERS

The right leaders can make a difficult operation work better. In Yasushi Akashi and General Sanderson, the United Nations chose well. Their diplomatic skills, perseverance, and ability to focus on an achievable goal—the holding of a UN-organized election in as neutral and free an environment as possible—were critical to UNTAC's success.

In choosing civilian and military heads of missions, the United Nations should consider leaders who can concentrate on the primary objective yet adapt as obstacles arise. It should choose military leaders who are politically adept and have as clear a vision of the mission's political goals as they do of its military ones. Wherever possible, the United Nations should draw on regional expertise to strengthen the regional players' commitments to the operation.

While there is no guarantee of who will do well, the United Nations should heed obvious warning signs. Though Admiral Jonathan Howe, the head of the Somalia operation in the summer of 1993, may have received an unwarranted share of the criticism for that mission's failure, putting an American military officer in charge of the civilian side of the mission should have made someone think twice. Howe's presence made the UN operation appear to be a U.S. venture—a recipe for potential trouble. In Cambodia, it was hardly coincidental that the top civilian and military leaders were from two of the most important regional players: Japan and Australia. The appointments of both Akashi and Sanderson were a recognition of the Asia/Pacific powers' commitment to a successful outcome for UNTAC.

While politics are important in choosing the senior heads of UN missions, it was Sanderson and Akashi's competence and capabilities that made them effective. Akashi made every effort to work through the Supreme National Council, even at the expense of delay, as was the case with the electoral law. He could have done far more on his own authority, particularly since Sihanouk, the Council's president, was absent from the country for most of UNTAC's tenure, but instead he chose to spare the United Nations the responsibility of imposing democracy on Cambodia. When Sihanouk asked Akashi to act in his stead, Akashi refused. Much of the action took place behind the scenes in a process of give and take. Akashi also maintained a nonconfrontational attitude toward the Khmer Rouge. It was not widely popular, but it kept the possibility of dialogue open and helped preserve the Security Council members' support.

Sanderson was ideally suited to head UNTAC's military side. He was steeped in the Paris Accords, knew the region well, and had experience dealing with the Thais. His experience in Vietnam had shaped his views about the limits on the use of force. That attitude and his belief, shared with Akashi, that the Cambodian endeavor was a peacekeeping—not a peace-enforcement—mission helped to keep UNTAC from derailing. More inclusive in his personal style than Akashi, Sanderson believed in the utility of a multinational force and structured his operation to ensure that all views were taken into consideration. While dealing with the sensitivities of many national units made his job more difficult, he felt that a multinational force was advantageous because it meant that the peacekeepers reflected the will of the international community. Future UN operations should seek out military commanders like Sanderson. He was a model diplomat-general; his political skills and clear vision of the mission's priorities contributed greatly to UNTAC's success.

PLANNING, PROCUREMENT, AND LOGISTICS

At the time UNTAC was on the drawing board, the United Nations had no experience planning a mission as large and complex as that envisioned for Cambodia. The UN Secretariat's Department of Peacekeeping Operations and its Field Operations Division shared the responsibility for planning. "U.N. officials stated that the peacekeeping department developed the overall implementation plan for UNTAC, but once the broad implementation plan was completed, logistical planning was turned over to the Field Operations Division. When plans had to be revised based on experience in Cambodia, the preparation of detailed operational plans with logistical specifications and deployment schedules was delayed because the two units could not agree on priorities, and there was no single authority short of the Secretary General to set the priorities for both units."[6]

Each component of UNTAC planned separately, rather than as part of an overall mission. The United Nations did not always send survey missions when needed, and much of the data used for planning purposes was out-of-date or useless. One such example was the satellite surveys used to identify land for repatriated refugees. When it became clear on the ground that the surveys were useless, the entire repatriation package had to be reconfigured, creating discontent among refugees with raised expectations. UNTAC's experience suggests that planning for multifaceted missions should be done in an integrated manner to ensure better coordination, that survey missions should be sent out as a matter of routine, and that missions should be planned to hit the ground running.

While the United Nations' haphazard planning process worked well for the electoral component, the repatriation effort, and the military unit, it did not serve UNTAC's other branches as well, particularly those most associated with peace-building activities: human rights, civil administration, and civil police. The electoral component drew on the UN Electoral Assistance Unit's experience in preparing a preliminary plan for the elections. The repatriation staff drew on the extensive expertise of the Office of the UN High Commissioner for Refugees (UNHCR). No similar UN units existed to help plan for UNTAC's other civilian components. Lack of Secretariat specialists in the areas of human rights, public administration, and policing, as well as a general lack of experience in carrying out these activities, impaired UNTAC's effectiveness. In addition to hiring such specialists, the Secretariat should also identify resources available worldwide for help in planning such missions, so the current depth of expertise in refugee and electoral affairs can be matched in other areas essential to peace-building.

The United Nations should also devise procedures for more quickly recruiting civilian personnel for missions. Slow deployment of personnel seriously impedes mission effectiveness. While geographic diversity should remain a consideration, the organization should give higher priority to getting qualified staff into the field quickly. Peace-building activities require expertise that may more often be found outside the UN system. Mission directors in the field should be given greater latitude to recruit staff and to go outside the United Nations' cumbersome hiring system.

For UNTAC, deployment delays meant more than just a slow start. In some instances, UNTAC missed significant opportunities. In June 1992, for example, the Phnom Penh bureaucrats awaited an UNTAC takeover. But by the time UNTAC's civil administrators arrived in force and determined what to do and how to do it, the SOC had become intransigent. UNTAC thus lost the chance to make significant inroads into the country's administrative apparatus.

While the sketchy UN planning process was detrimental to UNTAC in a number of ways, the lack of rigid, centralized control was not without its benefits. In a country as isolated and far from New York as Cambodia, UNTAC's authority to plan on the ground had clear advantages. It gave the mission flexibility and allowed faster response to changing situations. The delay in response time that affected the UN military command in Somalia and Bosnia was not an issue in Cambodia. That reflects, in part, the difference between peacekeeping and peace-enforcement missions. There also appears, however, to have been a tacit agreement by New York to give UNTAC leaders a freer hand in Cambodia than mission leaders may have had elsewhere. Planning for UN operations needs to be improved, but once in the field missions should retain significant local authority so that they can respond quickly and adjust tasks as obstacles arise.

Finally, the United Nations should streamline procurement procedures. While the current system may be reasonable for many missions, for large ones like UNTAC it has proved to be an almost intolerable burden. Coupled with inadequately developed and insufficiently coordinated logistics, uncertainty in requisitions made UNTAC's work far more difficult than it should have been. Among other things, UNTAC's civilian components pressured its peacekeepers for supplies. This not only strained military procurement and logistics, it irritated the commanders, who believed it was not their responsibility to have to take care of UNTAC's civilian side. Problems caused by procurement glitches were endemic. Telephones were in short supply, and even where they did exist they often did not work. At least one component lacked a working telephone system until mid-October 1992. UNTAC did not have enough computers until three to four months after the mission began. Some military contingents did not have safe drinking water for months because of delayed procurement of water purification plants. UNTAC also had a shortage of aircraft and fuel, a chronic shortage of vehicles, and the wrong type of vehicles for the civil police when the mission started. Given Cambodia's terrain and poor roads, they needed, but did not have, motorbikes and boats.[7] Clearly, the United Nations needs to devise streamlined procurement procedures for large missions.

The secretary-general recognized the chronic problem of slow start-up for UN operations. He recommended the establishment of a pre-positioned stock of basic peacekeeping equipment that would be immediately available to initiate an operation. Alternatively, he proposed that countries designate ready reserves of equipment for quick loan, donation, or sale to the United Nations. He also suggested that countries commit to standby arrangements of military personnel from which the United Nations could draw, noting in particular the difficulty of obtaining adequate logistics units.[8] The United Nations should implement these recommendations. It should press countries harder to designate ready reserves of standard equipment (vehicles, generators, office supplies, fuel, etc.). Civilian and military logistics should be integrated to prevent duplication, overlap, and competition for scarce supplies.

Although there has been little progress in implementing many of Secretary-General Boutros-Ghali's recommendations, there has been some progress in improving the organization's capacity to plan, logistically support, and deploy peacekeeping missions. As a result of its experience in Cambodia and Somalia, in September 1993 the Secretariat incorporated the Field Operations Division into the Department of Peacekeeping Operations. It also opened a twenty-four-hour situation room to improve communication with field headquarters.[9]

Member states' recent commitment of standby soldiers should help assemble peacekeeping forces more quickly. By April 15, 1994, eighteen countries had designated a total of 28,000 troops from which the United Nations can draw for peacekeeping missions. The organization expects thirty-one other countries to commit standby forces, which could raise the total to 70,000. Although designating military personnel for peacekeeping may reduce deployment time, commitments thus far do not cover the whole spectrum of resources needed to undertake UN operations. Deficiencies remain in the areas of communications, logistics, health services, supply, engineering, and transportation.[10] Logistics problems will be especially difficult to solve. While the proliferation of peacekeeping missions has increased demand, there is only a limited supply of trained logistics units. Few countries can spare them for extended periods of time. In May 1993, the General Assembly approved an increase of thirty-four positions in the Secretariat's permanent logistics staff that should help to improve planning capability.

COORDINATION

Large, multifaceted operations pose particular problems in terms of organization. UNTAC's experience demonstrated the necessity for devising better mechanisms for coordinating these large missions. Assigning specific staff responsibility for coordination and establishing a joint civilian-military staff both at headquarters and at the provincial or working level could help improve mission effectiveness.

The United Nations should place higher priority on managerial expertise and training in management techniques. While the head of the mission need not be skilled in management, the United Nations should designate a senior official, perhaps the deputy head of mission, as the mission's manager. Creating a new oversight position at the subnational level, provincial civil administrators could help ensure that mission objectives are carried out in a coordinated fashion and that the military and civilian sides of the mission's work are well integrated.

UNTAC's overall lack of coordination was, perhaps, most evident in each of its component's opinions about the performance of the others. The morale of UNTAC personnel was not uniformly high. Electoral staff members were unhappy with headquarters' unwillingness to crack down on the SOC. Provincial electoral staff also thought that headquarters paid insufficient attention to their safety. The civil administrators believed many of the civil police were incompetent and unreliable. Human rights staff believed that UNTAC did not pursue its rights mandate sufficiently aggressively. Civil administrators and human rights personnel did not work well together. Civilian staff thought some of the peacekeeping troops did little but cause trouble. Provincial staff generally felt ignored and slighted. Clearly, there was little sense of a unified effort working toward common objectives.

UNTAC should have been a tightly integrated operation. It needed formal mechanisms to coordinate its various activities. Specific timetables tying all its tasks to those of the electoral component would have helped to synchronize the mission, and prevent the branches from working at cross-purposes or duplicating efforts. The most critical deficiency was the tenuous linkage between military and civilian activities. A joint military-civilian staff at headquarters and at the local, working level would have helped. When Akashi and Sanderson redefined UNTAC's mission after the factions' failure to disarm, they partially rectified the problem. This resulted in enhanced security for civilian staff and improved logistical support for the electoral effort—without which the election might not have been accomplished. In addition, UNTAC's lines of authority ran independently from each component's district to its provincial level, and then to its headquarters in Phnom Penh. That gave each a great deal of autonomy, which may have been beneficial in some cases but was detrimental to UNTAC's overall effectiveness. Designating a civil administrator for each province, who would be responsible for ensuring accomplishment of all UNTAC's tasks in an integrated manner, could have improved coordination and mission performance.

REPATRIATION

Dealing with dislocated populations is likely to become an increasingly important job for the United Nations as ethnic and tribal conflicts become more pervasive. In Cambodia, the United Nations repatriated a long-standing and stable population of refugees that had resided on the

Thai-Cambodian border for nearly fifteen years. Repatriation was made easier because the refugees were in organized camps and were accustomed
to dealing with the United Nations and private voluntary agencies. On the
other hand, the Cambodian refugees were divided into political factions
and had been subject to intense political conflict.

Today's conflicts are causing sudden, massive displacement of populations—from Rwanda, from Bosnia, and from some of the former Soviet
republics. Kurds are still without permanent homes; Sudanese are on the
move; and Angolans remain unsettled. Increasingly, the United Nations will
be called on not only to feed, clothe, and shelter those displaced, but to move
them back when conflict winds down. The UN experience in Cambodia points
strongly to the necessity for working actively to depoliticize repatriation efforts
by seeking commitments to that effect from the involved parties and by the
United Nations itself maintaining strict neutrality to maximize the participants'
cooperation.

In Cambodia, repatriation succeeded not only in returning 365,000
refugees; it took place without a single accident or deliberately disruptive
incident. It is difficult to determine how much of this success should be
attributed to the refugees' overwhelming desire to return and how much
to UNTAC's efforts. Logistically, however, UNTAC and UNHCR made it possible for the refugees to return to Cambodia in safety. UNHCR had prior
experience in the region that gave repatriation a head start. UNHCR's
quasi-independent status also worked in its favor. Depoliticization of the
repatriation process was a critically important ingredient of success. The
consensus among all players—non-Cambodian as well as Cambodian—
from early in the negotiating process on the prerequisite of keeping refugee
issues isolated from factional quarrels ensured the four factions' cooperation. UNHCR's deliberate efforts to maintain impartiality, while time-consuming and occasionally torturous, prevented the process from being
subverted by any faction. While it may be difficult to achieve such balance
in future repatriation efforts, UNTAC's success suggests that it is possible
and worth the effort.

UN TROOP BEHAVIOR

The difficulties of melding forces from thirty-five different countries
into a peacekeeping force should not be underestimated. Establishing
and enforcing a common standard of behavior is difficult when cultural norms
differ and when the forces remain under the control of their national commanders. Culturally insensitive behavior can create severe impediments
to UN effectiveness, as well as erode or preclude the populace's goodwill
toward the peacekeepers. One way for the United Nations to minimize inap-
propriate comportment by its military and civilian personnel would be through
mandatory training sessions modeled on that used by Singapore to drill the

civil police contingent it contributed to UNTAC. Multidimensional training could help to instill a uniform code of conduct as well as an enhanced sense of shared mission.

The boorish behavior of some UN soldiers in Cambodia aroused local hostility toward UNTAC. Part of the problem stemmed from soldiers who were underutilized. UNTAC had effectively suspended disarmament and cantonment but had not yet reoriented its military mission toward support for the electoral process. "The breakdown of the cantonment process clearly has left many U.N. peace keepers with little to do. . . . [C]omplaints about the behavior of U.N. soldiers . . . have mounted amid a perception that some of them spend too much time in bars and brothels and drive their U.N. vehicles recklessly."[11]

UNTAC issued a number of directives emphasizing the necessity for appropriate behavior. Complaints diminished somewhat after the military mission's reorientation since the peacekeepers had less free time. Disciplinary problems did not disappear, however, and cases of sexually transmitted diseases, including HIV infection, which had been practically unknown in Cambodia prior to the United Nations' arrival, continued to increase.

LACK OF CONSENSUS ON WHEN TO USE FORCE IN SELF-DEFENSE

When UN peacekeepers should use force is a problem that has bedeviled many missions. There are two main issues: when peacekeepers should use force to defend themselves against attacks, and what level of force should be used to accomplish the mission's objectives.

Most peacekeeping operations in the past took occasional casualties, but missions today appear to entail greater risk. A clear understanding of when to use force entails more than just rules of engagement. It requires a pragmatic assessment of the degree of danger troops should be expected to face. It involves hard decisions during the mission's planning process about how to handle attacks on UN personnel. Deciding how to deal with potential attacks ought to be given high priority. The United Nations should be more conservative in assessing a mission's potential for danger, planning for the worst. Underestimating the level of danger can be costly—as it was for both civilian and military UNTAC personnel. Clearer and more uniform standards of when to use force can save lives.

In retrospect, Akashi concluded that UNTAC defined the right of self-defense too narrowly at the beginning of its mission. It broadened the definition as Khmer Rouge attacks intensified. Even so, standard operating procedures notwithstanding, there was no uniform interpretation of what constituted self-defense. Recruitment of UN troops inevitably results in contingents of uneven caliber, though this may have been a lesser problem for UNTAC than for other operations. Not only did the various national corps have different ideas about how to respond to attacks, they had different ideas about how aggressively to patrol, how to defuse potentially threatening situations, and how strongly armed they should be. Contingents came to UNTAC with differing levels of equipment that significantly affected their members' attitudes about when to use force.

UNTAC's personnel were vulnerable in part because the military units gave mixed signals about how they would respond to attacks. Those national contingents that were tough and aggressive in responding to attacks for the most part did not lose personnel. Those targeted, including the nine soldiers killed in April and May 1993 as well as those taken hostage in December 1992, tended to be from units that had a reputation for passivity. A clearer understanding of when to use force requires that the United Nations ensure that national contingent commanders agree on and then abide by whatever guidelines are set for the mission.

In preparing for missions, the United Nations should screen troop offers carefully. Once offers are accepted, it should ensure that national contingents are properly outfitted and equipped. This involves more than the contingents' operational readiness when they arrive. (In UNTAC's case, some contingents arrived without such necessary equipment as tents and sixty days' field rations.)[12] The level of danger to which UN troops may be exposed can vary throughout the deployment area; that can affect the type of equipment needed. Widely varying equipment levels, however, can lead local armies or factions to probe for soft spots in UN defenses, as did the Khmer Rouge.

One way to solve some of these difficulties would be to train military contingents jointly at a central location before embarking on the mission, instead of directly deploying to the field. While this may be impractical for all missions, it could enhance their effectiveness in the field. In lieu of joint training of all contingents, at minimum, the United Nations could require intensive joint training of the designated national commanders, to be supervised by each mission's force commander, prior to initial field deployment. Similarly, if the force commander is replaced during an operation's tenure, as often happens, bringing contingent commanders together for training could benefit all officers. Since national contingent commanders rotate as well, the force commander should ensure that all are routinely brought together to reiterate mission standards, priorities, objectives, and a common understanding of when to use force in self-defense.

ISSUES FOR FUTURE UN MISSIONS

As the first multidimensional, large, and complex mission, UNTAC brought to the fore a number of issues toward which the United Nations should devote attention. No issue is unique to UNTAC, and none is particularly amenable to resolution via specific recommendations. Some are, or should be, recognized as bearing significantly on most UN operations; others are new issues raised to prominence as the United Nations has undertaken more ambitious missions. These issues deserve further exploration and special consideration in the planning and conduct of future UN operations.

Views of the Populace

When peacekeeping is undertaken with the consent of all parties to a conflict, the views of the populace are of minimal importance. Peacekeepers may concern themselves with the people's welfare, but they seldom consider the effect, if any, of popular opinion on the political leaders with whom the United Nations must contend or on the overall success of the mission. For the most part, local leaders are what count.

UNTAC's experience, however, suggests that in situations where consent has been obtained, but where it may be suspect for one or more parties, the United Nations ought to take into consideration the views of the local populace. The people's support for the UN mission may substitute, in some instances, for the faltering commitment of a contending party's leaders, thus helping to keep the mission going.

In Cambodia, the people's overwhelming desire for peace was crucial to UNTAC's success. Through the means of a UN-organized election, the Cambodian people forced a political compromise between contending factions. Similarly, Salvadoran and Mozambican exhaustion with civil war lent support to UN peace-building efforts there. The people in all three countries acted as a check on the elites' tendency to drift back into armed conflict, and thus helped to keep the UN efforts from unraveling.

Popular opinion cannot always be relied on to play a meaningful or constructive role, however. In Angola, Jonas Savimbi repudiated the outcome of the country's UN-monitored election and then took his party and the country back into civil war. The sentiments of the Angolan majority have not been sufficient to counteract the appeal of a charismatic leader with numerous followers. Rwandans have been at the mercy of armed warfare between political elites whose conflict is rooted in rival tribes' power struggle. In the former Yugoslav republics, ethnic hatred that permeates the populace as well as the political leaders has fueled the conflict.

Instead of largely ignoring the masses, as it has in the past, the United Nations should look on the people as a potential asset that can help facilitate its mission. This goes beyond merely winning hearts and minds. When considering whether to undertake an operation, the organization should carefully analyze the situation to determine the extent to which the local populace is able to influence the political leaders' views and actions. It should assess whether the populace supports resolution of the underlying conflict, or whether it would actively undermine a UN operation, and to what extent it is at the mercy of political leaders who control most of the weapons. Obviously, developing accurate assessments may be difficult, if not impossible. To the extent such information is, or can be, made available, however, it should be an integral part of both the design and planning for UN operations.

CHARISMATIC LOCAL LEADERS

Because of the very nature of peacekeeping, most UN missions have paid little attention to the issue of charismatic local leaders. When all parties have agreed on the desirability of a UN presence, contending with charismatic leaders is a chore, but not a mission-breaker. As the United Nations increasingly contemplates operations where the contending parties' cooperation is either absent or suspect, however, the presence of one or more charismatic local leaders assumes far greater importance. They can pose serious problems for larger, more complex missions, whether they are Somalia-like Chapter VII peace-enforcement operations or Cambodia-like "Chapter VI and three-quarters" peacekeeping missions.

While it was not easy for UNTAC to deal with Sihanouk, it clearly benefited significantly from his support. Mercurial, vacillating, difficult to deal with, and often physically absent, Sihanouk was nonetheless the one figure around whom the country could rally. Only he had the stature to unify the Cambodian populace. He was pulled in all directions—by Hun Sen, the Khmer Rouge, and the West. His response was to remove himself from Cambodia during most of UNTAC's tenure. This allowed him to remain somewhat above the fray, forcing all contenders to compete for his support, and to keep his options open.

As president of the Supreme National Council, Sihanouk's voice carried weight when the United Nations needed decisions. His acquiescence smoothed the way for unilateral decisions by UNTAC in instances when the SNC deadlocked.

Sihanouk was the glue that kept the Cambodian peace process from breaking apart. By repudiating the short-lived coalition with the SOC in late 1991 and allowing the competitive electoral process to go forward, Sihanouk let the Cambodian people determine the composition of the new government. By the same token, had the Khmer Rouge not believed that Sihanouk would be its trump card, it might have resorted to a far more concerted campaign of violence against UN forces. As it was, UNTAC came close to unraveling under Khmer Rouge attacks in March-April 1993.

Charismatic leaders thus serve as a rallying point. They have the presence, and the strength of personality, to sway a populace. If they choose to target the United Nations as a detrimental, not beneficial, presence, peacekeepers can get killed. Many did in Somalia when clan leader Mohammed Farah Aideed turned his followers loose on UN troops. It would therefore behoove the United Nations to assess carefully with whom the local charismatic leaders will likely side. It should think twice about undertaking a mission if such leaders oppose or are even merely ambivalent about a UN presence. If the United Nations chooses to intervene under such conditions, the obstacles are increased, as is the potential for failure. Moreover, in an era of increasingly scarce reserves, the costs may exceed UN member nations' willingness to pay. On the other side of the coin, peace-building missions heavily reliant on a charismatic leader's support, as in Cambodia, risk failure if that leader dies or is removed from the scene. Sihanouk is elderly and in frail health. His son Prince Ranariddh has grown in stature, but he still lacks his father's following. Cambodia's long-term stability may be jeopardized if Sihanouk dies any time soon. Peace-building efforts need to be rooted in institutional reform and structural change if their effects are to be long lasting. Charismatic leaders can bolster a UN effort, but they cannot necessarily ensure its success.

SUPPORT OF EXTERNAL PARTIES

As William J. Durch has observed, "Peacekeeping operations require complementary political support from the Great Powers and the local parties. If either is missing or deficient, an operation may never get underway or may fail to achieve its potential once deployed."[13] In Cambodia, the external parties' support was perhaps the single most important force in keeping the peace process moving forward. The regional and extraregional players' commitment to ensuring that the election took place provided the momentum that overcame obstacles such as the general failure to disarm.

The Paris Accords were signed in October 1991 largely to allow the central players in the region—China and Vietnam—to disengage from Cambodia in a face-saving manner. Once the accords were signed, there was no serious deviation from the course set. Despite the problems that arose, the Security Council remained virtually united in backing the secretary-general's recommendations, including placing economic sanctions on the Khmer Rouge.

At three points, reaffirmation of that support was decisive: the summer of 1992, when the Khmer Rouge refused to disarm; November 1992, as UNTAC's mission was redefined; and April 1993, when UNTAC was under physical attack by the Khmer Rouge. Had external backing wavered at any of those points, UNTAC could have collapsed. The outside powers' confidence strengthened Akashi's hand in dealing with the four factions. It also undercut the factions' ability to derail the peace process.

The restraint imposed on the factions by their patrons allowed for a chafing against the parameters of the peace process, a testing of its stress limits, but prevented its outright collapse. Consequently, the Khmer Rouge could refuse to participate in disarmament and the election. It could even target UNTAC personnel. It could not, however, totally disrupt the peace process, or the election itself. Similarly, the SOC could harass, intimidate, and even kill some of its political opponents. But it found it could not refuse outright to cooperate with UNTAC.

Few recent UN missions have received such unified support. In Bosnia, the Europeans and Americans have been unable to agree on actions that would both protect the integrity of the UN mission and halt the conflict. The lack of effort by Somalia's African neighbors left a void that was filled by an international community whose interest in Somalia's problems was shallow and quickly eroded by casualties. As peace-enforcement operations, each faltered when external support waned, since the local contenders had little inclination to resolve their own problems.

Even after the systematic execution of more than 200,000 Rwandans in April and May 1994, the Security Council was unable to agree on whether the Rwandan mission, which was sharply scaled back after ten Belgian peacekeepers were killed, should be reconstituted for more forceful intervention. Compounding the problem, Rwanda's neighbors declined initially to raise troops for an African peacekeeping force, despite an American offer to fund it.[14] As the tribal slaughter continued into the summer, deployment of 5,500 new troops was repeatedly delayed by U.S. objections over the nature of the mission, pitfalls in the training of African peacekeepers, and haggling over U.S.-supplied equipment.[15] The result of multilateral inaction was the unilateral deployment of troops by France, previously a backer of one side of the conflict. Even that did not prevent a humanitarian crisis of nearly unparalleled proportions, and the subsequent dispatch of U.S. troops to aid relief efforts.

The El Salvador and Mozambique peace-building operations, however, have retained the commitment of both the contending parties and the external players. Neither operation has had to contend with extreme violence since getting under way; both missions were established following the conclusion of peace agreements to which all parties largely adhered.

The United Nations should be realistic in appraising the level of external support it can count on before embarking on a mission. Lack of such support can doom a mission, while firm commitments can help overcome obstacles that could cause it to fail. There is no guarantee that any appraisal will be an accurate gauge, particularly since unforeseen circumstances, such as the televised casualties from the Somalia mission, can erode support almost overnight. That does not mean, however, that the effort is without value. Evaluating the strength of commitments to an operation, and the potential for erosion of support, may help the United Nations to be more selective in the missions it undertakes.

PEACE AGREEMENTS

Of the nearly two dozen UN operations between 1948 and 1991, "about one-fourth resulted from Security Council initiatives to quell a conventional conflict. Another one-fourth originated with an independent request for UN assistance by the local parties to a conflict; all of these were made in the first half of the Cold War and involved situations best characterized as disputes over local political control. Fully one-half of all UN peacekeeping operations, some old, but most of them new, grew out of agreements brokered by third parties that sought UN assistance for implementation."[16]

The demise of U.S.-Soviet conflict allowed the resolution of a number of long-standing disputes in the late 1980s and early 1990s. Usually this took the form of agreements brokered by outside parties, which then sought implementation by the United Nations. Cambodia falls into this category, as does the settlement in El Salvador and operations to monitor Soviet withdrawal from Afghanistan and Cuban withdrawal from Angola.

According to Durch, these requests for UN implementation of a brokered agreement often involve political settlements where "the conflicting parties' objectives have changed from winning *everything* to a more modest objective, winning *something*. Openness to settlement may stem from stalemate on the battlefield or from the mutual exhaustion of the local parties, which leads them to look more favorably at alternatives to fighting. Movement toward a deal may also be a function of pressures exerted by outside powers who see their own interests placed at risk by continued conflict. Whatever the source of the shift, the parties reach the conclusion that pure victory is unattainable and, equally important, that settling for less than total victory does not mean risking total defeat."[17]

Cambodia's experience suggests that UN intervention to assist implementing such agreements are most successful when the agreement is designed to resolve disputes purely over political power. Situations exacerbated by ethnic or tribal conflict, such as Bosnia or Rwanda, appear less amenable to such agreements because the conflict may be rooted in centuries of hatred that is not easily resolved by negotiation. In such cases, contending parties appear less willing to settle for anything short of total victory.

The United Nations should carefully examine those agreements it is asked to implement. In cases where it had little hand in structuring the agreement, success or failure may depend on circumstances over which it has little control. It should look for flexibility in peace agreements: they should not be so tight that they preclude reinterpretation as the situation on the ground changes.

USE OF FORCE, POLITICAL OBJECTIVES, AND THE MISSION'S MANDATE

Although clarifying rules of engagement is important, as discussed earlier, the United Nations should be thinking more broadly about the proper role of force in its missions. Recent situations in which the organization has been asked to intervene have varied more than in the past. In addition to classic peacekeeping, missions now include disaster relief or humanitarian assistance (Somalia, also protection of the Iraqi Kurds); punishment or reversal of international aggression (the invasion of Kuwait); peace-building, often combined with traditional peacekeeping (El Salvador,

Mozambique); buffering to stop a civil or internecine war (Bosnia); and restoration of a democratically elected leader (Haiti). The United Nations may also be asked to intervene where there is a classic insurgency, but no current or recent operations fall into that category. This range of potential missions poses both definitional and policy problems for the United Nations. It has moved to deal with some of these situations by upgrading some missions to Chapter VII operations, for which extensive use of force is permissible.

The lessons from recent Chapter VII peace-enforcement missions, however, are not consistent. The Somalia and Bosnia missions indicate that even in operations where use of force has been fully authorized, it is difficult for the United Nations to determine what level of force will achieve the mission's objectives. Although the U.S.-led Somalia mission was able to provide security for the delivery of food aid, it did so not through force per se, but through an overwhelming demonstration of power. The operation adopted rules of engagement that would have allowed U.S. troops to crush anyone acting in a threatening manner. The mission did not, however, resolve the underlying clan conflict that had exacerbated the population's hunger. The successor operation in Somalia, UNOSOM II, had a far more ambitious objective of nation-building. The use of force was not intended to be a significant part of this operation. However, without a large U.S. presence to back it up, the UN force appeared less threatening to the Somalis, and it took significant casualties when it tried to create alternative political structures and marginalize the uncooperative Mohammed Farah Aideed.

In Bosnia, also a Chapter VII operation, the United Nations has been extremely hesitant to use the force that has been authorized. From the inception in February 1992, UN troops have acted largely as a peacekeeping, not a peace-enforcement, operation. They are outgunned and recognize that force alone is unlikely to halt the ethnic conflict. In neither Bosnia nor Somalia has the use of force been clearly coordinated with the missions' political objectives.

For Haiti, the United Nations authorized a 1300-person mission to train the Haitian police and army and help rebuild the country's infrastructure. The mission collapsed in the fall of 1993 when a ship carrying 200 American soldiers was prevented from docking by the de facto military regime. While the mission's political objective was designed to help restore the democratically elected President Jean-Bertrand Aristide, the level of force needed to achieve that objective was significantly underestimated. Although the fall 1994 U.S. operation in Haiti was authorized under Chapter VII, in cases when principal responsibility devolves on to the United Nations, the intervention is likely to take the form of a nation-building effort under peace-keeping—not peace-enforcement—parameters.

UNTAC's experience demonstrated the value of restraint in the use of force. Cambodia's mission was authorized under Chapter VI, whereby only peaceful means were to be used. UNTAC was not in Cambodia to enforce peace, or to impose it. Despite the Khmer Rouge's lack of cooperation, UNTAC achieved its political objectives. Refraining from using force was more effective in isolating the Khmer Rouge than any overt use of force against it would have been. UNTAC's military presence discouraged the parties from resuming combat and gave Cambodia nearly two years of breathing room for political development. By providing an internationally sanctioned time-out from fighting, UNTAC reinforced the people's desire for peace.

UN NEUTRALITY

While defining what constitutes neutrality can be tricky, impartiality nonetheless has traditionally been a hallmark of UN operations. The initiation of air strikes against Serbian attacks in Bosnia in April 1994 underscores how easily UN neutrality can be eroded in the pursuit of a larger objective. In Bosnia, the goal has been to press the Serbs toward a peace agreement that would end the fighting. In Cambodia, UN neutrality was undermined in more subtle ways.

It is probably fair to conclude that Akashi was not neutral in his approach to the factions. Some thought that the mission's leaders were biased in favor of the State of Cambodia, while others thought that UNTAC was insufficiently tough with the Khmer Rouge. If all parties believe the United Nations is biased in favor of their opponents, that may be an indicator of a balanced approach. A more accurate depiction, however, might be that Akashi leaned one way or the other as necessary.[18] He shied away from vigorous confrontation, whether the issue was Khmer Rouge noncooperation on disarmament or the Phnom Penh administration's disregard for human rights issues.

While UNTAC was expressly charged with creating a neutral political environment for the elections, that proved to be impossible. Akashi's solution was to create an approximation of a neutral political environment, or "neutral political acreages," through political rallies at which all parties could campaign freely. Akashi also favored the parties opposing the SOC by using UNTAC's civil police and military forces to protect political party candidates and offices from harassment.

Akashi's support for the SOC's opponents, as far as it went, does raise serious questions about how neutrality should be handled. Is the function of the United Nations in a peace-building mission to level the playing field by neutralizing the power that naturally accrues to the incumbent and buttressing opposition parties and candidates? This is a dangerous proposition. It lends the appearance of bias in favor of the challengers even as it attempts to make the overall political environment a fair one. This strategy was never challenged in Cambodia—and it worked there. Elsewhere, however, such a philosophy could easily backfire. A strategy in Somalia of actively opposing one powerful faction, that of Aideed, resulted in serious casualties to UN forces.

Strictly adhering to neutrality (in the sense of doing nothing that could be interpreted as assisting any party), even in non-peace-building missions, has its own problems. The United Nations can get physically over-run, as happened on numerous occasions to UNIFIL in Lebanon, when Israel pushed aside UN troops to attack PLO and other anti-Israeli forces. It can also become a target, as it did in Rwanda in April 1994, when ten Belgian peacekeepers were killed by government-aligned militias.

Peace-building involves more than the physical separation of for-merly fighting forces. It requires the nurturing of the institutions that are at the heart of a civil society. In some cases, those institutions have been completely destroyed; in others, they may never have existed. In the lat-ter case, peace-building requires the United Nations to walk a fine line as it imposes values on a society for which that society may have no histori-cal tradition or no understanding by the norms of the local culture. Those values, rooted in individual rights, democratic government, and free elec-tions, are generally Western ones. The United Nations needs to assess carefully the price it may pay for compromising its neutrality in pursuit of peace-building, particularly when some of the involved parties may not share its goal and may have no hesitation in resorting to violence in oppo-sition to it.

PEACEKEEPING IN TRANSITION

The United Nations has failed to live up to expectations raised by the cold war's conclusion that it could finally play the role designed for it as the cus-todian of world order. It has been unable to bring a halt to Bosnia's tragic eth-nic conflict; it was locked out of Haiti in October 1993 and deferred to near unilateral U.S. intervention in the fall of 1994; it effectively fled Rwanda after the death of several peacekeepers in April 1994; and it failed at nation-building in Somalia. Especially damaging to future UN efforts, the American casualties in Somalia caused the Clinton administration to pull back from its initial commitment to an expanded U.S. role in peacekeeping.

When the world turned to the United Nations in the late 1980s, it asked the organization to do too much with too little. There was no evaluation of the capability to carry out expanded missions. Clear and consistent parameters were not established for expanded UN peacekeeping. Nor were criteria set that could guide the decision as to when a peacekeeping operation should be undertaken. There were no major revisions to the United Nations' institutional structure or procedures. Worst of all, the international community failed to provide the resources necessary to meet the additional demands. The United Nations was simply expected to leap, headfirst, into each conflict that came its way.

It is hardly surprising that the United Nations itself did not critically assess its capabilities, make the necessary revisions, or develop criteria that could guide Security Council decisions about peacekeeping missions. It would have been difficult, if not impossible, for the organization to resist the tide of anticipation that swept over it in the late 1980s and early 1990s. It may have had inflated expectations itself about what it could accomplish. At the member states' insistence, it plunged into situations that defied solution and that constituted substantial departures from what it knew how to do well. The failure to produce miracles has led some to doubt whether it truly can play the role of the world's policeman and conscience combined.

Clearly, the international community forgot Clausewitz's maxim about the relationship between political and military objectives. Political objectives should be set first. They determine the military objectives, which in turn determine the military tactics. All too often in recent missions, the political aims have been unclear or unattainable by application of force. As one of Boutros-Ghali's top advisers, Alvaro de Soto, observed, "We only realized all the ramifications of getting involved in internal conflicts fairly late in the game."[19] The secretary-general himself commented in January 1994, "We are in a period of transition, and the world hasn't decided yet what will be the new rules of the game. . . . The member states haven't decided whether they really want a strong United Nations."[20]

The United Nations is experiencing growing pains with a proliferation of peace missions of increasing complexity. "New approaches such as peacebuilding and clearer peacekeeping enforcement mandates may prove effective. But these approaches are new and have yet to be completely tested. Moreover the new approaches must be balanced against a realistic assessment of the U.N.'s capability to implement them."[21]

The world community must reassess the fundamental question of what the United Nations can reasonably be expected to accomplish. "[T]he UN needs to think harder about the implications of its growing involvement in implementing political settlements and rebuilding countries, the ways in which such operations can go wrong, its options if they do, and the sorts of reserve capabilities that it will need in such cases."[22] The organization also needs to decide where to put the bulk of its peacekeeping money and how many long-term commitments it can actually afford. The proliferation of missions has dramatically expanded the peacekeeping budget, with correspondingly higher costs passed on to the member states. The result has been unpaid peacekeeping bills—at times, nearly $1 billion from the United States alone. The *Economist* complained,

> Those on the Security Council are self-deceivers of the first order. From one side of their mouths they call on a U.N. mission to accomplish more; from the other they nitpick about the bills. Peacekeepers can be extravagant in their ways but sending too few men is a false economy—and total costs do not compare with buying expensive weapons, let alone fighting wars. Governments,

if they want results, have to pay for them and, above all, pay for them on time.[23]

No one operation—including UNTAC—can serve as the model for all future peacekeeping efforts. In an October 1993 speech, Akashi admitted that there is no formula for achieving success in a UN mission, but said that common sense, dedication, flexibility, hard work, and persistence can improve the likelihood of it.[24] While Akashi can be proud of his accomplishments in Cambodia, UNTAC's real lesson is not that the world community can magically create peace out of conflict. Rather, it is that stubborn problems can be resolved if the correct solution is applied at the right time.

THE UNITED STATES AND PEACEKEEPING

Perhaps more than any other country, the United States has been responsible for increasing the burdens on the United Nations. When it became clear in the late 1980s that the Soviet Union no longer would act as an obstacle to using the organization to resolve regional or local conflicts, the United States took the lead in reinvigorating the United Nations in the hope that it could undertake the role originally envisioned for it. At the time, there was certainly no dearth of conflicts ripe for UN intervention. The end of the polarizing strategic competition between the United States and the Soviet Union unleashed a wave of ethnic and tribal conflicts, as well as solely political battles to fill the power vacuum left by the demise of communism.

Unfortunately, U.S. financial contributions did not keep pace with the country's consistent votes to establish new peacekeeping operations. Long-standing arguments about America's disproportionate share of UN costs were reignited at the same time that there was growing recognition of the need to tackle the U.S. budget deficit. A reluctant Congress, which had seldom mustered much enthusiasm for the United Nations, found it easy to stint on appropriations to meet the growing demands as peacekeeping costs soared. The backlog of unfulfilled U.S. financial obligations to the organization swelled.

The Clinton administration entered office in January 1993 firmly committed not only to peacekeeping, but to transferring the burden of keeping the global peace from the shoulder of the world's only remaining superpower to the United Nations. As one Defense Department official phrased it, the Clinton administration wanted to "make '911' ring in New York City, not Washington, D.C."[25]

Dubbed "assertive multilateralism" by the U.S. ambassador to the United Nations, Madeleine K. Albright, this policy was intended to demonstrate "a U.S. commitment to using military force in concert with other nations rather than unilaterally."[26] While the Clinton administration struggled to

define the circumstances under which U.S. military forces should be committed to overseas action, the policy was predicated on the premise that
UN capabilities could be strengthened by greater participation by the
United States. In a substantial departure from past practice, this entailed
greater willingness to permit U.S. military forces to participate in UN missions, including at times service under multinational rather than U.S.
command. In this way, it was initially hoped, less of the burden of intervention would fall on the United States.

That philosophy was not unrealistic, nor was it misguided. What was
unfortunate was that the first testing ground came in Somalia. After inher-
iting the Bush-initiated mission, the Clinton administration failed to recognize the difficulty of converting an invading force into neutral peacekeepers
or peace-builders. With the original mission of providing security for the
delivery of food aid accomplished, the Clinton administration fully intended to withdraw all U.S. forces from Somalia and turn the mission over to
the United Nations so that the latter could embark on nation-building.

The administration, however, yielded to pressure from Secretary-
General Boutros-Ghali to maintain a presence in Somalia. It then insisted on having a former U.S. admiral head the mission's civilian side. By drawing down its forces substantially at the same time as it maintained a
psychological dominance over the UN operation, the administration sent
the Somali warlords, particularly Mohammed Farah Aideed, mixed signals
about the U.S. commitment to Somalia. It failed to pay sufficient attention
to the deterioration of the political and military situation there. The October
1993 massacre should have come as no surprise.

In overreacting to that massacre, however, the Clinton administration
erred in generalizing from the specific. In its hasty retreat, instead of recognizing that its Somalia policy had been flawed, it concluded that its
entire approach to peacekeeping had been misguided. That amounts to throwing the baby out with the bathwater. In response to the debacle, the Clinton
administration spent months recrafting a presidential directive to set policy guidelines for the use of U.S. forces for peacekeeping purposes. After
extensive congressional consultations, the directive was signed and went
into effect in early May 1994. In its revised form, the directive "seeks to erase
the notion that peacekeeping is a central feature of Clinton's foreign policy, rather than a simple tool of it."[27]

Presidential Decision Directive (PDD) 25, which might more aptly be
termed a presidential *indecision* directive, represents a substantial retreat
for the Clinton administration from its previously stated aims of bolster-
ing U.S. capabilities to engage in peacekeeping and strengthening the United
Nations' ability to undertake operations in place of the United States. In
its final form, the PDD is "not intended to expand U.N. peacekeeping but
to help fix it."[28] Criteria for commitment of U.S. forces—already stringent—

were tightened to the point that few U.S. military personnel are likely to participate in any future UN operations.

A former Reagan administration official remarked that U.S. troops tend to "glow in the dark."[29] Because of their firepower, training, and reputation, the use of U.S. military forces, particularly in significant numbers, alters the coloration of a UN operation. By their very nature, they represent a physical challenge that cannot be ignored by local militia with ambitious leaders. As in Somalia, though, the presence of U.S. forces can make a UN mission appear to be an American one, which can have serious drawbacks if the degree of the U.S. commitment to the mission turns out to be limited.

These justifiable concerns, however, were not the primary basis for the change in policy. It was due instead to a fear of U.S. casualties during missions that might not be deemed vital to U.S. interests by either the Congress or the American public. While continuing publicly to maintain that "UN and other multilateral peace operations will at times offer the best way to prevent, contain or resolve conflicts that could otherwise be more costly and deadly," the Clinton administration had in fact reversed course.[30] As the white paper accompanying the PDD stated, "It is not U.S. policy to seek to expand ... U.S. involvement in such operations. Instead, this policy ... aims to ensure that our use of peacekeeping is *selective* and *more effective*."[31] That is a far cry from making 911 ring in New York instead of Washington.

More specifically, the Clinton administration repudiated support for a standing UN army or for the small, permanent rapid deployment force endorsed by Clinton during a campaign speech in April 1992.[32] Faced with substantial congressional opposition, it also retreated from efforts to earmark specific U.S. military units for participation in UN operations. Instead, it would "provide information about U.S. capabilities for data bases and planning purposes."[33] But this "in no way implies a commitment to provide those capabilities, if asked by the UN."[34]

While the presidential directive retains many of the original proposals for assisting the reorganization of the UN peacekeeping apparatus, it falls well short of the "assertive multilateralism" Albright spelled out at the beginning. Yet that policy was never really given a chance. It foundered on the Somalia casualties and Congressional opposition to UN command of U.S. forces.

The absence of foreign policy leadership, at a time when America's course in the world needs to be recharted, has resulted in wild swings of the pendulum. "From extolling the virtues of multilateralism ... the United States has retreated to defining its limits. The administration's focus is no longer to widen its U.N. options and increase the U.S. role in international peace-keeping and peacemaking. It is to demonstrate first of all to a nervous American electorate that Washington can avoid entrapment in

Somalia and Bosnia and can otherwise keep itself from going casually, naive-ly and perilously down the UN road."[35] Haiti this raises serious questions about whether the Clinton administration can apply those lessons to uni-lateral U.S. military intervention.

Such oscillations carry a large cost. They undermine U.S. credibility and erode confidence in U.S. leadership. The Clinton administration's inability to redefine U.S. national interests and its indecisiveness about the likes of Bosnia and Haiti have devolved into a collective shrugging of shoulders. It seems simply too hard to take a stance and stick with it for the long haul. The intellectual process of redefining the PDD to set criteria and guidelines for U.S. involvement in UN peacekeeping was carefully devel-oped. The failure lies in the interpretation by the executive branch. Paying lip service to the need for greater selectivity in the choice of UN missions while tacitly backing away almost entirely—this is not so much a retreat into isolationism as it is a withdrawal driven by fear into irresolution.

The United States should go back to the original policy of assertive mul-tilateralism, recognizing that, to make it work, it must be applied judiciously. But once a course of engagement is embarked upon, the commitment has to be decisive and undeterred by incidental setbacks, whether predictable or unexpected. No policy is successful 100 percent of the time. While the Clinton administration is learning when to say no, it must also learn when to say yes.

The international community is increasingly going to be faced with conflicts that rip apart the established order and shatter the institutions of civil societies. The vast majority of those conflicts are not going to take place in areas of first-tier interest to the United States. In the era beyond the cold war, the U.S. military will play a lesser, though still vital, role in coping with such primary dangers as threats to U.S. economic security, the possible fail-ure of democracy in Russia, and proliferation of nuclear and nonnuclear weapons of mass destruction. The greater challenge to U.S. policy will come from secondary dangers such as ethnic and religious nationalism and major humanitarian crises. These are conflicts or situations that do not direct-ly affect U.S. interests in significant ways but whose resolution often requires the use of force.

It makes far more sense, since these problems are not considered vital to the national interest, for the United States to seek multilateral solu-tions. The American contribution need not be in the form of military force. As the Cambodia experience suggests, there are many other ways to aid in the resolution of these problems. The United States is unparalleled in hav-ing a large number of the best-trained and -equipped logistics forces in the world and the most sophisticated transportation capability. Allowing the United Nations to make greater use of these assets would do much to assist in mul-tilateral solutions to conflicts. Similarly, implementing many of the policies laid out in the PDD such as providing the United Nations with an intelligence capability, designing a command, control, and communications system for the Operations Division, and helping to create and participate in a peacekeeper training program could substantially enhance the United Nations' ability to carry out peacekeeping operations.

What U.S. policy needs is a careful assessment of UN capabilities, leadership to implement measures that can improve those capabilities, and the wisdom to follow a policy whereby, as the white paper concludes, "peace operations can be one useful tool to advance American national interests and pursue our national security objectives."[36] A sober examination by Washington of UN operations to determine what has worked is called for. Among other things, greater attention needs to be paid to the issue of peace-building. Using force either to quell a conflict or to monitor an agreement that has been reached may work in some instances, but in many of the conflicts that have arisen since the cold war ended that approach is inadequate.

The world has seen, through the trials of Cambodia, that under the right circumstances peace operations can work. Reconstructing a shattered society can be a long and costly process. But the United States excels in the expertise needed to build up a country's criminal justice system, revamp its accounts to put the country on a sound financial basis, construct a comprehensive health system, and repair its physical infrastructure. U.S. contributions to and emphasis on these aspects of peacekeeping will be cheaper in the long run—particularly in terms of American lives—than trying to do it all alone or ignoring problems in the hope that they will just go away.

THE FUTURE FOR PEACE-BUILDING

Although UNTAC was designed as a peacekeeping mission, it was also charged with peace-building tasks. It was asked to refashion Cambodia in ways that would facilitate the transition to a freely elected government and would enhance the new government's stability. This kind of mission requires the use of civilians, from human rights monitors to civil administrators to police, who are critical to efforts to reestablish social cohesion. They are expensive, and the United Nations is only slowly gaining experience in integrating them into its operations.

Whether the United Nations continues in the direction charted by UNTAC will depend on its member states. Does the international community want the organization to continue to move away from its traditional missions of the past, which were relatively low in cost, limited in size, and had narrow mandates, in favor of those that are more complex and ambitious and almost open-ended in their commitments? Does it want to continue to engage in or expand efforts at peace-building?

If the answer is yes to these questions, the international community must be increasingly selective about the situations in which it asks the United Nations to intervene. It will have to ensure that peacekeeping missions' political objectives are clearly defined and that military plans are designed to help achieve the political objectives. It will also have to ensure that the missions' objectives are feasible and that international support is sufficiently strong that it will not evaporate at the first sign of casualties. It is a truism that a peacekeeping mission's mandate should be clear. But if the world community keeps handing the United Nations problems that are essentially unsolvable, or those for which the regional powers have no wish to exert the effort needed to bring about a solution, the organization will not succeed.

It is a sad, but realistic, commentary that some wars may have to go through the experience of the killing fields for there to be collective exhaustion and a willingness to give up and truly find peace. As Cambodia demonstrated, this is when the United Nations can be most effective. Peace-building does not by itself resolve conflict. Rather, in-country peace-building is designed to prevent the reoccurrence of conflict. It involves national and international efforts at economic development and institutional reform. It entails the creation or restoration of the conditions necessary to make countries stable and functioning after they have been torn apart by conflict. Peace-building seems to hold out more promise of success for the United Nations than peace-enforcement; imposing peace is far harder than helping those who already want it.

Australia's foreign minister, Gareth Evans, who was instrumental in the negotiation of the Paris Accords, wrote in his 1993 book, *Cooperating for Peace*, that the task of postconflict peace-building "will often be no less than the total reconstitution of broken and devastated societies."[37] To a large extent, UNTAC was asked to reconstruct Cambodia. Evans argued that it is essential, for "the people and their leaders to reach agreements about what sort of society and polity they wish to develop after the conflict."[38]

This precondition was not fully met in Cambodia, and UNTAC's achievement was as a result both flawed and fragile. "Still, Cambodia is in many ways better off today than it was before the peace agreements, and better off than it would have been without UN involvement. Foreign forces have been withdrawn, more than 360,000 refugees repatriated and millions of dollars in developmental aid committed."[39] Whether UNTAC's impact will be longer lasting now rests with the Cambodian people.

As for the United Nations, it did rather well.

NOTES

CHAPTER 1

1. "Cambodia: A Vote Worth Defending," *New York Times*, June 2, 1993, p. A18.

2. *Report of the Secretary-General Pursuant to Paragraph 7 of Resolution 840 (1993)*, United Nations Security Council S/26090, July 16, 1993, paragraphs 6 and 8, p. 2.

3. Philip Shenon, "Khmer Rouge Hint They May End Rebellion," *New York Times*, July 14, 1993, p. A5.

4. William Branigin, "Cambodia Adopts Constitution Restoring Monarchy; Sihanouk to Be King," *Washington Post*, September 22, 1993, p. A25.

5. William Branigin, "UN Ends Cambodian Operation," *Washington Post*, September 27, 1993, p. A12.

6. "UN Begins Pullout of 20,000 Soldiers in Cambodia Force," *New York Times*, August 3, 1993, p. A5; telephone interview with Jeanne Dixon, librarian, United Nations Information Centre, Washington, D.C., March 1, 1994, for information on information on UNTAC's final troop withdrawal.

7. Philip Shenon, "UN Preparing to End Its Operation in Cambodia," *New York Times*, August 12, 1993, p. A6.

8. Thomas W. Lippman, "Aid Is Out if Khmer Rouge Is In, U.S. Tells Cambodia," *Washington Post*, July 19, 1993, p. A9.

9. William Branigin, "Thais Scramble to Explain Weapons Cache," *Washington Post*, December 19, 1993, p. A35; "How to Help Cambodia," *New York Times*, December 23, 1993, p. A16.

10. Philip Shenon, "Khmer Rouge Violence Said to Signal Goals," *New York Times*, August 4, 1993, p. A5.

11. Philip Shenon, "In Big Threat to Cambodia, Thais Still Aid Khmer Rouge," *New York Times*, December 19, 1993, section 1, p. 16.

12. Marjorie Ann Browne, "United Nations Peacekeeping: Issues for Congress," CRS Issue Brief IB90103, Congressional Research Service, updated February 2, 1993, p. 1.

13. United States General Accounting Office, *UN Peacekeeping: Lessons Learned in Managing Recent Missions*, GAO/NSIAD-94-9, December 1993, p. 10.

14. "Mr. Clinton's UN Reality Test," *New York Times*, September 29, 1993, p. A20; telephone interview with Jeanne Dixon, March 1, 1994, for information on 1993 UN peacekeeping expenditures.

15. Richard Bernstein, "Sniping Is Growing at UN's Weakness as a Peacekeeper," *New York Times*, June 21, 1993, p. A6; telephone interview with Jeanne Dixon, March 1, 1994, for information on 1992 UN peacekeeping expenditures.

16. William J. Durch, ed., *The Evolution of UN Peacekeeping: Case Studies and Comparative Analysis* (New York: St. Martin's Press, in association with the Henry L. Stimson Center, 1993), pp. 3–4.

17. Gareth Evans, *Cooperating for Peace: The Global Agenda for the 1990s and Beyond* (St Leonards, Australia: Allen & Unwin, 1993), p. 99.

18. For technical accuracy, it should be noted that the UN Iraq-Kuwait Observation Mission (UNIKOM), although a traditional peacekeeping mission, was authorized under Chapter VII. This reflects its genesis as part of the comprehensive provisions to end the Gulf war in 1991. Evans, *Cooperating for Peace*, p. 144.

19. Ibid., p. 143.

20. Ibid., p. 104.

21. Boutros Boutros-Ghali, *An Agenda for Peace—Preventive Diplomacy, Peacemaking and Peace-keeping*, Report of the Secretary-General, United Nations General Assembly and Security Council, A/47/277, S/24111, June 17, 1992, paragraph 55, p. 16.

22. Virginia Page Fortna, "United Nations Transition Assistance Group," in Durch, *The Evolution of UN Peacekeeping*, pp. 353–75, especially pp. 359–61.

23. Ibid., pp. 361–62.

24. UNTAC was budgeted at roughly $1.9 billion over eighteen months. Slow deployment of peacekeeping forces and slow recruitment of civilian personnel resulted in reduced costs. The final cost was $1.7 billion. Paul Lewis, "UN Given Cambodia Troop Proposal," *New York Times*, February 21, 1992, p. A3; telephone interview with James A. Schear, policy consultant to the special representative of the secretary-general for Cambodia, November 16, 1993; Branigin, "UN Ends Cambodian Operation."

25. UNPROFOR in the former Yugoslav republics is running at roughly $1.5 billion annually—so, too, is UNOSOM II in Somalia. David B. Ottaway, "UN Officials in Croatia Call Peace Mission Unviable, Recommend Its End," *Washington Post*, November 10, 1993, p. A32; Julia Preston, "No Mission to Burundi, UN Says," *Washington Post*, November 3, 1993, p. A10.

26. A detailed examination of the internal workings of the UN peacekeeping machinery, however, lies outside the scope of this work. While this paper touches on some of the issues related to the United Nations' peacekeeping apparatus, they are more fully evaluated in the General Accounting Office report *UN Peacekeeping: Lessons Learned in Managing Recent Missions.*

27. Daniel Williams, "Clinton Peacekeeping Policy to Set Limits on Use of U.S. Troops," *Washington Post,* February 6, 1994, p. A24.

CHAPTER 2

1. Interview with a senior U.S. government official (anonymous), Washington, D.C., September 21, 1993.

2. William S. Turley, "The Khmer War: Cambodia after Paris," *Survival* 32 (September-October 1990): 437, cited in Frank Frost, "The Cambodia Conflict: The Path towards Peace," *Contemporary Southeast Asia* 13, no. 2 (September 1991): 139.

3. Douglas Pike, "The Cambodian Peace Process: Summer of 1989," *Asian Survey* 29, no. 9 (September 1989): 847, cited in Frost, "The Cambodia Conflict."

4. Gerard, Hervouet, "The Cambodian Conflict:The Difficulties of Intervention and Compromise," *International Journal* 45 (Spring 1990): 264–65.

5. Ibid., pp. 266–67.

6. Robert Delfs, "Reapeating the Lesson," *Far Eastern Economic Review,* September 28, 1989, p. 23.

7. Hervouet, "The Cambodian Conflict," p. 278.

8. Frost, "The Cambodian Conflict," p. 135; Steven Erlanger, "Vietnam Promises Troops Will Leave Cambodia by Fall," *New York Times,* April 6, 1989, p. A1.

9. Members of Congress conveniently overlooked the history of U.S. support for the Khmer Rouge. In fact, as Elizabeth Becker pointed out, a democratically controlled Congress had given carte blanche to President Jimmy Carter to make a deal in 1979 with China and Thailand to rebuild the Khmer Rouge in order to prevent a permanent Vietnamese occupation of Cambodia. She reported that Carter's national security adviser, Zbigniew Brzezinski, told her: "I encouraged the Chinese to support Pol Pot. I encouraged the Thais to help." She noted further that the United States made sure the Khmer Rouge retained Cambodia's UN seat while Washington, as she quoted Brzezinski saying, "winked semipublicly" at Chinese and Thai direct aid to the Khmer Rouge. Elizabeth Becker, "Up from Hell," *New Republic,* February 17, 1992, pp. 33–34.

10. Steven Erlanger, "Britain Sticks to Cambodia Plan," *New York Times,* December 1, 1989, p. A8.

11. Elizabeth Becker, "Cambodian Blueprint for Peace Approved," *Washington Post,* August 2, 1989, p. A16; Becker, "Conference on Cambodia Appears Deadlocked," *Washington Post,* August 29, 1989, p. A16; Becker, "Cambodia Conference Suspended," *Washington Post,* August 31, 1989, p. A1.

12. Estimates differ on the number of Vietnamese troops in Cambodia at its peak. "US-Cambodia Relations," *Gist*, a publication of the U.S. Department of State, October 1989, p. 2, cited 200,000 troops. Robert G. Sutter cited more than 100,000 troops in *Cambodian Crisis: Problems of a Settlement and Policy Dilemmas for the United States*, CRS Issue Brief IB89020, Congressional Research Service, updated May 9, 1989, p. 2. Jacques Bekaert, in "Cambodia: A Nasty Little War," *International Defense Review* 22 (March 1989): 290, wrote that "Hanoi has never disclosed how many troops it sent to Cambodia in 1978–79. Up to 200,000 men were probably involved in the initial offensive, with 160,000 remaining in the country after 1979. By 1988 about 10 to 12 divisions, many undermanned, were still stationed in Cambodia. . . . Six divisions were officially withdrawn in December 1988." Bekaert reported that after a May 1988 announcement by Hanoi that it would withdraw 50,000 troops from Cambodia by the end of the year, a Pentagon source told him that from "30,000 to 35,000 bo doi (vietnamese infantrymen) had effectively left Cambodia in 1988, leaving a total force of 80,000–100,000 still in the country" (p. 292). Sutter also reported that international observers judged that more than 30,000 troops had departed by the end of 1988 (*Cambodian Crisis*, p. 4).

13. Daniel Southerland, "Cambodian Resistance Issues Plan," *Washington Post*, February 10, 1989, p. A30.

14. Lorna Hahn, "No Deals with the Butchers of Cambodia," *Washington Post*, January 9, 1989, p. A11.

15. "Cambodia's Agony," *Washington Post*, September 3, 1989, p. C6.

16. The Solarz proposal is noted in David B. Ottaway, "Solarz Urges U.S. Military Aid for Sihanouk," *Washington Post*, April 8, 1989, p. A13; Elizabeth Becker, "Cambodian Asks Truce, More Talks," *Washington Post*, December 5, 1989, p. A20.

17. Gareth Evans, minister for foreign affairs and trade, "Prospects for a Cambodian Peace Settlement," *The Australian Senate Hansard*, Canberra, December 6, 1990, p. 5160.

18. Steven Erlanger, "Diplomats Step Up Drive in Cambodia," *New York Times*, December 17, 1989, p. A15.

19. In response to the announcement by Hun Sen that the Phnom Penh government would accept the Evans proposal, Khieu Khanarith, editor of the weekly magazine *Kampuchea*, said that "the Government was confident of victory in any election. 'If we lose, we are ready to step aside. . . . During the last 10 years, the Phnom Penh Government has learned how to conduct an election campaign. If we lose, it is our own fault.'" "Cambodia Agrees to UN-Controlled Election," *New York Times*, December 14, 1989, p.A21.

20. Valerie Strauss and David Hoffman, "U.N. to Offer Peace Plan for Cambodia," *Washington Post*, August 28, 1990, p. A12.

21. Telephone interview with Richard Bush, director for committee liaison, Committee on Foreign Affairs, U.S. House of Representatives, December 22, 1993.

22. Steven Erlanger, "Cambodia Will Talk Again, But Listeners Are Scarce," *New York Times*, February 25, 1990, section 4, p. 3.

23. Steven Erlanger, "Peace Talks on Cambodia Break Down," *New York Times*, March 1, 1990, p. A3.

24. Ibid.

25. Ibid.

26. Don Oberdorfer, "China Offers Two Proposals for Settling Cambodian War," *Washington Post*, June 15, 1990, p. A30.

27. Steven Erlanger, "Cambodian Factions to Meet Today," *New York Times*, June 4, 1990, p. A3; "Thai Reports Accord on Cambodian Truce," *New York Times*, May 24, 1990, p. A15.

28. Stephen J. Solarz, "Cambodia and the International Community," *Foreign Affairs* 69, no. 2 (Spring 1990): 106.

29. "Cambodia: U.S. Opposes Cease-fire and Neutral Camp," *Indochina Digest*, Indochina Project, Vietnam Veterans of America Foundation, Washington, D.C., May 13–19, 1990, p. 1.

30. Oberdorfer, "China Offers Two Proposals for Settling Cambodian War."

31. Ibid.

32. Interview with a senior U.S. government official (anonymous), Washington, D.C., September 21, 1993.

33. Patrick G. Marshall, "Cambodia's Never-Ending Civil War," *Editorial Research Reports* (Congressional Quarterly Inc.) 2, no. 11, (September 22, 1989): p. 532.

34. Interview with a senior U.S. government official (anonymous), Washington, D.C., September 21, 1993.

35. Oberdorfer, "China Offers Two Proposals for Settling Cambodian War."

36. Ibid.

37. Steven Erlanger, "Cambodian Talks Quickly Collapse with Boycott by the Khmer Rouge," *New York Times*, June 5, 1990, p. A10.

38. "Two Factions in Cambodia Sign Truce," *Washington Post*, June 6, 1990, p. A18.

39. Alan Riding, "5 Powers Report Gains on Cambodia," *New York Times*, July 18, 1990, p. A5.

40. Frank J. Prial, "Five U.N. Powers Announce Accord on Cambodia War," *New York Times*, August 29, 1990, p. A9; Trevor Rowe, "Cambodian Peace Plan Announced," *Washington Post*, August 29, 1990, p. A14.

41. *Statement of the Five Permanent Members of the Security Council of the United Nations on Cambodia*, with *Annex: Framework for a Comprehensive Political Settlement of the Cambodia Conflict*, August 28, 1990, contained in "Letter Dated 30 August 1990 from the Permanent Representatives of China, France, the Union of Soviet Socialist Republics, the United Kingdom, and the United States, to the United Nations, addressed to the Secretary General," United Nations Security Council S/21689, August 31, 1990.

42. *Framework for a Comprehensive Political Settlement of the Cambodia Conflict*, paragraph 10, p. 9.

43. Prial, "Five U.N. Powers Announce Accord on Cambodia War," Rowe, "Cambodian Peace Plan Announced."

44. "U.N. Plan on Cambodia Reported," *New York Times*, August 28,1990, p. A3.

45. "Agreement on Cambodia," *Washington Post*, August 29, 1990, p. A24.

46. Ibid. An extended discussion of the shift in U.S. policy toward Cambodia and Vietnam is beyond the scope of this paper. For details, see Thomas L. Friedman, "U.S. Shifts Cambodia Policy, Ends Recognition of Rebels, Agrees to Talk to Hanoi," *New York Times*, July 19, 1990, p. A1; David Hoffman, "U.S. Shifts Policy toward Cambodia," *Washington Post*, July 19, 1990, p. A1; Al Kamen, "Domestic Politics a Factor in U.S. Shift," *Washington Post*, July 19, 1990, p. A28. The Bush administration was under pressure from Congress to alter policy toward Cambodia, which was reflected in a June 28, 1990, vote by the Senate Select Intelligence Committee to terminate more than $15 million in annual covert aid to the non-Communist resistance, a bipartisan letter from influential senators to Bush asking for a change in policy, and the inclusion in May of $5 million in humanitarian aid for children *inside* Cambodia in the supplemental appropriations bill. In response, the Bush administration announced on July 18, 1990, that it would open a dialogue with Vietnam about Cambodia and P.O.W.-M.I.A. issues. The policy shift, motivated as well by a concern about Khmer Rouge gains on the ground, also included a withdrawal of support for the CGDK holding Cambodia's UN seat and a loosening of restrictions on humanitarian aid for Vietnam and Cambodia. See also Robert S. Greenberger and Walter S. Mossberg, "U.S., in Policy Shift, Will Begin Talks with Vietnam on Cambodia," *Wall Street Journal*, July 19, 1990, p. A7; Clifford Krauss, "Behind U.S. Reversal: Gains by the Khmer Rouge," *New York Times*, July 19, 1990, p. A10; press release by the U.S. Department of State, Office of the Assistant Secretary/Spokesman, "Remarks of Secretary of State James A. Baker III and Soviet Foreign Minister Eduard Shevardnadze at the Conclusion of Bilateral Meeting," Paris, July 18, 1990. See Dan Morgan, "'Concern' on Aid to Children in Cambodia," *Washington Post*, May 12, 1990, p. A6, for information on congressional aid to Cambodian children.

47. William Branigin, "Cambodians Agree to Share Power," *Washington Post*, September 11, 1990, pp. A1, 15.

48. Jim Hoagland, "Vietnam's Vietnam," *Washington Post*, March 13, 1990, p. A25. Hoagland uses the figure of $2 billion in Soviet aid. Steven Erlanger cites a Soviet diplomat for the figure of $2.5 billion in his article, "East Europe Considers Cutting Aid to Indochina," *New York Times*, April 6, 1990, p. A10.

49. Lena Sun, "Leaders of Vietnam, China Held Secret Talks," *Washington Post*, September 19, 1990, p. A16.

50. Interview with a senior U.S. government official (anonymous), Washington, D.C., September 21, 1993.

51. "U.S. to Open an M.I.A. Office in Hanoi," *New York Times*, April 21, 1991, section 1, p. 3.

52 David Hoffman, "Baker Repeats Terms for U.S.-Vietnam Ties," *Washington Post*, July 25, 1991, p. A29.

53. Steven Erlanger, "Khmer Rouge Get More China Arms," *New York Times*, January 1, 1991, p. A3.

54. Copy of statement presented by the State of Cambodia to the U.S. government in Vientiane on April 18, 1991, p. 5. Spelling and punctuation as in original.

55. Frost, "The Cambodia Conflict," p. 153.

56. Ibid., p. 154.

57. "Slogging On in Cambodia," *Washington Post*, June 17, 1991, p. A8.

58. Frost, "The Cambodia Conflict," p. 154.

59. William Branigin, "4 Factions, Including Khmer Rouge, to Take Roles in Cambodian Capital," *Washington Post*, June 26, 1991, p. A9.

60. "Cambodian Factions Agree to Halt Arms Imports," *New York Times*, June 25, 1991, p. A3; William Branigin, "Cambodians Fail to Agree on Implementation of Cease-fire and Arms Cutoff," *Washington Post*, June 27, 1991, p. A37.

61. Sheryl WuDunn, "Cambodian Factions Agree to Share Seat at U.N.," *New York Times*, July 18, 1991, p. A7.

62. "Beijing-Hanoi Ties Warm," *New York Times*, August 11, 1991, section 1, p. 10. See also Philip Shenon, "Peace's Prospects in Cambodia Grow," *New York Times*, July 14, 1991, section 1, p. 9; Clifford Krauss, "U.S. Is Encouraged by Hanoi Cabinet," *New York Times*, August 18, 1991, section 1, p. 9.

63. William Branigin, "Cambodians Agree on Peace Keepers," *Washington Post*, August 27, 1991, p. A7.

64. *Framework for a Comprehensive Political Settlement of the Cambodia Conflict*, section 2: Military Arrangements during the Transitional Period, paragraphs 18–19, p. 11.

65. "Cambodian Factions Agree on Troop Cuts," *New York Times*, August 27, 1991, p. A9; William Branigin, "Cambodian Armed Factions Agree to Demobilize 70 Percent of Forces," *Washington Post*, August 28, 1991, p. A20.

66. Michael Leifer, "Power-Sharing and Peacemaking in Cambodia?" *SAIS Review* 12, no. 1 (Winter/Spring 1992): 148.

67. William Branigin, "Big Powers Endorse Cambodians' Proposal," *Washington Post*, August 31, 1991, p. A25.

68. Leifer, "Power-Sharing and Peacemaking in Cambodia?" p. 151.

69. Ibid., p. 147.

70. Robert H. Miller, "Historical Sources of Conflict in Southeast Asia: Cambodia at the Vortex," *Conflict* 10, no. 3 (July-September 1990): 207, 8.

71. Ibid., p. 212.

72. "Cambodia Abolishes Communism," *Washington Post*, October 19, 1991, p. A16.

73. Ibid.
74. Ibid.

CHAPTER 3

1. Philip Shenon, "4 Parties in Cambodian War Sign UN-Backed Peace Pact; Khmer Rouge Shares Rule," *New York Times*, October 24, 1991, p. A1.

2. United States General Accounting Office, *UN Peacekeeping: Lessons Learned in Managing Recent Missions*, GAO/NSIAD-94-9, December 1993, p. 33.

3. William Branigin, "Cambodians Facing Deadly Threat: Mines," *Washington Post*, November 22, 1991, pp. A35, 38.

4. William Branigin, "Mob Attacks Leader of Khmer Rouge," *Washington Post*, November 28, 1991, p. A61.

5. William Branigin, "Cambodians Hail Sihanouk's Return," *Washington Post*, November 15, 1991, p. A33; Philip Shenon, "Khmer Rouge Left outside Coalition," *New York Times*, November 24, 1991, section 1, p. 23.

6. Philip Shenon, "Sihanouk Backs Trials in Khmer Rouge Terror," *New York Times*, November 17, 1991, section 1, p. 18.

7. William Branigin, "Khmer Rouge to Resume Peace Role," *Washington Post*, December 4, 1991, p. A27.

8. "Make Room for the Cambodians," *New York Times*, December 25, 1991, p. A30.

9. *Report of the Secretary-General on Cambodia*, United Nations Transitional Authority in Cambodia (UNTAC) S/23613, February 19, 1992, referred to hereafter as the Secretary-General's Implementation Plan; United Nations Security Council Resolution S/RES/745 (1992), February 28, 1992; Trevor Rowe, "UN Security Council Approves Peace-Keepers for Cambodia," *Washington Post*, February 29, 1992, p. A18. For details of costs, see *Report of the Secretary-General on Cambodia: Addendum*, United Nations Security Council S/23613/Add.1, February 26, 1992.

10. Rowe, "UN Security Council Approves Peace-Keepers for Cambodia"; *The Secretary-General's Consolidated Appeal for Cambodia's Immediate Needs and National Rehabilitation*, United Nations Transitional Authority in Cambodia (UNTAC), May 1992, p. i.

11. Paul Lewis, "UN Given Cambodia Troop Proposal," *New York Times*, February 21, 1992, p. A3; Secretary-General's Implementation Plan, para. 65, p. 10.

12. Secretary-General's Implementation Plan, paragraph 65, p. 10; paragraph 85, pp. 13–14; paragraph 90, pp. 15–16.

13. Rowe, "UN Security Council Approves Peace-Keepers for Cambodia."

14. Paul Lewis, "U.S. Peacekeeping Arrears at UN Near a Billion," *New York Times*, October 22, 1993, p. A5.

15. Robert G. Sutter, *The Cambodian Peacekeeping Operations: Background, Prospects and U.S. Policy Concerns*, Congressional Research Service, report 93-286-S, March 3, 1993, pp. 3–4.

16. Michael Leifer, "Power-Sharing and Peacemaking in Cambodia," *SAIS Review* 12, no. 1 (Winter/Spring 1992): 139–40.

17. Ibid., p. 140.

18. Elizabeth Becker, "Up from Hell," *New Republic*, February 17, 1992, p. 37.

19. Barbara Crossette, "Cambodia Mission Chief Sees Team as a Catalyst," *New York Times*, March 7, 1992, p. 6.

20. Ibid.

21. Ibid.

22. Ibid.

23. David E. Sanger, "Seeking Stature in Cambodia, Japan Gets Deathly Dilemma," *New York Times*, May 13, 1993, p. A7.

24. William Branigin, "1st Japanese Troops Arrive in Cambodia," *Washington Post*, September 26, 1992, p. A15.

25. Philip Shenon, "Japanese Sun Again Rises Overseas," *New York Times*, September 27, 1992, section 1, p. 10.

26. William Branigin, "Japanese Killed During Ambush in Cambodia," *Washington Post*, May 5, 1993, p. A23; Philip Shenon, "Khmer Rouge Campaign to Sabotage Elections," *New York Times*, May 9, 1993, section 4, p. 2.

27. David E. Sanger, "Japan Grows Wary of Cambodia Role," *New York Times*, April 29, 1993, p. A3.

28. Paul Blustein, "UN Eases Risk for Japanese in Cambodia," *Washington Post*, May 11, 1993, p. A12. Blustein notes as well the deployment of a fifty-three-man unit to the UN peacekeeping effort in Mozambique (p. A16).

29. Philip Shenon, "Actions of Japan Peacekeepers in Cambodia Raise Questions and Criticism," *New York Times*, October 24, 1993, section 1, p. 8.

30. Ibid.

31. Paul Lewis, "UN Presses for $300 Million to Begin Moves in Cambodia," *New York Times*, November 9, 1991, p. A4.

32. Shenon, "Actions of Japan Peacekeepers in Cambodia Raise Questions and Criticism."

33. Elizabeth Becker, *When the War Was Over: The Voices of Cambodia's Revolution and Its People* (New York: Simon & Schuster, 1987), p. 83.

34. Philip Shenon, "Cambodia Pact Founders on Attacks and Distrust," *New York Times*, August 18, 1992, p. A5.

35. Mary Kay Magistad, "UN Troops Mark Time in Cambodia," *Washington Post*, July 25, 1992, p. A17.

36. Yasushi Akashi, special representative of the secretary-general for Cambodia, third annual Charles Rostow Lecture on Asian Affairs, The Nitze School of Advanced International Studies, Johns Hopkins University, Washington, D.C., October 14, 1993.

37. Dinah PoKempner and Sidney Jones, "An Exchange on Human Rights and Peace-Keeping in Cambodia," *News from Asia Watch*, 5 no. 14, (September 23, 1993): 3.

38. When the General Accounting Office circulated for comments a report it had undertaken for the U.S. Congress on lessons from peacekeeping missions, Akashi responded in a letter about the importance of the Information and Education division's activities to UNTAC's mission. ". . . I can find no mention in your draft of the Information/Education Division, whose contribution to the success of the mission was invaluable. The assembling of a concentration of Khmer-speaking experts provided UNTAC with indispensable information about the thinking of the Cambodian people, especially in the provinces, while the establishment of a Khmer-language radio station and TV studio made it possible for us to get the UNTAC message across to the whole population and to convince voters that democracy was vital and the ballot was secret. No useful discussion of the UNTAC mission would be complete without making these points." Letter from Yasushi Akashi, special representative of the secretary-general for Cambodia, to Tetsuo Miyabara, United States General Accounting Office, August 5, 1993, p. 2.

39. United States General Accounting Office, *UN Peacekeeping: Lessons Learned in Managing Recent Missions*, pp. 13–14.

40. Lois McHugh, *United Nations Operations in Cambodia*, CRS Issue Brief IB92096, Congressional Research Service, updated January 25, 1993, p. 6; Secretary-General's Implementation Plan, p. 7.

41. United States General Accounting Office, *UN Peacekeeping: Lessons Learned in Managing Recent Missions*, p. 27.

42. McHugh, *United Nations Operations in Cambodia*, p. 11.

43. United States General Accounting Office, *UN Peacekeeping: Lessons Learned in Managing Recent Missions*, p. 36.

44. Ibid., pp. 36–37.

45. Briefing Report, internal analysis prepared by United States General Accounting Office investigators, February 18, 1993, p. 2.

46. United States General Accounting Office, *UN Peacekeeping: Lessons Learned in Managing Recent Missions*, p. 35.

47. Interview with a senior U.S. government official (anonymous), Washington, D.C., September 21, 1993.

48. The SNC was composed of twelve members until December 20, 1992, when a thirteenth member was added to give FUNCINPEC a second representative. Until then, Sihanouk had served in the dual capacity as president and as the second FUNCINPEC member. *Third Progress Report of the Secretary-General on the United Nations Transitional Authority in Cambodia*, United Nations Security Council S/25124, January 25, 1993, paragraph 13, p. 3.

49. Magistad, "UN Troops Mark Time in Cambodia."

CHAPTER 4

1. Philip Shenon, "Khmer Rouge Said to Harass Refugees," *New York Times*, March 26, 1992, p. A3.

2. William Branigin, "Cambodians Launching Offensive," *Washington Post*, March 30, 1992, p. A12.

3. Quoted in Ron Moreau, "The Perilous Road Home," *Newsweek*, April 13, 1992, p. 37.

4. *Report of the Secretary-General on Cambodia*, United Nations Transitional Authority in Cambodia (UNTAC) S/23613, February 19, 1992, paragraph 137, p. 23. Referred to hereafter as the Secretary-General's Implementation Plan.

5. Ibid., paragraph 138, p. 23; Moreau, "The Perilous Road Home," p. 36.

6. Philip Shenon, "UN Starts Cambodia Refugee Return," *New York Times*, March 31, 1992, p. A12.

7. William Branigin, "UN Starts Cambodian Repatriation," *Washington Post*, March 31, 1992, p. A14.

8. Henry Kamm, "Return of Refugees to Cambodia to Take Longer than Planned," *New York Times*, April 12, 1992, section 1, p. 22.

9. William Branigin, "Missteps on the Path to Peace," *Washington Post*, September 22, 1992, p. A14.

10. William Branigin, "Khmer Rouge Balks, Halts Peace Process," *Washington Post*, June 13, 1992, p. A15.

11. Kamm, "Return of Refugees to Cambodia to Take Longer than Planned."

12. *Fourth Progress Report of the Secretary-General on the United Nations Transitional Authority in Cambodia*, United Nations Security Council S/25719, May 3, 1993, paragraph 89.

13. Lois B. McHugh, *United Nations Operations in Cambodia*, CRS Issue Brief IB92096, Congressional Research Service, updated January 25, 1993, p. 7.

14. Ibid.

15. *Fourth Progress Report of the Secretary-General on the United Nations Transitional Authority in Cambodia*, paragraph 88.

16. Ron Moreau, "Cambodia: 'This Is My Home,'" *Newsweek*, February 22, 1993, p. 38.

17. U.S. Congress, Senate, Committee on Foreign Relations, *Reform of United Nations Peacekeeping Operations: A Mandate for Change*, S. Prt. 103–45, 103rd Cong., 1st sess., August 1993, p. 29.

18. *The Secretary-General's Consolidated Appeal for Cambodia's Immediate Needs and National Rehabilitation*, United Nations Transitional Authority in Cambodia (UNTAC), May 1992, p. i.

19. Ibid.

20. *Report on UNTAC's Activities: The First Six Months, 15 March–15 September 1992*, September 15, 1992, paragraph 135, p. 29.

21. *Declaration on the Rehabilitation and Reconstruction of Cambodia*, United Nations Security Council S/23177, October 30, 1991, Annex, section IV, paragraph 10.

22. Secretary-General's Implementation Plan, paragraph 153, p. 26.

23. *Cambodia: An Economic Assessment of Rehabilitation Needs*, United Nations Transitional Authority in Cambodia (UNTAC), June 22, 1992, foreword. The information contained in the report was gathered in March 1992,

although the report was not issued until June. It served as the basis for *The Secretary-General's Consolidated Appeal for Cambodia's Immediate Needs and National Rehabilitation*.

24. William Branigin, "UN Peace-Keeping Efforts Criticized in Cambodia, Bosnia: Khmer Rouge Charges Tilt toward Phnom Penh," *Washington Post*, June 19, 1992, p. A30.

25. David E. Sanger, "880 Million Pledged to Cambodia but Khmer Rouge Pose a Threat," *New York Times*, June 23, 1992, p. A2.

26. *Tokyo Declaration on Cambodia Peace Process*, Ministerial Conference on Rehabilitation and Reconstruction of Cambodia, Tokyo, June 22, 1992, reprinted in *Japan Times*, June 23, 1992, p. 13.

27. *Report on UNTAC's Activities: The First Six Months*, paragraphs 139–40, p. 30; *Second Progress Report of the Secretary-General on the United Nations Transitional Authority in Cambodia*, United Nations Security Council S/24578, September 21, 1992, paragraph 52, p. 12.

28. Proposal for discussion, Ministerial Conference on Rehabilitation and Reconstruction of Cambodia, Tokyo, June 1992, paragraph 11, as cited in *Second Progress Report of the Secretary-General on the United Nations Transitional Authority in Cambodia*, paragraph 53, p. 12.

29. Sanger, "880 Million Pledged to Cambodia but Khmer Rouge Pose a Threat."

30. Ibid.

31. *Second Progress Report of the Secretary-General on the United Nations Transitional Authority in Cambodia*, paragraph 54, p. 13.

32. Ibid., paragraph 55, p. 13.

33. *Report on UNTAC's Activities: The First Six Months*, paragraph 136, p. 29.

34. United States General Accounting Office, "Subject: Multilateral and Bilateral Donors who Have By Passed Approved Channels for Project Endorsement by the SNC," internal memorandum, no date.

35. Ibid.

36. Ibid.

37. Ibid.

38. *Appendix II: Multilateral Humanitarian and Development Assistance to Cambodia*, document provided to the United States General Accounting Office by Michael Feldstein, desk officer for Indochina, Agency for International Development, dated by GAO October 20, 1992, p. 12. The main report to which the Appendix belongs could not be located by GAO. The $85 million figure was also cited in the donors' review meeting of February 25, 1993, *Rehabilitation and Development in Cambodia: Achievements and Strategies*, report prepared by United Nations Transitional Authority in Cambodia (UNTAC) in collaboration with UNDP and the UN specialized agencies, p. 3.

39. *Third Progress Report of the Secretary-General on the United Nations Transitional Authority in Cambodia*, United Nations Security Council S/25124, January 25, 1993, paragraph 86, p. 18.

40. *Report of the Secretary-General on the Implementation of Security Council Resolution 792 (1992)*, United Nations Security Council S/25289, February 13, 1993, paragraph 31, p. 8.

41. *Multilateral Humanitarian and Development Assistance to Cambodia*, p. 12.

42. Donors' review meeting of February 25, 1993: *Rehabilitation and Development in Cambodia*, p. 3.

43. Ibid.

44. Philip Shenon, "Most Cambodians See Nothing of Aid," *New York Times*, February 21, 1993, section 1, p. 10.

45. Ibid.

46. Ibid.

47. Donors' review meeting of February 25, 1993: *Rehabilitation and Development in Cambodia*, p. 22.

48. Ibid., p. 24.

49. Ibid., pp. 24–25.

50. *Report of the Secretary-General Pursuant to Paragraph 7 of Resolution 840 (1993)*, United Nations Security Council S/26090, July 16, 1993, paragraph 30, p. 6.

51. *Tokyo Declaration on Rehabilitation and Reconstruction of Cambodia*, Ministerial Conference on Rehabilitation and Reconstruction of Cambodia, Tokyo, June 22, 1992, paragraph 5 and Annex: "Framework of ICORC."

52. "First Meeting of the International Committee on the Reconstruction of Cambodia," press release, Paris, September 9, 1993, paragraph 17, p. 9, available from UNCTAD.

53. Ibid., paragraph 18, p. 9.

54. "IMF Chief Visits Indochina," *Indochina Digest* 6, no. 41, (October 15, 1993): 1.

55. *Second Progress Report of the Secretary-General on the United Nations Transitional Authority in Cambodia*, paragraphs 57–58, p. 13.

56. Trevor Rowe, "UN Council Penalizes Khmer Rouge," *Washington Post*, December 1, 1992, p. A32.

57. *Report of the Secretary-General on the Implementation of Security Council Resolution 792 (1992)*, paragraph 25, p. 7.

58. *Impact of UNTAC on Cambodia's Economy*, report prepared by the Economic Adviser's Office, UNTAC, Phnom Penh, December 21, 1992, p. 15.

59. Ibid., p. 14.

CHAPTER 5

1. U.S. Congress, Senate, Committee on Foreign Relations, *Reform of United Nations Peacekeeping Operations: A Mandate for Change*, S. Prt. 103–45, 103d Cong., 1st sess., August 1993, pp. 6–7.

2. Tom Masland with John Barry and Joshua Hammer, "The Pitfalls of Peacekeeping," *Newsweek*, July 26, 1993, p. 33.

3. Judy McCloskey, record of interview with Lieutenant General John Sanderson, UNTAC force commander, Phnom Penh, December 12 and 19, 1992, United States General Accounting Office, I/M-1, p. 1.

4. *Report of the Secretary-General on Cambodia*, United Nations Transitional Authority in Cambodia (UNTAC) S/23613, February 19, 1992, paragraph 53, p. 8, referred to hereafter as the Secretary-General's Implementation Plan.

5. Ibid., paragraph 54, pp. 8–9.

6. Ibid., paragraph 55, p. 9.

7. Countries contributing military personnel to UNTAC included Algeria, Argentina, Australia, Austria, Bangladesh, Belgium, Brunei, Bulgaria, Cameroon, Canada, Chile, China, France, Germany, Ghana, India, Indonesia, Ireland, Japan, Malaysia, Netherlands, New Zealand, Pakistan, Philippines, Poland, Russia, Senegal, Thailand, Tunisia, United Kingdom, United States, and Uruguay. United States General Accounting Office, *UN Peacekeeping: Lessons Learned in Managing Recent Missions*, GAO/NSIAD-94-9, December 1993, "Appendix II: Countries Contributing Military Personnel to UNTAC or UNO-SOM II," p. 63.

8. Countries contributing infantry battalions were the Netherlands, Bangladesh, Pakistan, Uruguay, India, Indonesia, France, Malaysia, Bulgaria, Tunisia, and Ghana. U.S. Congress, *Reform of United Nations Peacekeeping Operations*, p. 34.

9. Ibid.

10. Kimberly Gianopoulos, record of meeting with Colonel K. Mat Yusuf, desk officer for UNTAC, Military Adviser's Office, UN Secretariat, New York, April 7, 1993, United States General Accounting Office, I/M-23, p. 2.

11. *UN Peacekeeping: Lessons Learned in Managing Recent Missions*, p. 39.

12. Record of interview with John Sanderson, p. 4.

13. Record of meeting with K. Mat Yusuf, p. 4.

14. United States General Accounting Office, "Point Paper: Military Component," internal document, no date, p. 3.

15. *Third Progress Report of the Secretary-General on the United Nations Transitional Authority in Cambodia*, United Nations Security Council S/25124, January 25, 1993, paragraph 10, p. 3.

16. *Fourth Progress Report of the Secretary-General on the United Nations Transitional Authority in Cambodia*, United Nations Security Council S/25719, May 3, 1993, paragraphs 46–47.

17. "Point Paper: Military Component," p. 2.

18. *Special Report of the Secretary-General on the United Nations Transitional Authority in Cambodia*, United Nations Security Council S/24090, June 12, 1992, paragraph 2, p. 1. Paul Lewis reports that Akashi said in an interview that the United Nations wanted to begin disarmament on June 1, but that it might slip until no later than June 15 if there weren't enough troops in Cambodia by then. Paul Lewis, "Showdown Is Set on Cambodia Arms," *New York Times*, May 9,

1992, p. 7. In *Report on UNTAC's Activities: The First Six Months, 15 March–15 September 1992*, September 15, 1992, UNTAC reported that the date for the beginning of disarmament was moved from June 1 to June 13 (paragraph 73, p. 17).

19. Judy McCloskey, "Analysis of UNTAC's Military, Human Rights, and Civilian Police Mandates," memo, United States General Accounting Office, I/O-3, April 30, 1993, p. 1.

20. *Second Progress Report of the Secretary-General on the United Nations Transitional Authority in Cambodia*, United Nations Security Council S/24578, September 21, 1992, paragraph 22, p. 5.

21. Judy McCloskey, record of interview with Colonel Aris Salim, UNTAC military chief of operations, Phnom Penh, December 11, 1992, United States General Accounting Office, I/M-2, p. 2.

22. "Point Paper: Military Component," p. 1.

23. Letter from Yasushi Akashi, special representative of the secretary-general for Cambodia, to Tetsuo Miyabara, United States General Accounting Office, I-32, August 5, 1993, pp. 1–2.

24. William Branigin, "Missteps on the Path to Peace," *Washington Post*, September 22, 1992, p. A14.

25. United Nations Department of Public Information, "Fact Sheet: United Nations Transitional Authority in Cambodia (UNTAC)," DPI/1217, May 1992, p. 1.

26. John Ryle, "The Invisible Enemy," *New Yorker*, November 29, 1993, p. 126.

27. Branigin, "Missteps on the Path to Peace," p. A14.

28. Judy McCloskey, record of interview with Col.onelN. Bradley, force engineer, UNTAC Engineering Branch, Phnom Penh, December 10, 1992, United States General Accounting Office, I/M-11, p. 6.

29. Note from Colonel N. Bradley, force engineer, UNTAC Engineering Branch, dated December 10, 1992, forwarded to United States General Accounting Office staff, C/F-2.

30. Ryle, "The Invisible Enemy," p. 124.

31. Record of interview with N. Bradley, p. 7.

32. Ryle, "The Invisible Enemy," p. 125.

33. Record of interview with N. Bradley, p. 7.

34. Ibid. Notes from this GAO record use June 10, 1992, as the date the SNC reestablished the CMAC as a Cambodian organization. In the *First Progress Report of the Secretary-General on the United Nations Transitional Authority in Cambodia*, United Nations Security Council S/23870, May 1, 1992, Boutros Boutros-Ghali reports that at its meeting on April 20, 1992, the SNC agreed to the establishment of the CMAC under the presidency of Sihanouk and the vice-presidency of Akashi. The CMAC was to assist in long-term programs of mine awareness, mine marking, and mine clearance. It was to be managed by a ten-member Governing Council, which was established by the end of April 1992, with five Cambodian members to be appointed by Sihanouk and five other members to be appointed by Akashi (paragraph 26, page 6).

35. Ryle, "The Invisible Enemy," pp. 125–26.

36. *UN Peacekeeping: Lessons Learned in Managing Recent Missions*, p. 25.

37. *Further Report of the Secretary-General Pursuant to Paragraph 7 of Resolution 840 (1993)*, United Nations Security Council S/26360, August 26, 1993, paragraph 25.

38. Telephone interview with Robert Muller, executive director, Vietnam Veterans of America Foundation, Washington, D.C., March 21, 1994.

39. *UN Peacekeeping: Lessons Learned in Managing Recent Missions*, p. 49.

40. Ibid.

41. Ibid., pp. 49–50.

42. Tetsuo Miyabara, record of meeting with Colonel Raji Arshad, sector and contingent Commander, Malaysian Battalion National Contingent; Lieutenant Colonel Goh, contingent commander, Thai Engineering Battalion; Colonel Waxin, chief liaison officer, UNTAC Civilian Police; and Major Doma, liaison officer, UNTAC Civilian Police, Phnom Penh, December 21, 1992, United States General Accounting Office, IX-2, p. 2.

43. *UNTAC Standard Operations Procedures*, "Section 4: Use of Force," paragraph 76, p. 2. This extract of UNTAC's standard operating procedures was provided to the United States General Accounting Office by Colonel Aris Salim, UNTAC military chief of operations.

44. Tetsuo Miyabara, record of meeting with Colonel J. F. Carter, sector head, and chief liaison for United Nations military observers, Phnom Penh, December 8, 1992, United States General Accounting Office, I-19, p. 2.

45. Tetsuo Miyabara, record of meeting with Prince Norodom Sirivudh, vice president of FUNCINPEC, and General Thon Penh, head of FUNCINPEC security, Phnom Penh, December 8, 1992, United States General Accounting Office, IEL-8.

46. William Branigin, "Bulgarians Put Crimp in Peace Keeping," *Washington Post*, October 29, 1993, p. A33.

47. Tetsuo Miyabara, record of meeting with Judy Leland, director in Cambodia, American Red Cross, Phnom Penh, December 8, 1992, United States General Accounting Office, IEL-5.

48. Tetsuo Miyabara, record of meeting with Kathy Hopper, director, Holt International Children's Services; Ms. Galbreaux; Sok Sananee; Phnom Penh, December 8, 1992, United States General Accounting Office, IEL-4.

49. "Point Paper: Military Component," p. 16.

50. Branigin, "Bulgarians Put Crimp in Peace Keeping."

51. Paul Lewis, "UN Gives Warning to Khmer Rouge," *New York Times*, October 14, 1992, p. A6. See also United Nations Security Council Resolution 783 (1992).

52. Paul Lewis, "UN Curbing Trade with Khmer Rouge," *New York Times*, December 1, 1992, p. A9. See also United Nations Security Council Resolution 792 (1992).

53. *Third Progress Report of the Secretary-General on the United Nations Transitional Authority in Cambodia*, paragraph 39, p. 9.

54. *Report of the Secretary-General on the Implementation of Security Council Resolution 783 (1992)*, United Nations Security Council S/24800, November 15, 1992, paragraph 31, p. 8.

55. "Point Paper: Military Component," p. 4.

56. Ibid.

57. U.S. Congress, *Reform of United Nations Peacekeeping Operations*, p. 26.

58. Secretary-General's Implementation Report, paragraphs 114, 117, and 118, pp. 20–21.

59. Judy McCloskey, record of interview with Brigadier-General Klaas Roos, commissioner, UNTAC Civilian Police, Phnom Penh, December 11, 1992, United States General Accounting Office, I/C-S, pp. 1–2.

60. Judy McCloskey, record of interview with Colonel Detlef Buwitt, chief of staff, UNTAC Civilian Police, Phnom Penh, December 11, 1992, United States General Accounting Office, I/C-2, p. 5; United States General Accounting Office, "Briefing Paper: Civilian Police Component," internal document, no date, p. 1.

61. Record of interview with Detlef Buwitt, p. 4.

62. Judy McCloskey, record of interviews with Colonel Bleem, commander, Battambang Civilian Police, and six representatives of nongovernmental organizations, Battambang, Cambodia, December 14, 1992, United States General Accounting Office, I/C-4, pp. 1–2.

63. U.S. Congress, *Reform of United Nations Peacekeeping Operations*, p. 26.

64. "Requirements for and Testing of UN Civilian Police Monitors," memo, United Nations Secretariat, November 30, 1992, pp. 3–4.

65. Tetsuo Miyabara, record of meeting with Jennifer Hills, UN district electoral supervisor; Tony Ho and John Lee, UNTAC Civilian Police from Singapore, Battambang, Cambodia, December 15, 1992, United States General Accounting Office, IEL-2, p. 3.

66. Ibid.

67. Record of interview with Detlef Butwitt, p. 7.

68. Judy McCloskey, record of interview with Saroop Grewal, CARE, Battambang, Cambodia, December 14, 1992, United States General Accounting Office, I/C-4, pp. 3–4.

69. Judy McCloskey, record of interviews with Colonel Waxin, chief liaison officer, Major Laval, liaison officer, UNTAC Civilian Police; and Major Doma, liaison officer to the Ministry of National Security, Phnom Penh, December 11, 1992, United States General Accounting Office, I/C-3, pp. 3–4.

70. *CIVPOL Standard Operating Procedures: Human Rights Matters*, obtained by the United States General Accounting Office from Stephen Marks, human rights officer, Education and Training Section, UNTAC Human Rights Component, Phnom Penh.

71. Record of interviews with Waxin, Laval, and Doma, p. 2.

72. "Briefing Paper: Civilian Police Component," p. 2.

73. *UN Peacekeeping: Lessons Learned in Managing Recent Missions*, p. 28. Based on Tetsuo Miyabara, record of meeting with Dieter von Samson, provincial director (Kampong Cham), and Dominique Laronde, assistant director (Kampong Cham), Phnom Penh, December 18, 1992, United States General Accounting Office, ICA-6, p. 1.

74. U.S. Congress, *Reform of United Nations Peacekeeping Operations*, pp. 27–28.

75. Record of interviews with Waxin, Laval, and Doma, pp. 2–3.

76. Record of interview with Detlef Buwitt, pp. 3–4.

77. William Drozdiak, "Cambodian Peace Pact Is Signed: UN to Run Nation until Vote; Officials Warn Khmer Rouge," *Washington Post*, October 24, 1991, p. A1.

78. United Nations Transitional Authority in Cambodia, outline of speech to UN Volunteers, no. 3, July 30, 1992, p. 2. Copy obtained from United States General Accounting Office.

79. Hanne Sophie Greve, mediator, United Nations Transitional Authority in Cambodia, Civil Administration Complaints and Investigation Unit, "Guidelines: Practical Procedures," internal document, November 1, 1992, p. 2. Annex 2: "Background Information for the Handling of Complaints and Investigation." Copy obtained from United States General Accounting Office.

80. Secretary-General's Implementation Plan, paragraph 94, p. 17.

81. United Nations Transitional Authority in Cambodia, outline of speech to UN volunteers, pp. 9–10.

82. *Second Progress Report of the Secretary-General on the United Nations Transitional Authority in Cambodia*, paragraph 38, p. 9.

83. United Nations Transitional Authority in Cambodia, outline of speech to UN Volunteers, p. 10.

84. Ibid., p. 4.

85. United Nations Transitional Authority in Cambodia, Cvil Administration, "Logistics Problems," December 13, 1992, p. 3. Copy obtained from United States General Accounting Office.

86. *Second Progress Report of the Secretary-General on the United Nations Transitional Authority in Cambodia*, paragraphs 26 and 29, pp. 6–7.

87. Tetsuo Miyabara, record of meeting with Gerard Pourcell, director, UNTAC Civil Administration, Phnom Penh, December 16, 1992, United States General Accounting Office, ICA-1, p. 1.

88. Tetsuo Miyabara, record of meeting with John Ryan, inspector, and Dominique Gureut, director, Defense Section, UNTAC Civil Administration, Phnom Penh, December 16, 1992, United States General Accounting Office, ICA-5, p. 1.

89. Tetsuo Miyabara, record of meeting with Gantcho Ganchev, provincial director, Defense Section, UNTAC Civil Administration, Battambang, Cambodia, December 14, 1992, United States General Accounting Office, ICA-4, p. 1.

90. *Second Progress Report of the Secretary-General on the United Nations Transitional Authority in Cambodia*, paragraph 29, p. 7; record of meeting with Gerard Pourcell, p. 1.

91. United Nations Transitional Authority in Cambodia, outline of speech to UN Volunteers, p. 12.

92. Record of meeting with Gerard Pourcell, p. 1.

93. Secretary-General's Implementation Plan, paragraph 95, p. 17.

94. Statement by UNTAC to the Cambodian people, June 26, 1992. Copy obtained from United States General Accounting Office.

95. Mary Kay Magistad, "UN Chief: Khmer Rouge Should Stay in Peace Plan," *Washington Post*, April 8, 1993, p. A36.

96. Statement by UNTAC to the Cambodian people.

97. Record of meeting with Dieter von Samson and Dominque Laronde, p. 1.

98. *Second Progress Report of the Secretary-General on the United Nations Transitional Authority in Cambodia*, paragraph 33, p. 8.

99. Tetsuo Miyabara, record of meeting with Ok Serei Sopheak, vice president, external affairs, Cambodian Liberal Democratic Party, Phnom Penh, December 8, 1992, United States General Accounting Office, IEL-7.

100. Mary Kay Magistad, "Cambodian Rulers Cited in Anti-Voting Violence," *Washington Post*, June 10, 1993, p. A29. Text of UN document included as "Part III: Text of Undisclosed UN Report on Undercover Units Formed by the Phnom Penh Regime to Oppose Political Rivals," in "An Exchange on Human Rights and Peace-Keeping in Cambodia," *News from Asia Watch* 5, no. 14 (September 23, 1993).

101. *Fourth Progress Report of the Secretary-General on the United Nations Transitional Authority in Cambodia*, paragraphs 57–59.

102. "An Exchange on Human Rights and Peace-Keeping in Cambodia," p. 3.

103. U.S. Congress, *Reform of United Nations Peacekeeping Operations*, p. 20.

104. Ibid., p. 21

105. Yasushi Akashi, special representative of the secretary-general for Cambodia, third annual Charles Rostow Lecture on Asian Affairs, The Nitze School of Advanced International Studies, Johns Hopkins University, Washington, D.C., October 14, 1993.

106. Interview with James A. Schear, policy consultant to the special representative of the secretary-general for Cambodia, Washington, D.C., October 18, 1993.

CHAPTER 6

1. *Report of the Secretary-General on Cambodia*, United Nations Transitional Authority in Cambodia, (UNTAC) S/23613, February 19, 1992, paragraph 8, p. 2. Referred to hereafter as the Secretary-General's Implementation Plan.

2. Ibid., paragraph 9, p. 2.

3. Ibid., paragraph 19, p. 4.

4. Yasushi Akashi, special representative of the secretary-general for Cambodia, United Nations Transitional Authority in Cambodia, the third annual Charles Rostow Lecture on Asian Affairs, The Johns Hopkins University Nitze School of Advanced International Studies, Washington, D.C., October 14, 1993.

5. U.S. Congress, Senate, Committee on Foreign Relations, *Reform of United Nations Peacekeeping Operations: A Mandate for Change,* S. Prt. 103–45, 103rd Cong., 1st sess., August 1993, p. 22.

6. Ibid.

7. *Second Progress Report of the Secretary-General on the United Nations Transitional Authority in Cambodia,* United Nations Security Council S/24578, September 21, 1992, paragraph 7, pp. 2–3.

8. U.S. Congress, *Reform of United Nations Peacekeeping Operations,* p. 23.

9. *Second Progress Report of the Secretary-General on the United Nations Transitional Authority in Cambodia,* paragraph 8, p. 3; *Report on UNTAC's Activities: The First Six Months, 15 March–15 September 1992,* September 15, 1992, paragraph 37, p. 9; *Report of the Secretary-General on the Implementation of Security Council Resolution 783 (1992),* United Nations Security Council S/24800, November 15, 1992, paragraph 13, p. 3.

10. *Report on UNTAC's Activities: The First Six Months,* paragraphs 40 and 41, p. 10.

11. Ibid., paragraph 42, p. 10.

12. Judy McCloskey, record of interview with Dennis McNamara, director, UNTAC Human Rights, Phnom Penh, December 18, 1992, General Accounting Office, I/H-1, p. 6.

13. *Second Progress Report of the Secretary-General on the United Nations Transitional Authority in Cambodia,* paragraph 11, p. 3; presentation by Dinah PoKempner, staff counsel, Human Rights Watch, at American University, Washington, D.C., February 4, 1994.

14. United States General Accounting Office, *U.N. Peacekeeping: Lessons Learned in Managing Recent Missions,* GAO/NSIAD-94-9, December 1993, p. 26.

15. *Report of the Secretary-General on the Implementation of Security Council Resolution 792 (1992),* United Nations Security Council S/25289, February 13, 1993, paragraph 13, p. 3.

16. "An Exchange on Human Rights and Peace-Keeping in Cambodia," *News from Asia Watch* 5, no. 14 (September 23, 1993):1. Earlier report referred to "Cambodia: Human Rights before and after the Elections," *Asia Watch* 5, no. 10 (May 1993).

17. Comments on the Asia Watch report of May 1993 are from a letter written by Special Representative Yasushi Akashi, printed in "An Exchange on Human Rights and Peace-Keeping in Cambodia," paragraphs 6–7, p. 2.

18. "An Exchange on Human Rights and Peace-keeping in Cambodia," p. 2.

19. Ibid., pp. 2–3.

20. Ibid., p. 4.

21. Judy McCloskey, record of interview with Basil Fernando, senior officer, Investigations and Monitoring Section, UNTAC Human Rights, Phnom Penh, December 18, 1992, General Accounting Office, I/H-2, p. 2.

22. Ibid., pp. 2–3.

23. Ibid., pp. 3–4; *Report of the Secretary-General on the Implementation of Security Council Resolution 792,* paragraph 15, p. 4.

24. Tetsuo Miyabara, record of meeting with Tony Bambridge, officer, UNTAC Human Rights, Battambang, Cambodia, December 13, 1992, General Accounting Office, ICA-3.

25. Statement by the director of UNTAC Human Rights Component on Political violence, Phnom Penh, May 23, 1993. Copy obtained from United States General Accounting Office.

26. U.S. Congress, House, Committee on Foreign Affairs, Subcommittee on Asia and the Pacific, "Safeguarding Human Rights in Cambodia in the Wake of the U.N. Mission," testimony of Dinah PoKempner, Human Rights Watch, 103d Cong., 1st sess., October 27, 1993, p.4.

27. Statement by the director of UNTAC Human Rights Component on Political Violence, pp. 5–7.

28. "An Exchange on Human Rights and Peace-Keeping in Cambodia," p. 1.

29. Statement by the director of UNTAC Human Rights Component on Political Violence, p. 7.

30. Ernest Doring, record of interview with Padmasiri Nanayakkara, UNTAC special prosecutor, Phnom Penh, June 18, 1993, General Accounting Office, p. 2.

31. "Cambodia: The Critical Tests," *New York Times,* May 19, 1993, p. A18.

32. Secretary-General's Implementation Plan, paragraph 49, p. 8.

33. Ibid., paragraphs 23 through 40, pp. 5–7.

34. *U.N. Peacekeeping: Lessons Learned in Managing Recent Missions,* p. 21; Lois B. McHugh, "United Nations Operations in Cambodia," CRS Issue Brief IB92096, Congressional Research Service, updated January 25, 1993, p. 6. Although a number of sources indicate that there were 400 UN Volunteers in Cambodia, the director of the electoral component told the GAO in December 1992 that there were 470 involved with this outfit. Tetsuo Miyabara, record of meeting with Reginald Austin, director, UNTAC Electoral Component, and staff, Phnom Penh, December 9, 1992, General Accounting Office, IEL-1, p. 2.

35. Record of meeting with Reginald Austin and staff, p. 2.

36. *U.N. Peacekeeping: Lessons Learned in Managing Recent Missions,* pp. 31–32.

37. Ibid., pp. 33–34.

38. Kimberly Gianopoulos, record of interview with Horacio Boneo, director, Electoral Assistance Unit, Department of Political Affairs, UN Secretariat, March 2, 1993, General Accounting Office, I-25, p. 3.

39. *Report Analyzing the UNTAC Cambodia Election Plan,* prepared by Richard W. Soudriette, director, International Foundation for Electoral Systems, for the

United States Agency for International Development, June 1992; *Report of the United Nations Survey Mission on Elections in Cambodia*, undated, chapters 3 through 5, pp. 9–21, provided to the United States General Accounting Office. Horacio Boneo, director of the Electoral Assistance Unit, at the UN Secretariat, told GAO that the effective date of the report was December 1991.

40. *Report Analyzing the UNTAC Cambodia Election Plan; Report of the United Nations Survey Mission on Elections in Cambodia*, chapters 6 and 7, pp. 22–33.

41. Record of meeting with Reginald Austin and staff, p. 2.

42. *Report on UNTAC's Activities: The First Six Months*, paragraph 54, p. 13.

43. Yasushi Akashi, special representative of the secretary-general for Cambodia, remarks at a National Press Club Morning Newsmaker Session, Reuter transcript, Washington, D.C., October 6, 1992, pp. 2–3.

44. R*eport of the Secretary-General on the Implementation of Security Council Resolution 783*, paragraphs 25 and 26, p. 6.

45. Akashi, third annual Charles Rostow Lecture on Asian Affairs.

46. Mary Kay Magistad, "Cambodian Regime Harassing Opposition Leaders, Diplomats and Parties Say," *Washington Post*, November 27, 1992, p. A41.

47. "An Exchange on Human Rights and Peace-Keeping in Cambodia," Part III, "Text of Undisclosed UN Report on Undercover Units Formed by the Phnom Penh Regime to Oppose Political Rivals."

48. *Report of the Secretary-General on the Implementation of Security Council Resolution 792*, paragraph 17, p. 4.

49. Interview with James A. Schear, policy consultant to the special representative of the secretary-general for Cambodia, Washington, D.C., October 18, 1993.

50. *Report of the Secretary-General on the Implementation of Security Council Resolution 792*, paragraph 36, p. 9.

51. *Fourth Progress Report of the Secretary-General on the United Nations Transitional Authority in Cambodia*, United Nations Security Council S/25719, May 3, 1993, paragraph 21.

52. *Third Progress Report of the Secretary-General on the United Nations Transitional Authority in Cambodia*, United Nations Security Council S/25124, January 25, 1993, paragraph 29, p. 6.

53. *Report of the Secretary-General on the Implementation of Security Council Resolution 792*, paragraph 38, p. 9.

54. Mary Kay Magistad, "U.N. Workers in Cambodia Give Ultimatum," *Washington Post*, April 16, 1993, p. A19; Akashi, third annual Charles Rostow Lecture on Asian Affairs.

55. Ron Moreau, "A Vote—But Not for Peace," *Newsweek*, May 24, 1993, p. 40.

56. Mary Kay Magistad, "Khmer Rouge Quit Phnom Penh," *Washington Post*, April 14, 1993, p. A25.

57. Secretary-General's Implementation Plan, paragraph 160, p. 27.

58. Ibid., paragraph 163, p. 27.

59. *Report of the Secretary-General on the Implementation of Security Council Resolution 783*, paragraph 10, p. 3.

60. *Second Progress Report of the Secretary-General on the United Nations Transitional Authority in Cambodia*, paragraph 62, p. 14.

61. *Third Progress Report of the Secretary-General on the United Nations Transitional Authority in Cambodia*, paragraph 91, p. 19.

62. U.S. Congress, *Reform of United Nations Peacekeeping Operations*, p. 40.

63. *Report on UNTAC's Activities: The First Six Months*, paragraph 153, p. 33.

64. *Fourth Progress Report of the Secretary-General on the United Nations Transitional Authority in Cambodia*, paragraphs 75 through 77.

65. *Third Progress Report of the Secretary-General on the United Nations Transitional Authority in Cambodia*, paragraph 92, pp. 19–20.

66. *Fourth Progress Report of the Secretary-General on the United Nations Transitional Authority in Cambodia*, paragraph 8.

67. Philip Shenon, "U.N. Vows to Hold Vote in Cambodia," *New York Times*, May 19, 1993, p. A5.

68. Ibid.

69. Philip Shenon, "Cambodia Factions Use Terror Tactics in Crucial Election," *New York Times*, May 10, 1993, p. A6.

70. Ibid.

71. Ibid.

72. Shenon, "U.N. Vows to Hold Vote in Cambodia."

73. William Branigin, "Losses Add to Japan's Tension in Cambodia," *Washington Post*, May 7, 1993, p. A26.

74. *Report of the Secretary-General on the Conduct and Results of the Elections in Cambodia*, United Nations Security Council S/25913, June 10, 1993, paragraph 5, p. 2.

75. Philip Shenon, "Cambodia Voting Seems to Lure Hard-Line Rebels," *New York Times*, May 25, 1993, p. A3.

76. Ibid.

77. Philip Shenon, "Defying Rebels, Voters Throng Cambodia Polls," *New York Times*, May 24, 1993, p. A6.

78. *Report of the Secretary-General on the Conduct and Results of the Elections in Cambodia*, paragraph 5, p. 2.

79. Ibid., paragraph 8, p. 2.

80. Ibid., paragraph 13, p. 3.

81. Philip Shenon, "Cambodian Rulers Ask for New Vote," *New York Times*, June 2, 1993, p. A9.

82. William Branigin, "Vote Count in Cambodia Is Criticized," *Washington Post*, June 1, 1993, p. A13.

83. Philip Shenon, "Sihanouk Role Seems Crucial to Cambodia's Fate," *New York Times*, May 31, 1993, p. A3.

84. Helen R. Chauncey, *On Watch in Cambodia: Notes of an Election Observer*, report to the Center for National Policy, Washington, D.C., June 1993, p. 2.

85. Ibid.

86. Ibid., p. 1.

87. Ibid., p. 2.

88. Shenon, "Cambodia Voting Seems to Lure Hard-Line Rebels."

89. U.S. Congress, *Reform of United Nations Peacekeeping Operations*, p. 40.

CHAPTER 7

1. William Shawcross, "The Nightmare Is Over," *New York Times*, October 12, 1993, p. A23.

2. *Report of the Secretary-General on Cambodia: Addendum*, United Nations Security Council S/23613/Add.1, February 26, 1992, p. 2.

3. Alvaro de Soto and Graciana del Castillo, "Obstacles to Peacebuilding," *Foreign Policy* 94 (Spring 1994): 69–83.

4. "Civic Action Plan for the Malaysian Battalion in Sector 8," memo from Colonel Mohd Arshad Bin Mohd Raji, contingent commander, Malaysian battalion, Battambang, to UNTAC Headquarters, September 12, 1992, p. 3, General Accounting Office copy provided by Colonel Aris Salim, chief of operations, UNTAC Military Component.

5. Comments on the General Accounting Office's draft report on UNTAC by Lieutenant General John Sanderson, UNTAC force commander, contained in a letter from Mary Eliza Kimball, senior political affairs officer, Department of Peace-keeping Operations, United Nations Secretariat, New York, to Tetsuo Miyabara, General Accounting Office, August 18, 1993, p. 2.

6. United States General Accounting Office, *U.N. Peacekeeping: Lessons Learned in Managing Recent Missions*, GAO/NSIAD-94-9, December 1993, p. 33.

7. United States General Accounting Office, Far East Office, "Summary: Military, Human Rights, and Civilian Police Operations of the United Nations Transitional Authority in Cambodia," undated, pp. 28–29. Partial report used in preparing the General Accounting Office's *U.N. Peacekeeping: Lessons Learned in Managing Recent Missions*.

8. Boutros Boutros-Ghali, *An Agenda for Peace: Preventive Diplomacy, Peacemaking and Peace-keeping*, Report of the Secretary-General, United Nations General Assembly and Security Council, A/47/277, S/24111, June 17, 1992, paragraphs 51 and 53, pp. 15–16.

9. United States General Accounting Office, *U.N. Peacekeeping: Lessons Learned in Managing Recent Missions*, pp. 33, 47.

10. "The United Nations Standby Forces System," paper used for press briefing, Office of the Secretary-General's Spokesman, UN Secretariat, April 14, 1994, pp. 8–9. Briefing paper provided by Joan Luke Hills, information officer, United Nations Information Centre, Washington, D.C. Information also reported on National Public Radio, April 15, 1994.

11. William Branigin, "Key Phases of U.N. Peace Operation in Cambodia Seen Breaking Down," *Washington Post*, October 4, 1992, p. A34.

12. United States General Accounting Office, *U.N. Peacekeeping: Lessons Learned in Managing Recent Missions*, p. 44.

13. William J. Durch, "Getting Involved: The Political-Military Context," in *The Evolution of UN Peacekeeping: Case Studies and Comparative Analysis*, ed. William J. Durch (New York: St. Martin's Press, in association with the Henry L. Stimson Center, 1993), pp. 22–23.

14. Julia Preston, "Rwandans Confound U.N. Security Council," *Washington Post*, May 8, 1994, p. A25; Keith Richburg, "Witnesses Describe Cold Campaign of Killing in Rwanda," *Washington Post*, May 8, 1994, p. A1.

15. Joshua Hammer, "Inside a War Zone: 'The Situation Is Desperate,'" *Newsweek*, June 20, 1994, p. 46.

16. Durch, "Getting Involved," p. 16.

17. Ibid., pp. 21–22.

18. Interview with Maureen S. Steinbruner, president, Center for National Policy, Washington, D.C., October 1, 1993.

19. Julia Preston, "Vision of a More Aggressive U.N. Is Dimming," *Washington Post*, January 5, 1994, p. A24.

20. Ibid.

21. U.S. Congress, Senate, Committee on Foreign Relations, "U.N. Peacekeeping: Observations on Mandates and Operational Capability," Statement of Frank C. Conahan, assistant comptroller general, National Security and International Affairs Division, United States General Accounting Office, before the Subcommittee on Terrorism, Narcotics, and International Operations, Senate hearing 103-330, 103rd Cong., 1st sess., June 9, 1993, p. 11.

22. Durch, "Getting Involved," p. 36.

23. "The United Nations," *Economist*, December 26, 1992, p. 57.

24. Yasushi Akashi, special representative of the secretary-general for Cambodia, third annual Charles Rostow Lecture on Asian Affairs, Nitze School of Advanced International Studies, The Johns Hopkins University, Washington, D.C., October 14, 1993.

25. "Rethinking Peacekeeping in the Post–Cold War Era," internal paper, U.S. Department of Defense, December 1, 1993, p. 1.

26. R. Jeffrey Smith and Julia Preston, "U.S. Plans Wider Role in U.N. Peace Keeping," *Washington Post*, June 18, 1993, p. A1.

27. Daniel Williams, "Clinton Peacekeeping Policy to Set Limits on Use of U.S. Troops," *Washington Post*, February 6, 1994, p. A24.

28. Ann Devroy, "Clinton Signs New Guidelines for U.N. Peacekeeping Operations," *Washington Post*, May 6, 1994, p. A30.

29. Kenneth L. Adelman, former director, U.S. Arms Control and Disarmament Agency, presentation before students in American University's Washington Semester and World Capitals Program, Washington, D.C., February 2, 1994.

30. "The Role of Peace Operations in U.S. Foreign Policy," *Key Elements of the Clinton Administration's Policy on Reforming Multilateral Peace Operations*, white paper accompanying Presidential Decision Directive 25, no date, introduction, p. 2. Made available May 5, 1994.

31. Ibid., p. 3.

32. Elaine Sciolino, "U.S. Narrows Terms for Its Peacekeepers," *New York Times,* September 23, 1993, p. A8.

33. *Key Elements of the Clinton Administration's Policy on Reforming Multilateral Peace Operations,* introduction, p. 3.

34. Ibid., p. 9.

35. Stephen S. Rosenfeld, "Who'll Be the Global Cop?" *Washington Post,* September 24, 1993, p. A23.

36. *Key Elements of the Clinton Administration's Policy on Reforming Multilateral Peace Operations,* introduction, p. 15.

37. Gareth Evans, *Cooperating for Peace: The Global Agenda for the 1990s and Beyond* (St Leonards, Australia: Allen & Unwin, 1993), p. 55.

38. Ibid.

39. "Cambodia: The Critical Tests," *New York Times,* May 19, 1993, p. A18.

INDEX

About the Author

Janet E. Heininger has been assistant professor of U.S. foreign policy in the Washington Semester Program at American University since September 1993. She is also a member of the faculty of American University's School of International Service. Previously, she spent seven years on Capitol Hill and four years in the State Department. From 1986 to 1991, she worked for Senator Robert C. Byrd (D.-WV), covering regional foreign policy issues and foreign aid appropriations subcommittee issues and serving as his legislative director. From 1991 to 1992, she covered foreign policy issues as administrative assistant for Congresswoman Barbara B. Kennelly (D.-CT). In the State Department, from 1983 to 1986, Dr. Heininger served as senior analyst for international organizations in the Office of Global Issues, Bureau of Intelligence and Research. Prior to that, she was an analyst of internal Chinese political developments in the Bureau of Intelligence and Research and served in the department's Office of the Historian.

FOR A **FREE CATALOG**
OF ALL
TWENTIETH CENTURY FUND
PUBLICATIONS

RETURN THIS CARD

Note: If you are reading this in a library copy, kindly leave the card in place and send us your name and address.

PLEASE SEND ME A FREE CATALOG
OF ALL TWENTIETH CENTURY FUND PUBLICATIONS

NAME

COMPANY

ADDRESS

CITY _____ STATE _____ ZIP

TELEPHONE

TWENTIETH CENTURY FUND
41 East 70th Street, New York, New York 10021 (212) 535-4441

The Twentieth Century Fund sponsors and supervises timely analyses of economic policy, foreign affairs, and domestic political issues. Not-for-profit and nonpartisan, the Fund was founded in 1919 and endowed by Edward A. Filene.

For a FREE CATALOG of all Twentieth Century Fund publications, please fill out and return this card. If you are reading this in a library copy, kindly leave the card in place and send us your name and address.

NO POSTAGE
NECESSARY
IF MAILED
IN THE
UNITED STATES

BUSINESS REPLY MAIL

FIRST CLASS MAIL   PERMIT NO 1851   NEW YORK NY

POSTAGE WILL BE PAID BY ADDRESSEE

TWENTIETH CENTURY FUND

41 EAST 70TH STREET

NEW YORK NEW YORK 10131–0770